Protecting the Global Environment

Mark A. Boyer and Shareen Hertel, Series Editors

International Studies Intensives (ISI) is a book series that springs from the desire to keep students engaged in the world around them. Books in the series address a wide array of topics in the international studies field, all devoted to getting students involved in the ways in which international events affect their daily lives. ISI books focus on innovative topics and approaches to study that cover popular and scholarly debates and employ new methods for presenting theories and concepts to students and scholars alike. ISI books pack a lot of information into a small space—they are meant to offer an intensive introduction to subjects often left out of the curriculum. ISI books are relatively short, visually attractive, and affordably priced.

Editorial Board

Robin Broad, *American University*
Michael Butler, *Clark University*
Dan Caldwell, *Pepperdine University*
Mary Caprioli, *University of Minnesota, Duluth*
Robert Denemark, *University of Delaware*
A. Cooper Drury, *University of Missouri Columbia*
Doug Foyle, *Wesleyan University*
H. Richard Friman, *Marquette University*
Jean Garrison, *University of Wyoming*
Vicki Golich, *Metropolitan State College of Denver*
Jeffrey Hart, *Indiana University*
Jonathan Wilkenfeld, *University of Maryland*
Jeanne Hey, *Miami University*
Steve Hook, *Kent State University*

Valerie Hudson, *Brigham Young University*
David Kinsella, *Portland State University*
Robert Kudrle, *University of Minnesota*
Lynn Kuzma, *University of Southern Maine*
Steve Lamy, *University of Southern California*
Jeffrey Lantis, *College of Wooster*
James McCormick, *Iowa State University*
James Mittelman, *American University*
Lisa Prugl, *Graduate Institute of International and Development Studies, Geneva*
Paul Sharp, *University of Minnesota, Duluth*
David Skidmore, *Drake University*
Jennifer Sterling-Folker, *University of Connecticut*
Emek Ucarer, *Bucknell University*

Titles in the Series

Barcode in Back

Protecting the Global Environment

Gary C. Bryner
Foreword by Mark A. Boyer

Paradigm Publishers
Boulder • London

DISCARD

HUMBER LIBRARIES LAKESHORE CAMPUS
3199 Lakeshore Blvd West
TORONTO, ON.   M8V 1K8

All rights reserved. No part of this publication may be transmitted or reproduced in any media or form, including electronic, mechanical, photocopy, recording, or informational storage and retrieval systems, without the express written consent of the publisher.

Copyright © 2011 by Paradigm Publishers

Published in the United States by Paradigm Publishers, 2845 Wilderness Place, Suite 200, Boulder, Colorado 80301 USA.

Paradigm Publishers is the trade name of Birkenkamp & Company, LLC, Dean Birkenkamp, President and Publisher.

Library of Congress Cataloging-in-Publication Data
Bryner, Gary C., 1951-2010
    Protecting the global environment / Gary C. Bryner.
        p. cm. — (International studies intensives)
    Includes bibliographical references.
    ISBN 978-1-59451-674-0 (hardcover : alk. paper) — ISBN 978-1-59451-675-7 (pbk. : alk. paper)   1. Environmental policy—Political aspects.   2. Global environmental change—Political aspects.   3. Environmental protection—Political aspects.   I. Title.
    GE170.B79 2011
    363.7'0526—dc22
                                        2010035325

Printed and bound in the United States of America on acid-free paper that meets the standards of the American National Standard for Permanence of Paper for Printed Library Materials.

Designed and Typeset by Mulberry Tree Enterprises.

14   13   12   11   10   5   4   3   2   1

In Memory of Gary C. Bryner, 1951-2010

CONTENTS

FOREWORD

This is a very special book. It's special in several quite distinctly different ways. First and most importantly, it represents the culmination of Gary Bryner's distinguished academic career, one focusing on environmental issues from international, legal, and policy perspectives. But it is not just that this book comes near the end of his career. The final manuscript was submitted to the publisher after Gary passed away in March 2010. In a very real sense, these are among Gary's last scholarly words, and they are insightful, thought-provoking and valuable ones indeed.

Second, this book is distinct for its emphasis on using the lenses of international relations theory to help us better understand the dilemmas of global environmental politics. Throughout the book, Gary introduces the reader to many of the fundamental theories and concepts of political science and international relations as ways of analyzing the political problems that face the countries of the world today. And he does this in exceedingly readable, accessible, and practical ways. By infusing his discussion of global environmental politics with theoretical richness, he challenges the reader to make choices for action and not just intellectual exercise. In very direct ways, he leaves us with agendas for thought and action that seek to link this generation to those that will follow. Put simply, without action today, we risk leaving those who come after us with truly insurmountable problems. The theme that ultimately jumps from this book is the need for current citizens and policymakers to make environmental choices that are ethical, moral, and just in transgenerational ways. At the risk of sounding trite, the future is now, and we must act.

A third way in which this book is special stems from the collective enterprise that was necessitated during its production. This book is part of the International Studies Intensives series, a highly collaborative series with an active Editorial Board. This Board gave Gary input into his project from the beginning and followed the manuscript's development with great interest. When Gary became ill, we realized the project might not come to fruition. But we were surprised and delighted when Gary's wife, Jane Bryner, submitted a nearly complete manuscript directly following Gary's death.

As series editor and also as a scholar who has recently jumped into environmental research, I seemed a logical choice as the one to assume the role of "editor of last resort" for the copy-edited manuscript. More than anything else, I figured I might learn something from Gary's work, especially as I am slated to teach Global Environmental Politics for the first time next semester. And learn things, I did. But I also want to express my sincere appreciation to several others who helped me through the production process.

First and foremost, M. J. Peterson graciously agreed to read and review the entire manuscript after we noticed that Gary had left some of her comments in "track changes" in several of the chapters. She filled in a lot of information and did an excellent job helping us answer some remaining questions in the text. She assiduously maintained the spirit of Gary Bryner as author while helping bring the manuscript into near final form. The end result is much better for her efforts. Second, Jerry Rice, graduate student extraordinaire, did a terrific job of tracking down loose citations in the manuscript. The work of Kay Mariea and Josephine Moore was also invaluable in making this book come to print. Their careful editing and production work is much appreciated, as well as their patience with me as I took longer to get through the copy editing than was optimal from a production perspective. Jennifer Knerr is, as always, a joy to work with as our editor at Paradigm and continues to have a great sense of our field and how we can address curriculum needs in new and creative ways. She saw such things early in discussions with Gary about this project and should take a lot of credit for helping shape the early structure of this book. And last, we all owe very special thanks to Jane Bryner for taking the time and effort to send us this text during what must have been a very difficult time in her life. We are truly thankful that she did so, as all who read this book will take away much of value.

So as you read the pages that follow, think about Gary's mission in writing this book and how you can take your own mission away from it and into the world, as you seek to change it and to protect the global environment.

Mark A. Boyer
University of Connecticut

Introduction:
Protecting the Global Environment

The twentieth century was a period of tremendous human achievement and remarkable progress in so many areas. The world's population increased fourfold while the global economy increased twentyfold. Revolutions in medical technologies, transportation, electronics, and a host of other areas transformed life in unimaginable ways for billions of people. But the century also left daunting challenges for us, including a host of environmental problems that threaten the well-being of current and future generations as well as persistent poverty that afflicts billions of people left behind by the century's remarkable surge of wealth and consumption. A series of reports issued during the first decade of the twenty-first century by think tanks, environmental groups, individual scholars, the United Nations along with other global and national government agencies, and others have outlined a sobering set of environmental threats, risks, and challenges.

We have made considerable progress in reducing some forms of pollution, such as air and water contaminants, especially in the developed countries, thereby causing some to suggest that the solution to environmental problems is economic growth (Hollander 2003; Lomborg 1998, 2004). Wealthier countries have the resources to clean up toxic wastes, purify polluted water, scrub air pollutants from power plants, and adapt to disruptive climate change. However, many problems, such as greenhouse gas emissions, the loss of biodiversity, and the accumulation of chemicals in the environment, are growing worse. These threats have largely been fueled by production and consumption in the industrialized world, although the rapid growth of developing nations like China, India, Brazil, and Mexico is an increasingly important driver of global environmental conditions. Those who believe that we can grow our way out of environmental problems ignore the widely held conclusions that environmental scientists and others have drawn—that the planet cannot sustain current levels of consumption of raw materials, energy use, and production of waste, particularly if developing countries follow the same model of economic growth that the wealthy, industrialized nations pursued (Daily 1997; Brown 2001; Princen, Maniates, and Conca 2002; Ehrlich and Ehrlich 2004; Princen 2005; Simpson, Toman, and Ayers 2005; Pirages and Cousins, 2005).

The most immediate environmental problems are typically found in the less developed countries, where poverty and environmental decline are inextricably intertwined. People who struggle to survive often engage in environmentally unsustainable practices, and those people are particularly affected by environmental problems such as water and air pollution, lack of clean drinking water and sanitation, loss of local biodiversity, and disruptive climate changes like increased flooding, longer droughts, greater severity and frequency of hurricanes, and melting of glaciers. Climate change will likely make managing the other environmental problems plaguing the developing world more difficult. Reports from the United Nation's Intergovernmental Panel on Climate Change (IPCC Feb., Mar., Apr., Oct., and Nov. 2007, 2007a, b, and c) provide dramatic evidence that the earth and its inhabitants have already begun to experience the effects of disruptive climate change and that the impacts are much greater in some areas, such as Arctic communities, than in others. Just as serious are the threats to the supply of clean water, which is a concern throughout the developing world (De Villiers 2000; Rothfeder 2001; Blatter and Ingram 2001; Conca 2006).

Developing effective policy options for significantly reducing the magnitude of the threat of global environmental decline and for adapting to likely environmental changes are among the most ambitious and challenging tasks now facing the residents of the planet. Climate change, for example, is being driven by emissions from the generation and use of energy that powers virtually every aspect of modern economic life and by land use decisions made in every community on earth. Action to reduce the risk of climate change and other global environmental threats requires an unprecedented level of coordinated and complex policy making and a greater collective commitment to political change than has ever occurred.

The prospects for a transformation in politics and policy making to effectively address global environmental threats are hardly promising. The reports and studies that warn of current, impending, and future environmental problems and crises—including loss of species, spread of disease, reduced agricultural output, declining fisheries, water shortages, and toxic chemicals in human tissue—have made only a little dent in public policy making. The health of ecosystems on which all human life depends is a precondition for human life and activity, yet protecting them rarely becomes a high political priority. Although the dynamism of environmental research has produced a massive expansion of knowledge about environmental problems during the past four decades, effective policy making has languished (Speth 2005; Speth and Haas 2006; Bryner 1997, 2001; Harrison and Bryner 2004). There are dozens of major global environmental treaties and agreements but little evidence that they are contributing significantly to reducing the threats that seem to be more serious each year. Governments struggle mightily in global forums to devise effective solutions to the problems that threaten their collective well-being (Kuehls 1996; Litfin 1998; Florini 2005; Paehlke 2003; Jasanoff and Martello 2004).

The contrast between rising environmental threats and stagnant policy, therefore, forces us to consider what kinds of political changes are required to generate the support necessary to bring about the kinds of political transformations required for effective responses to global environmental threats. How can societies make the kinds of fundamental changes that are required so as to ensure that those societies are ecologically sustainable? What are the political factors that contribute to such dramatic policy shifts? Under what conditions are those kinds of political, economic, and social changes possible? What can be learned from other eras of fundamental transformation in politics and public policies that could suggest how progress could be made in order to deal with the host of environmental threats we face around the world? The purpose of this book is to explore answers to these and related questions and also to suggest what might be required to generate the kind of political support necessary for effective policies to reduce environmental threats and to promote an ecologically sustainable global economy.

Answering these questions essentially requires flows of ideas between general political science and international relations theory on one side and knowledge of environmental issues on the other. Theories, concepts, and ideas from political science and international relations can help illuminate the nature of the challenges involved in efforts to develop political agreements that define goals to be pursued and actions to be taken as well as to ensure effective implementation of those agreements. The literature on international environment policy is dominated by economics, and although that perspective is obviously essential to assessing costs and benefits of policy options, understanding how broad changes in economic preferences, economic behavior, social values, and political imperatives develop and change is central to successfully meeting the environmental challenges facing us. Whereas global environmental politics and policy is an important focus of the literature on international relations, studies of national security, trade and economics, and diplomacy also provide insights needed to address environmental challenges effectively. At the same time, studying environmental issues can contribute to international relations and political science scholarship. The extensive body of global environmental treaties and agreements, for example, provide a useful set of data to help examine alternative explanations for why countries cooperate and why they agree to binding accords that are not necessarily consistent with their economic self-interest. The diversity and energy reflected in environmental nongovernmental organizations and the level of participation in grassroots groups provide material for reassessing theories of democratic politics. Environmentalism as a political movement may contribute to democratic governance even if it doesn't actually solve environmental problems. Furthermore, the complexity of the scientific issues surrounding environmental problems can help clarify the challenges that science and technology pose for democratic decision making.

This book treats the needed flow of ideas as bidirectional, focusing on how international relations theory can inform environmental policy making and how exploring environmental issues can help refine and develop political science scholarship. Thus, the first task here is to briefly summarize the existing literature on environmental politics and international relations and then go beyond that to integrate theories, themes, and concepts from the broader political science literature for a general audience, one that is interested in global environmental problems but largely unfamiliar with that scholarship. As the scientific consensus becomes firmer and the policy imperatives become clearer, the political questions about how to bring about transformational political change put political science at the heart of environmental debates. The second task, then, is to provide students and scholars in environmental studies with clear and concise explanations of how theories and analytical frameworks developed in international relations and political science can help them understand what kinds of political arrangements and agreements can promote the transformations needed to attain ecological sustainability. Hence the book is designed to help students and scholars in environmental studies use theories and frameworks from international relations to identify the kinds of political agreements and arrangements to help ensure that countries reduce their impact on the global environment and to help students and scholars of international relations see how environmental issues provide empirical and conceptual examples that can help them refine their theories and models.

Outline of the Book

Chapter 1 briefly discusses and summarizes global environmental threats, the current scientific research regarding those threats, and the gap between the scientific consensus over the nature of global environmental threats and the kinds of political change required to design and implement policies that will effectively address those threats (World Resources Institute n.d.; United Nations Environment Programme 2002; United Nations Development Programme 2007; WorldWatch Institute 2007, 2008; American Association for the Advancement of Science 2000; Kennedy 2006; World Scientists' Warning to Humanity 2003). The chapter focuses on three problems that are particularly serious and capture much of the concern with the state of the global environment: water scarcity, climate change, and loss of biodiversity.

Chapter 2 examines how theories from political science in general and international relations in particular help us understand and explain the challenges in producing the kinds of policy changes required for effectively addressing these environmental problems and threats. The goal here is to explore how these individual environmental problems and the policy-making efforts responding to them can be understood and explained as part of a pattern of global politics. Different theories of international relations provide alternative analytic frameworks through which environmental policy making can be explained and understood. Much like different lenses of a camera, from telephoto to wide angle, can be used to illuminate different aspects of a scene, different theories of international relations can be used to identify various patterns and key elements of environmental cooperation. Similarly, different levels of analysis, from the individual to the nation-state to world systems, can be helpful for understanding environmental problems from different perspectives (Sterling-Folker 2005).

The next three chapters focus on critical issues that form essential parts of the agenda that need to be addressed in order to develop more effective environmental cooperation: making markets work, fostering ecologically sustainable forms of development, and ensuring fairness and justice in the distribution of environmental harms and risks. These chapters lay out the basic contours of the concern, identify the political challenges involved in facilitating cooperative efforts, and consider how leading theories of international politics can help understand the challenges and possible solutions to global environmental problems in general and protecting water quality, securing biodiversity, and reducing the threat of climate change in particular.

Chapter 3 takes up the first of the three—making markets operate in ways that contribute to addressing environmental threats by establishing an effective system of regulation for global environmental protection policies. This approach rests on the presumption that the pervasiveness of globalization and the expansion and reach of markets mean that remedies for environmental problems will be designed and implemented within the framework of markets. Yet accepting the market as a social ordering device does not obviate the need for public policies, particularly when there are market failures that require corrective political action. Remedying environmental problems here are framed as making markets work for society as a whole by making sure market transactions reflect more of the true costs of producing, transporting, using, and disposing of goods and services. The task of international regimes, transnational NGOs, domestic policies aimed at implementing environmental accords, and other institutions and processes is to design ways to make markets work better and to generate support for the higher prices and increased regulatory interventions required to make that happen. This is to a great extent a question of institutional design—identifying the kinds of institutions required to make markets work in ways that will protect the ecological systems and services on which those markets depend (Lindblom 1977; Heilbroner 1991; Group of Green Economists 1992; Heal 2000; McMillan 2002; Nadeau 2003; Cashmore, Auld, and Newsom 2004; Keohane and Olmstead 2007).

Chapter 4 takes up the second concern by exploring the challenges of integrating environmental sustainability into development. Reducing global poverty and addressing the demands of poor countries for economic growth and development can clash with the environmental protection agenda of the wealthy world. Although the cooperation of both Northern and Southern Hemispheres are required to effectively address climate change, biodiversity preservation, and other issues, securing the Southern Hemisphere's cooperation requires a commitment to development. Because countries of the South possess some things that countries of the North desire, such as protected forests and habitat for assuring biodiversity preservation and carbon sequestration, the Southern Hemisphere's emerging bargaining leverage creates an opening for raising the visibility of development. Though the discussions of these issues are often quite contentious, the prospects for cooperation are in some ways quite promising because the developing countries have a great interest in ensuring that development occurs in ways that are consistent with global ecological constraints. Promoting sustainable development requires addressing another set of institutional design questions, including issues of how to make sure aid or investments from developed countries both address developing countries' immediate needs to improve their populations' quality of life and remedy immediate environmental problems such as water and air pollution as well as the long-term issues of climate stabilization and preservation of biodiversity (Milbrath 1989; Panayotou 1993; Kirkby, O'Keefe, and Timberlake 1995; Daly 1996; Prugh, Costanza, and Daly 2000; Lafferty and Meadowbrook 2000; Harris et al. 2001; Lafferty and Hovden 2003; Lafferty 2004; Hossay 2006).

Chapter 5 completes the tour of substantive challenges by examining the issues of justice and fairness that have become central to environmental policy making. The distributional consequences of environmental policy are critically important, and conceptions of environmental justice posit intra- and intergenerational equity and fairness as key aspirations of environmental policy making. These aspirations find one expression in the notion that environmental justice is a human right. However, the impact of human rights discourses is uncertain; although they can impel action, they run up against strong limits when they challenge the prerogatives of powerful nation-states. But notions of environmental rights, combined with the broader family of human rights ideals, may be able to play a powerful role in generating support for more effective global environmental governance. Here, too, institutions are important. Transnational human rights movements, the UN family of institutions seeking to promote human rights and environmental protection, and international tribunals all have roles in identifying global norms and values relevant to addressing environmental threats (Nickel 1987; Camacho 1998; Pogge 2002; Donnelly 2003; Pellow and Brulle 2005; Adger et al. 2006; Roberts and Parks 2007; Sandler and Pezzullo 2007; Carruthers 2008; Gibney 2008).

The final chapter summarizes the main themes of the book and draws some conclusions about the prospects for the kinds of political changes required to develop effective policies to address global environmental threats. It highlights the role that theories and concepts from political science can play in illuminating global environmental policy making and the compelling need that these international challenges present for more creative thinking, studying, and theorizing about global politics. The contemporary environmental challenges, most fully indicated by issues of climate change, biodiversity, and water, may well combine to produce unprecedented global crises and disruptions.

As these crises unfold in ways that are impossible to forecast or predict, they will place even greater strains on global politics. If climate changes occur as rapidly as some scientists fear, thereby overwhelming efforts to mitigate them, then massive flooding, food and energy shortages, rapidly spreading disease, refugee flows, and other consequences will overpower our ability to adapt. If environmental change does occur so quickly that the human ability to adapt is overwhelmed, international politics will degenerate into a struggle for survival in the face of resource shortages, hunger, environmental decline, and violent conflict. If we could be sure that environmental change will unfold slowly enough to permit incremental change, we could be more confident about the future; after all, humans have constantly made incremental change to their societies, cultures, beliefs, collective policies, and individual behavior. However, the signs point to more rapid change, thus requiring a massive transformation.

Massive transformation requires effective change along three related dimensions. The first is to make markets work for the environment and sustainability by adopting public policies that force even the least environmentally minded market actors to take the full cost of their activities into account. The second is to help developing countries achieve sustainable development, a project that involves rethinking the whole pattern of economic development. The third is to create a just society based on respect for human rights and intergenerational equity. Beginnings have been made in all three areas, but the changes needed are more fundamental than have yet been accomplished. Thus the task before citizens, experts in political science and environmental affairs, and governments alike is creative theorizing about how to shape science, technology, economics, and political imperatives in ways that will foster all three transformations and ensure an ecologically sustainable future for all of the inhabitants of Earth.

Chapter One
GLOBAL ENVIRONMENTAL TRENDS

Scientists are deeply concerned by environmental trends. "A Warning to Humanity" (1993), written more than a decade ago by more than a thousand of the world's leading scientists, summarized the situation in sobering terms:

> Human Beings and the Natural World are set on a collision course. If not checked, many of our current practices put at serious risk the future that we wish for human society and the plant and animal kingdoms, and may so alter the living world that it will be unable to sustain life in the manner that we know.

A series of reports by the World Resources Institute, the United Nations Environment Programme, the WorldWatch Institute, and a host of scientists in research institutes, universities, and government agencies have outlined a sobering set of environmental threats, risks, and challenges (United Nations Environment Programme 2002; American Association for the Advancement of Science 2000; World Resources Institute 2005; WorldWatch Institute 2008).

These reports indicate that many of the most serious environmental problems, such as greenhouse gas emissions, the loss of biodiversity, and the accumulation of chemicals in the environment, have grown worse. These reports also indicate that the planet cannot sustain current levels of consumption and pollution occurring in the wealthy, industrialized nations and that the problem becomes far worse if people in the developing world increase their resource use to similar per capita levels. The most immediate environmental problems are typically found in the less developed countries, where poverty and environmental decline are inextricably intertwined. People who struggle to survive often engage in environmentally unsustainable practices, and those people are particularly affected by environmental problems such as water and air pollution, lack of clean drinking water and sanitation, and loss of biodiversity.

Longer-term environmental threats such as disruptive climate change are a concern in both the industrialized and developing world. Global warming has already been associated with significant changes in the climate of some regions and is expected to exacerbate problems of drought and severe storms that are already plaguing the developing world. Consumption of nonrenewable resources is similarly a global problem. Box 1.1 summarizes trends in some natural resources. Perhaps the most familiar resource consumption issue involves oil. Many petroleum engineers and analysts argue that we have or will soon reach "peak oil"—the point at which we have used half of the world's recoverable oil—and production will begin an inexorable decline. With demand for oil continuing to grow steadily, decline in production will produce a tremendous gap between supply and demand, thus creating profound economic disruptions as prices skyrocket and growth no longer becomes possible (Goodstein 2004; Roberts 2004; Simmons 2005). For those who regard the current patterns of resource use and pollution as unsustainable, environmental degradation not only threatens people alive today but will also create pressures severely limiting the opportunities of succeeding generations to pursue their life choices.

Although there is wide agreement among environmentalists and ecological scientists that the world faces a grim future unless fundamental changes in consumption patterns occur, this conclusion is not as widely shared among the general public or those engaged in environmental politics. There are two primary reasons for this discrepancy. First, some measures of environmental quality show significant improvement over time. Air pollution, the kind of pollution that generally has the greatest impact on human health, has been reduced throughout the developed world. In the United States, emissions of total suspended particles peaked around 1950. Controls on burning and greater use of cleaner fuels induced steady declines until the 1980s. Carbon monoxide emissions peaked in about 1970 and have fallen noticeably since then, largely a result of motor vehicle emission controls. Emissions of volatile organic compounds (the primary constituent of ozone pollution) and of

Box 1.1
Trends in Global Natural Resources

	Global Trends
Biodiversity	Around 24 percent of mammals and 12 percent of birds are classified as threatened.
Deforestation	The net loss in global forest area during the 1990s was about 94 million hectares (ha), about 2.4 percent of total forests. This was the combined effect of a deforestation rate of 14.6 million ha annually and a rate of reforestation of 5.2 million ha annually.
Desertification	Desertification affects as much as 1/6 of the world's population, 70 percent of all drylands, and 1/4 of the world's total land area and costs the world approximately US$42 billion a year.
Energy	Global energy use, which has increased nearly 70 percent since 1971, is projected to increase at more than 2 percent annually for the next fifteen years.
Fish Stocks	3/4 of all fish stocks are being exploited at or above their sustainable limits.
Land Degradation	By 1990 poor agricultural practices had contributed to the degradation of 562 million hectares, about 38 percent of the roughly 1.5 billion ha in cropland worldwide. Since 1990 an additional 5 to 6 million hectares have been lost to severe soil degradation annually.
Water	1/3 of the world's population lives in countries experiencing moderate to high water stress.
Wetlands	50 percent of wetlands are estimated to have been lost since 1900.

Sources: World Resources Institute, www.wri.org/trends/index.html; UNESCO. *World Water Assessment Programme*, www.unesco.org/water/wwap/facts_figures/protecting_ ecosystems.shtml; UNEP, *GEO-3*. p. 4, www.unep.org/geo/geo3/english/pdfs/synthesis .pdf; United Nations Division for Sustainable Development, www.un.org/esa/sustdev/ sdissues/desertification/desert.htm; United Nations Commission on Sustainable Development, *Agriculture, Land, and Desertification 2001*, p. 2, http://ods-dds-ny.un.org/doc/ UNDOC/GEN/N01/312/96/PDF/N0131296.pdf?OpenElement; World Bank. *World Development Report 2003: Sustainable Development in a Dynamic World*, p. 164, www-wds .worldbank.org/servlet/WDSContentServer/WDSP/IB/2002/09/06/000094946_ 02082404015854/Rendered/PDF/multi0page.pdf; Wetlands International, *The Socio-economics of Wetlands*, www.wetlands.org/pubs&/pub_online/SocioEcs/Part1.pdf.

nitrogen oxide also peaked around 1970 but have only declined slightly in subsequent decades. Economic growth, technological modernization, and environmental regulation have combined to improve environmental quality (Bryner 1995, 54–56). Air quality data from other industrialized countries show a similar pattern of dramatic improvement over the past three decades in air quality, even as population increased by more than a third and gross domestic product has more than doubled (Lomborg, 1998, 177). There is considerable evidence showing that as countries become wealthier, their citizens demand more protection of environmental quality and have the resources to invest in cleaner technologies and in pollution control. Yet it remains unclear whether these effects are sufficient to have more than local impact.

Second, some advocates of economic growth argue that future generations will be better off if we leave them greater wealth to adapt to whatever problems they face rather than trying to prevent specific problems from occurring (Wildavsky 1997). Although not opposed to investments in developing new technologies and new sources of clean energy, which will benefit future as well as current generations, they are skeptical of investing large sums in efforts to prevent potential environmental changes that may not occur or have the effects that ecological scientists anticipate.

Thus, there is a yawning gap between two views of the planet's future, with many economists arguing that wealth is the key to the future because it can be used to solve whatever environmental problems occur, whereas ecologists warn that irreplaceable natural processes and ecological services on which life depends are directly threatened by the continuation of current consumption and pollution patterns (Daily 1997).

Until recently, assessing such claims was difficult because there were no clear indicators for evaluating the severity of measuring environmental threats. In 2009 the journal *Nature* published a paper by a group of scientists proposing a way to gauge threats by identifying boundaries for human activity that should not be transgressed if people want to prevent unacceptable global environmental changes and preserve the environmental stability the planet has enjoyed during the past 10,000 years (Rockström et al. 2009). They argued that during the Holocene era, environmental changes were ubiquitous but nonetheless within the regulatory capacity of earth systems to maintain stable, human development–friendly conditions. However, the industrial revolution opened a new era, called the Anthropocene, dominated by the growing use of fossil fuels and industrialized agriculture. In their view, these patterns are pushing earth systems beyond the bounds of the stable environmental state enjoyed during the Holocene and could result in "irreversible and, in some cases, abrupt environmental change, leading to a state less conducive to human development."

The scientists defined the thresholds dividing sustainable from unsustainable activity through physical indicators such as the concentration of carbon dioxide or the number of species going extinct beyond the natural or background level. Using those indicators, they estimated that three of the nine planetary systems—climate change, biodiversity loss, and the nitrogen cycle—have exceeded safe boundaries and that others are close to doing so. They identified the climate threshold as 350 parts per million of CO_2 in the atmosphere, and noted that the current level is 387. They defined the rate of biodiversity loss boundary as no more than ten per million species, and observed that the current rate is more than one hundred. They set 35 million tons a year as the limit for the amount of nitrogen removed from the earth to produce fertilizer for agriculture and other products, and reported that the current volume is 121 million tons. Excess nitrogen ends up polluting waterways and coastal regions, and nitrous oxide is a potent greenhouse gas. They also indicated that the boundaries may soon be reached for global freshwater use, the amount of land converted to cropland, and ocean acidification. They also regarded the boundaries as intertwined, stating, "we do not have the luxury of concentrating our efforts on any one of them in isolation from the others. If one boundary is transgressed, then the other boundaries are under serious risk."

Although they provided easily stated targets that can serve as focal points in policy debates, their approach does not end disagreement about the likelihood of catastrophic environmental change. They acknowledged that there are many uncertainties about how long it will take to produce dangerous environmental changes or to trigger feedbacks that "drastically reduce the ability of the Earth system, or important subsystems, to return to safe levels" (Rockstrom et al. 2009, 474–75).

Yet their work reinforces other studies emphasizing that environmental and natural resource challenges have increasingly become global in scope. Some challenges, such as the threat to the stratospheric ozone layer and to the global climate as well as the decline of oceanic fisheries and degradation of the oceans, center on the global commons—the ecosystems on which all life depends. Other challenges, such as acid rain, hazardous wastes, and river pollution, are environmental problems that cross national boundaries and implicate international relationships in devising solutions. Another set of global threats arise from the globalization of markets and trade, which has greatly increased cross-border interactions and international flows of pollution and wastes as well as chemicals, genetically modified organisms, and other products. Additional challenges are primarily local in nature, such as the health effects of polluted air and water, the exhaustion of local nonrenewable resources, and damage to natural systems that provide important environmental services like watersheds and wildlife habitat. These problems reach virtually every part of the planet and affect communities almost everywhere. Cooperation, technology sharing, and other interactions can improve efficiency and effectiveness, particularly in policy areas in which more developed nations can assist developing ones to foster the technical and regulatory problem-solving capacity. Distributing global resources requires collective efforts so as to ensure there is some fair distribution of access and use as well as preservation for future generations. All countries have a stake in preserving the Arctic, the Antarctic, and other unique areas that are part of the common heritage of humankind.

Consequently, as environmental and natural resource problems have become international challenges, the scope of necessary response also broadened. The developed countries, although they are responsible for disproportionate contributions to the threats to the global commons, cannot protect and restore them without the help of the developing countries, whose economic growth is now also contributing emissions that threaten the biosphere. Countries are much less able to export their environmental pollution and problems to others today because they are constrained by a host of treaties and agreements aimed at managing international environmental relations. Local environmental problems in the developing world often overwhelm local resources, and technical and financial resources from elsewhere are required for timely and effective remediation. Poverty and environmental degradation are intimately intertwined: the struggle to survive leads to unsustainable use of resources, and environmental decline threatens livelihoods that are closely tied to the health of the land and water.

Three problems—loss of biodiversity, scarcity of fresh water, and disruptive climate change—are particularly difficult and emblematic of the global environmental challenges we face.

Biodiversity

Biological diversity represents the variety of ecosystems on earth, the species that inhabit them, and the genes that make up those species.

Ecosystems, species, and genes can be described as three levels of living things on Earth. Each level interacts with and affects the others, but preserving each also represents distinct challenges. Ecosystems are formed by both living and nonliving components of an environment. The interactions among these elements are critical in determining the health of the system overall as well as individual species. Ecosystems range from complex tropical forests and coral reefs to estuaries and ponds, savannas and prairies, deserts and mountain tops, and neighborhood parks and backyards (Alonso, et al. 2007, 4–7). Species are groups of individual organisms sharing a set of unique characteristics. Some species can be found throughout the world, whereas others, endemic species, are only found in certain regions and require unique habitats. If these habitats are destroyed, the species are lost. Keystone species, such as kelp and corals in coastal ecosystems, are particularly important because they affect the health and well-being of other species; if they are damaged, others are endangered. Some 1.75 million species have been identified out of the 10–30 million species scientists estimate exist. The number of species of mammals (4,900), birds (9,800), amphibians and reptiles (13,000), and fish (28,000) is relatively small compared to the 360,000 species of beetles and 400,000 species of noninsect invertebrates identified so far (Alonso et al. 2007, 4–5). Genetic diversity—differences in the genetic makeup of individual members of a species—is essential for the flourishing of the species. The interaction between genetic makeup and local environments determines how well species can adapt to changing conditions, diseases, and other threats. Isolated species typically lack the access to genetic diversity that is essential for adapting to changing conditions.

Biodiversity produces a host of ecological goods and services that are essential for life, including food, medicines, fuel, and materials. It is also central to the spiritual, cultural, and aesthetic lives of people around the world. Ecosystem services include pollination necessary for food production, purification of air and water, stabilization of local and globalwide climates, drought and flood control, and recycling of nutrients. Because they are essential for physical life or spiritual and mental well-being, many people regard them as priceless. Others are willing to estimate a monetary value so that ecosystem services can be incorporated into economic analysis. One such study estimated the value of some of the world's ecoservices at US$33 trillion a year, twice the value of all the goods and services produced by people. Some indicators of ecosystem services include the value of drugs containing ingredients from wild plants, the value of fisheries and fish catch, products from natural and managed forests, and soil bacteria that convert nitrogen into a form that can be used to produce crops and natural vegetation (Alonso et al. 2007, 8–13).

Naturally caused extinction is part of biodiversity: there have been five major mass extinctions in earth's history, occurring about every 26 million years. Their causes are still debated, with explanations being offered that range from meteorites and comets to climate change to the loss of keystone species (Mackay 2009, 14). Natural processes result, on average, in the extinction of two species a year. These natural extinctions need to be distinguished from the extinctions resulting from human actions, including the loss and fragmentation of habitat to agriculture, human settlements, quarrying and mining, intentional or inadvertent introduction of invasive species that overwhelm ecosystems, unsustainable harvesting of plants and animals, air and water pollution, release of toxic chemicals, and global climate change. Together, these contribute to an extinction rate several hundred times greater than the natural rate. The extinction rate for specific species varies greatly, depending on their size, distribution, and characteristics. Habitat loss is the leading threat to biodiversity, a function of human population growth and growing consumption. Invasive species introduced into freshwater systems pose a separate threat by spreading disease, damaging power plants and other equipment, and requiring massive pesticide use in agriculture. Nine of the world's fisheries are declining because of overfishing, pollution, and habitat destruction. Climate change is a threat to biodiversity in general because of the way it disrupts patterns of rainfall and alters temperature as well as magnifies the problem of biodiversity loss in a variety of specific ecosystems, such as corals, alpine meadows, barrier islands, southern temperate forests, deserts, and arctic coastal areas. As the European Environment Agency warns (EEA n.d.), "As we understand more about the ways that climate change is impacting biodiversity, it becomes clear that we cannot tackle the two crises separately. Their interdependence requires us to address them together." Thus, loss of biodiversity directly translates into economic decline as harvesting of fish, timber, and other products decline; food production drops; and a host of other benefits, including medicines, aesthetic and spiritual well-being, and recreation opportunities becomes sparse. Loss of biodiversity is also irreversible—a permanent loss to humankind of part of the richness of planet earth (Alonso et al. 2007, 14–19).

Globally, some 24 percent of mammals and 12 percent of birds have been classified as threatened. In the United States 120 of 822 freshwater fish species are considered threatened, representing 15 percent of total fish species (UNESCO n.d.). Globally, scientists estimate that more than 20 percent of the world's 10,000 recorded freshwater fish species have become extinct, threatened, or endangered in recent decades. This number, however, may well be an underestimate (World Resources Institute n.d., A). Although insufficient information is available to determine precisely how many species have become extinct in the past three decades, about 24 percent (1,130) of mammals and 12 percent (1,183) of bird species are currently regarded as globally threatened (UNEP n.d., 5). In its 2007 Red List, the International Union for the Conservation of Nature listed 16,306 species that are threatened or endangered, and 785 that have become extinct (IUCN 2007). It also concluded that 1 in 4 mammals face extinction because of habitat loss, hunting, and climate change (IUCN 2008). In 2008 the U.S. Fish and Wildlife Service (2008) listed 447 animal and 598 plant species as endangered and 162 animals and 146 plants as threatened. Plantlife International publicized estimates that some 15,000 of the approximately 50,000 plant species that have medicinal value for humans also face extinction (Plantlife International 2008).

Changes in land cover also threaten biodiversity. A UN Food and Agricultural Organization analysis concludes that the leading causes of deforestation are the extension of subsistence farming and government-backed conversion of forests to other land uses, such as large-scale ranching that is most common in Latin America and Asia (UN Food & Agricultural Organization n.d.). The deforestation rate is highest in Africa, at over 7 percent per decade, and Latin America, at somewhat under 5 percent per decade (UNEP n.d.). Deforestation is also widespread in Southeast Asia, with Indonesia losing some 14 million hectares of forest a year in the late 1990s (ASEAN 2000). Yet forests harbor about two-thirds of known terrestrial species, and many forest-dwelling large mammals, half of the large primates, and nearly 9 percent of all known tree species are at some risk of extinction (UNEP n.d., 12). The world has lost half its forests over the past 8,000 years through conversion to farms, pastures, and human settlements or commercial sites (World Resources Institute n.d., B). Tropical and southern temperate regions are losing biodiversity the fastest, whereas northern temperate regions appear to be more stable or in slower decline since 1970. Deforestation has several adverse consequences: the loss of sustainable supply of forest products, increased flooding in areas where forests formerly retained water, reduced biodiversity, and increased net greenhouse gas emissions (World Bank n.d., 134).

Desertification is another source of biodiversity loss. Desertification is land degradation in arid, semi-arid, and dry subhumid areas that results from various factors, including climatic variations and human activities. It affects as much as one-sixth of the world's population, 70 percent of all dry lands (amounting to 3.6 billion hectares), and one-quarter of the total land area of the world. It results in widespread poverty as well as the degradation of billion hectares of rangeland and cropland (United Nations Division for Sustainable Development n.d.). The United Nations Environment Programme (UNEP) estimates that desertification costs the world approximately US$42 billion a year (United Nations Commission on Sustainable Development 2001a, 2). The most obvious physical impact of desertification is the degradation of 3.3 billion hectares of the total area of rangeland, constituting 73 percent of the rangeland with a low potential for human and animal carrying capacity; decline in soil fertility and soil structure on about 47 percent of the dry land areas constituting marginal rain-fed cropland; and the degradation of irrigated cropland, amounting to 30 percent of the dry land areas with a high population density and agricultural potential (United Nations Division for Sustainable Development, n.d., ch. 12).

Loss of wetlands is also severe. Worldwide, 50 percent of wetlands are estimated to have been lost since 1900. Initially these losses occurred mainly in the northern temperate zone. However, since the 1950s tropical and subtropical wetlands, particularly swamp forests and mangroves have also been disappearing rapidly. Agriculture is considered the principal cause for wetland loss worldwide (Wetlands International n.d., 2, 7). Erosion, salinization, compaction, and other forms of soil degradation affect 30 percent of the world's irrigated lands, 40 percent of rain-fed agricultural lands, and 70 percent of rangelands (World Bank 2003b, 85).

Water

The total amount of water in the world is immense, but the vast majority of it (97.5 percent) is seawater. Another 1.75 percent is contained in ice caps, leaving only 0.75 percent of the total available for human use using current technologies and at current prices. The amount of freshwater available for human needs has largely remained constant while the population has grown exponentially for more than a century. Securing sufficient water to meet human needs and protecting its quality are tremendous challenges worldwide, particularly in arid and semi-arid regions. More than a billion people lack access to sufficient amounts of safe water. Nearly 3 billion lack access to adequate sanitation services. Groundwater levels are falling around the world. The water delivery infrastructure is aging and in need of major improvements.

Water also faces a problem of quality. Surface water quality has improved in most developed countries during the past twenty years, but nitrate and pesticide contamination remain persistent issues. Data on water quality in other regions of the world are sparse, but water quality appears to be degraded in almost all regions that have intensive agriculture and rapid urbanization. Every day 2 million tons of human waste are disposed of in water courses. In Europe only the upper sections of the fourteen largest rivers retain "good ecological status," and in Asia all rivers running through cities are badly polluted (UNESCO n.d.). An estimated 90 percent of wastewater in developing countries is still discharged directly to rivers and streams without any waste processing treatment. In developing countries 70 percent of industrial wastes are dumped untreated into waters, where they pollute the usable water supply (UNESCO n.d.). Pollution forces 3.3 billion people to use contaminated water, causing about 250 million cases of water-related diseases each year, with some 5 to 10 million deaths (World Wildlife Fund 2002b, 18). The level of nutrients such as nitrates and phosphorous in freshwater ecosystems is also a problem worldwide. In most areas the major cause of this contamination is the increased use of manure and manufactured fertilizer in agriculture (Revenga and Mock 2000).

On a global basis, water withdrawals amount to only 10 to 20 percent of total renewable water resources. Water supplies, however, are very unequally distributed and cannot be moved long distances cost effectively. Assuming that current water consumption patterns continue unabated, projections show that at least 3.5 billion people, or 48 percent of the world's projected population, will live in "water-stressed" river basins (basins subject to frequent shortages) in 2025. Even regions where per capita water availability appears sufficient when averaged over the year may actually face water shortages in the dry season. The World Commission on Water predicts that water use will increase by 50 percent over the coming thirty years and that 4 billion people—half of the world's population—will live under conditions of severe water stress in 2025 (World Bank 2003b, 85). The areas under greatest stress are in North Africa, the Middle East, China, and India. Water shortages contributed to the Darfur genocide, as drought caused agriculture and cattle grazing to collapse. Groundwater withdrawal is currently exceeding the natural recharge rate of groundwater by 70 to 90 percent in Yemen, Egypt, Libya, and Sudan (Gleick 2003). By some estimates, India will exhaust 60 percent of its aquifers by 2030 (Schaefer 2008). In 2008–2009 the worst drought in half a century left 4 million people and 2 million cattle facing serious water shortages (Torchia 2009). About 40 percent of the world's population already lives in river basins with less than 2,000 cubic meters of water per person per year for all purposes, including maintenance of natural ecosystems. In such areas, water shortages are increasingly limiting development options (United Nations 2007, 11).

Water use varies across different countries. In low-income and developing nations, agricultural uses take 82 percent of all water; industry uses take 10 percent, and household use takes 8 percent; in high-income countries, industry is the big water user at 59 percent, whereas agricultural uses take 30 percent and household use is 10 percent (World Bank 2001). Data from the World Bank reveals China as the most water-stressed country in East Asia, exploiting 44 percent of its usable water (in the aggregate), and is projected to exceed 60 percent by 2020. Primary withdrawal of more than 60 percent is widely considered by water experts to exceed the environmental carrying capacity of a river basin system (World Bank 2003b, 85).

Water pollution and reduced biodiversity are often connected. Coral reefs are among the most biologically diverse ecosystems on our planet and also some of the most ancient. Although they occupy less than one quarter of one percent of the marine environment, coral reefs are home to more than a quarter of all known marine fish species. Globally, more than 400 marine protected areas contain coral reefs; however, at least forty countries lack any marine protected areas for conserving their coral reef ecosystems (United Nations Commission on Sustainable Development, 2001b). Studies have emphasized the threats to coral reefs, including overexploitation and destructive fishing techniques, coastal development, inland pollution and sedimentation, marine-based pollution and coral bleaching (World Bank 2003b, 164). The reefs in Southeast Asia, noted for their extraordinarily high levels of biodiversity, are also among the most threatened (United Nations Commission on Sustainable Development, 2001b). The *Status of Coral Reefs of the World: 2000 Report* confirms that data collected from the world's coral reefs predicted that over half of the coral reef areas may be lost in thirty years if efforts to conserve them are not enhanced (Wilkinson 2000).

The geographic location of water greatly complicates policy making. Nearly half of the world's land surface is within international watersheds. There are 261 transboundary waterways, making water policy a primary subject of international law and agreements. Although water law and policy is a major challenge in international relations, there is a lively debate among academics and policy makers over whether water shortages and limited supplies have caused or will cause armed conflict. Some analysts believe that competition for scarce resources like water inevitably leads to war. They find evidence of water wars throughout history, particularly in arid regions such as the Middle East. Rivers that serve as international boundaries are chronic sources of conflict. Peter Gleick and colleagues (2002, 194) reported that water resources "have rarely been the sole source of violent conflict or war" but then identified a "long and highly informative history of conflicts and tensions over water resources, the use of water systems as weapons during war, and the targeting of water systems during conflicts caused by other factors."

Others argue that water conflicts have never been the cause of an international conflict and that water wars are irrational, ineffective in securing water, and thus rarely if ever occur. Gleick and colleagues listed eighty-one conflicts between 1504 and 2001 as involving water (2002, 196–206). However, the Transboundary Freshwater Dispute Database (2007) found only seven cases where water conflicts led to mobilizing military forces and some form of armed confrontation, but the only war attributed to water conflicts occurred 4,500 years ago when two Sumerian city-states fought over Tigris River waters. The database identified more than 3,600 treaties concerning international waters. The number of treaties and the scarcity of water conflicts suggest that water is better viewed as a promising arena of international cooperation and may present opportunities for countries to work out differences peacefully. The difference between these two assessments of water conflicts, as Gleick and colleagues suggested, is whether water is involved in the conflict or whether it is the sole or even primary source of conflict. For example, seven of the eighty-one conflicts counted as involving water took place during World War II when, for example, dams were bombed and rivers flooded to impede the advance of armies (Gleick et al. 2002, 197). Water was clearly not a primary factor in the war, but water resources clearly have security implications.

Climate Change

There is an enormous amount of literature on climate science, and non-scientists face a tremendous challenge when trying to answers the question of how serious climate change is and what kinds of actions should be taken. One way to try to make some sense of this remarkably complex issue is to look for conclusions drawn by groups of scientists after efforts to develop consensus among relevant experts. Their reports are a much more helpful guide in developing policy responses than relying on a few individual or small-group studies or even the most recent study because the synthesis reports are based on studies that have undergone additional peer review and scrutiny.

A number of scientific bodies have produced reports emphasizing the seriousness of the threat of climate change and the importance of developing policies to reduce emissions. The American Association for the Advancement of Science, the American Geophysical Union, and the American Meteorological Society all argue that carbon emissions have changed the climate. Eleven national science academies, including the U.S. National Academy of Science, issued a statement in 2005 that said, "The scientific understanding of climate change is now sufficiently clear to justify nations taking prompt action. It is vital that all nations identify cost-effective steps that they can take now, to contribute to substantial and long-term reductions in net global greenhouse gas emissions." (Joint Science Academies' Statement 2005, 1).

The most important scientific consensus-building body is the United Nation's Intergovernmental Panel in Climate Change, or IPCC. Its creation was inspired by a UN General Assembly request that the World Meteorological Organization and the UN Environment Programme create a panel of scientists to study the risk of anthropogenic climate change and to provide "balanced, objective policy advice" to governments of the world in order to address the threat in 1988 (IPCC Oct. 2007). Three working groups were established to examine (1) climate science, (2) likely impacts of climate change, and (3) options for mitigating or reducing the threat. It was awarded the Nobel Peace Prize in October 2007, along with former U.S. Vice President Al Gore, for its work in raising public awareness of the threat of climate change.

Thousands of scientists from around the world have contributed reports and research findings, and thousands more have served as reviewers. These scientists are nominated by their country's government to serve on IPCC panels. All the scientists have donated their time, and no one has been paid for the work completed. IPCC reports are written by a team of authors who are recognized as leading experts in the field. Reports are themselves subject to broad peer review and produced through a transparent process that also involves government officials from countries around the world agreeing to the summary language. Each report includes a "summary for policymakers" forcing the authors to make clear the report's implications for the policy-making process. This combination of peer-reviewed science and political efforts to secure broad acceptance of the major conclusions has allowed the IPCC to bridge the worlds of science and politics.

The first IPCC report, submitted to the UN General Assembly in 1990, led to negotiations that culminated in the 1992 Framework Convention on Climate Change that was signed by attendees of the Rio Earth Summit (virtually every nation in the world, including the United States). That report argued that there is a significant likelihood that human emissions of carbon dioxide and other heat-trapping greenhouse gas emissions were warming the average temperature of the earth and that climate-based disruptions are already occurring in different regions and will become even more disruptive in the future. Additional reports were issued in 1995 and 2001. Issued in 2007, the fourth assessment, like the earlier versions, was based on the work of some 600 contributing authors from forty countries, more than 30,000 comments from external reviewers, and representatives from 113 governments edited the summary report for policy makers (Kerr 2007, 1413). It concluded that scientific research leads to a "very high confidence that the globally averaged net effect of human activities since 1750 has been one of warming" and that "[w]arming of the climate system is unequivocal" (IPCC Feb. 2007, 5). The conclusion that evidence for warming is "unequivocal" was based on measurements of air and ocean temperatures, widespread melting of snow and ice, and rising global average sea level. "Observational evidence from all continents and most oceans," the authors of the report wrote, "shows that many natural systems are being affected by regional climate changes, particularly temperature increases" (IPCC Nov. 2007, 1). The IPCC concluded that emissions from humans have *very likely* contributed to sea level rise; *likely* contributed to changes in wind patterns and extratropical storm tracks and temperature patterns; increased temperatures of extreme hot nights, cold nights, and cold days; and *more likely than not* contributed to the increased risk of heat waves, droughts, and the frequency of heavy precipitation events. Particularly significant is the conclusion that "discernible human influences now extend to other aspects of climate, including ocean warming, continental-average temperatures, temperature extremes and wind patterns" (IPCC Feb. 2007, 5). Box 1.2 summarizes the current evidence concerning the effects of global warming.

Box 1.2
Current Evidence of Global Climate Change

- Average Arctic temperatures increased at almost twice the global average rate in the past one hundred years (although a warm period was also observed from 1925 to 1945).
- Satellite data since 1978 show that annual average Arctic sea ice extent has shrunk by 2.7 percent (ranging from 2.1 to 3.3 percent) per decade, with larger decreases in summer of 7.4 percent (ranging from 5.0 to 9.8 percent) per decade.
- Temperatures at the top of the permafrost layer have generally increased since the 1980s in the Arctic (by up to 3°C). The maximum area covered by seasonally frozen ground has decreased by about 7 percent in the Northern Hemisphere since 1900, with a decrease in spring of up to 15 percent.
- Long-term trends from 1900 to 2005 have been observed in the amount of precipitation over many large regions. Significantly increased precipitation has been observed in eastern parts of North and South America, northern Europe, and northern and central Asia. Drying has been observed in the Sahel, the Mediterranean, southern Africa, and parts of southern Asia.
- More intense and longer droughts have been observed over wider areas since the 1970s, particularly in the tropics and subtropics. Increased drying linked with higher temperatures and decreased precipitation have contributed to changes in historical drought patterns. Changes in sea surface temperatures (SST), wind patterns, and decreased snowpack and snow cover have also been linked to droughts.
- The frequency of heavy precipitation events has increased over most land areas, consistent with warming and observed increases of atmospheric water vapor.
- Widespread changes in extreme temperatures have been observed over the last fifty years. Cold days, cold nights, and frost have become less frequent, whereas hot days, hot nights, and heat waves have become more frequent.
- There is observational evidence for an increase of intense tropical cyclone activity in the North Atlantic since about 1970, which is correlated with increases of tropical sea surface temperatures; there are also suggestions of increased intense tropical cyclone activity in some other regions, where concerns over data quality are greater.

Source: IPCC Feb. 2007, 8.

More significant for policy debates than aggregate, global impacts is the tremendous variation in local and regional impacts that might occur. These are the projected consequences of climate change in North America:

- Warming in western mountains is expected to cause decreased snowpack, more winter flooding, and reduced summer flows, exacerbating competition for overallocated water resources.
- In the early decades of the century, moderate climate change is projected to increase aggregate yields of rain-fed agriculture by 5 to 20 percent, but with important variability among regions. Major challenges are projected for crops that are near the warm end of their suitable range or that depend on highly utilized water resources.
- During the course of this century, cities that currently experience heat waves are expected to be further challenged by an increased number, intensity, and duration of heat waves, with potential for adverse health impacts.
- Coastal communities and habitats will be increasingly stressed by climate change impacts interacting with development and pollution.

The greatest impacts are expected to be in the Arctic, where high rates of warming will affect natural and human communities; in Africa, because of the limited capacity of societies to adapt to climate change; in the small island states, where people are highly exposed to sea level rise and storms; and in the Asian and African megadeltas, with high populations particularly susceptible to sea level rise and flooding from rivers and storm surges. Projected impacts in Africa are particularly threatening to human well-being. By 2020 between 75 and 250 million people are projected to be exposed to increased water stress due to climate change. By 2020 in some countries, yield from rain-fed agriculture could be reduced by up to 50 percent. In many African countries agricultural production, including access to food, is projected to be severely compromised. This would further adversely affect food security and exacerbate malnutrition. Toward the end of the twenty-first century, projected sea level rise will affect low-lying coastal areas with large populations. The cost of adaptation could amount to at least 5 to 10 percent of a country's Gross Domestic Product (GDP). By 2080 an increase of 5 to 8 percent of arid and semi-arid lands in Africa is projected under a range of climate scenarios (IPCC Mar. 2007, 14–15).

The magnitude, timing, location, and distribution of these impacts are not well understood and difficult to predict. A NASA study in 2008 concluded that half of Arctic warming between 1890 and 2007 was the result of black carbon rather than carbon dioxide (Shindell and Faluvegi 2009). The likelihood is *virtually certain* that over most land areas, there will be "warmer and fewer cold days and nights, warmer and more frequent hot days and nights." This will likely result in some positive impacts, such as increased agricultural and forestry yields in colder environments, a reduction in the number of people who die from cold weather episodes, reduced use of heating fuels, and reduced disruption of transportation due to snow. Likely negative impacts include increased insect outbreaks, reduced supplies of water that rely on snowpack for storage, and increased demand for energy to fuel air conditioning. It is *very likely* that warm spells and heat waves will increase in frequency throughout most of the earth. Impacts will be significant, including reduced agricultural yields due to heat stress, increased demand for water, a rise in heat-related deaths, and a general reduction in the quality of life for many people. It is also *very likely* that heavy precipitation events will become more frequent, producing a host of problems such as contaminated water supplies, soil erosion, waterlogging of soils, damage to crops, increased death and injury rates and cases of respiratory and skin diseases, disruption of commerce and damage to communities, and loss of property (IPCC Mar. 2007, 14–15).

The IPCC Fourth Assessment concludes that it is *likely* that droughts will increase, resulting in land degradation, reduced crop yield and livestock populations, decreased water supplies, decreased hydropower electricity production, increased risk of wildfire, and greater problems of food and water shortages, malnutrition, disease, and migration. It is also *likely* that the intensity of cyclones will increase, resulting in damage to crops, trees, and coral reefs as well as more power outages and disruptions of water supplies, more injuries and deaths due to water- and food-borne diseases, more damage due to high winds and storms, and more forced migration. Increases in sea levels are also *likely*, accompanied by salinization of drinking and agricultural water, damage to estuaries and freshwater ecosystems, increased deaths and injuries due to flooding, and increased migration (IPCC Mar. 2007, 14–15).

What Constitutes "Dangerous Interference with the Climate System"?

Moderate climate change threatens to exacerbate the problems of inadequate water supplies and loss of biodiversity, but the possibility of dramatic climate disruption is the greatest global environmental threat we face and overwhelms all others in terms of the risks it poses. Scientists do not agree on what concentration level would ensure meeting the goal of preventing "dangerous anthropogenic interference with the climate system," as stated in the 1992 UN Framework Convention on Climate Change, but leading climate scientists argue that, given the evidence that global change is already doing damage, it is not likely that "any level equivalent to more than a doubling of the pre-industrial CO_2 concentration could plausibly be considered compliant with the convention" (Holdren 2001, 13). Some scientists have argued that an atmospheric CO_2 concentration of 450 parts per million (ppm) would likely be required in order to satisfy the FCCC goal. They have concluded that stabilizing the CO_2 concentration at 450 ppm would require cutting emissions by 60 to 80 percent of 1990 levels by midcentury. If that goal is to be achieved, emissions would presumably continue to rise over the next few years until an agreement is in place, and then they would begin to fall rapidly, bringing down the concentration to the target range by 2050. Although one can debate the seriousness of the impacts of a doubling of CO_2, "any basis for optimism shrinks when the postulated CO_2 level moves to a tripling or quadrupling." At a quadrupling of CO_2, the mean surface temperature could rise from 3 to 9°C; increases in some areas would be even higher (Holdren 2001, 13).

The goal of a 60 to 80 percent reduction in GHG emissions is fraught with uncertainties because of feedback mechanisms that are not well understood or difficult to predict. However, if the average temperature increases by more than 2°C, scientists fear that the planet will become hotter than it has been for hundreds of thousands of years, which will create an environment much different than the one in which current life has evolved. Some climate scientists illustrate this concern by using the idea of a "tipping point," popularized by Malcolm Gladwell's (2000) book of that title. They fear that warming could reach a point at which it irretrievably changes the climate by melting the Arctic sea ice or Greenland, altering the ocean conveyor belt and/or the high altitude jet stream, and causing a dramatic rise in sea levels. Some scientists argue that an average global temperature rise of 3.1°C would trigger an ice-free Greenland (Walker 2009). The 60 to 80 percent emissions cut is also a tremendous challenge because even simply stabilizing emissions at current levels—a virtual impossibility—would not lead to stabilizing atmospheric concentrations. Some estimate that the impacts of current high levels of carbon dioxide emissions would persist for a thousand years even if emissions levels are reduced soon (Solomon 2009).

Even as the IPCC reports were being completed and published in 2007, some scientists were warning that a 60 to 80 percent reduction by midcentury would not be enough, and the goal should be 90 percent or more. This debate will be taken up in the next IPCC assessment. In a March 2008 paper, leading atmospheric scientist James Hansen and colleagues argued that the target of no more than a 1°C temperature rise relative to the 2000 average global temperature, which itself represented a 0.7°C increase since pre-industrial times, was too high. "Our current analysis," the scientists wrote, "suggests that humanity must aim for an even lower level of GHGs." The climate feedback mechanisms, "such as ice sheet disintegration, vegetation migration, and GHG release from soils, tundra or ocean sediments, may begin to come into play on time scales as short as centuries or less." As a result, they concluded, stabilizing the climate "requires that net CO_2 emissions approach zero, because of the long life time of CO_2." The current level of 385 ppm, increasing about 2 ppm a year, is already in the danger zone and must be reduced (Hansen et al. 2008, 1).

Reducing the concentration to 350 ppm has become the target of a national campaign led by Hansen and others. In testimony to the U.S. Congress in June 2008, Hansen warned that although a two degree Fahrenheit increase may almost seem innocuous, "amplifying feedbacks spur large rapid changes." For example, as warming melts sea ice, the darker ocean that absorbs more sunlight is exposed, thus causing more ice melt. As a result, the Arctic will soon be ice free in the summer even if no additional GHGs were emitted. Similarly, West Antarctic and Greenland ice sheets initially respond slowly to warming, but once they begin to disintegrate, that becomes unstoppable. If emissions continue to rise, sea level rise of at least two meters is likely to occur by the end of this century, producing hundreds of millions of refugees from coastal areas. Mass extinctions of species would likely occur as ecosystems collapse, as have occurred in the earth's earlier warming eras. Mountain glaciers that provide fresh water for hundreds of millions of people are receding worldwide, reducing rivers to trickles. Coral reefs that are home to one-third of the ocean's species are threatened by warming. "A level of no more than 350 ppm is still feasible," Hansen warned, "but just barely—time is running out" (Hansen 2008).

The Challenge of Climate Science Uncertainty

Although the IPCC Assessments indicate a widespread consensus regarding the threat posed by GHG emissions, consensus is not universal. Some climate scientists offer three distinct arguments against adopting extensive policy measures now. The first is that the evidence of climate change is insufficient to justify developing expensive mitigation strategies. The second is that humans are largely powerless to affect climate trends. The third is that warming is beneficial. This last argument starts with the observation that the warming during the last part of the twentieth century was associated with the greatest increases in food supply, health, and human well-being the world has ever seen, and the argument continues by projecting that the beneficial trend will likely continue throughout this century. It would be impossible, they argue, for a modest increase in the global average temperature to reverse the progress of the past century (Michaels 2005). Colder than average temperatures in the winter of 2008 in the United States quickly spawned articles and op-ed pieces proclaiming the end of global warming (Revkin 2008). Richard Lindzen (2006), another atmospheric scientist who is skeptical of the fear of climate change, agrees that global temperature and CO_2 levels have risen, but models show that warming reduces the temperature differences between the poles and the equator, which should produce fewer additional tropical storms rather than more.

Lindzen and other skeptics argue that IPCC and other consensus reports have been used by some politicians to hype fears and by scientists to pressure policy makers for more research funds. They further claim that scientists who "dissent from alarmism" are unable to get funding for their research, so few studies are published in leading scientific journals that challenge the consensus position. "Alarm rather than genuine scientific curiosity," Lindzen argues, "is essential to maintaining funding." An iron triangle of "climate scientists, advocates, and policymakers" dominates climate science and media reports, and this, according to Lindzen, has produced a reluctance to find out how the climate really works (Lindzen 2006).

Skeptics who are not atmospheric scientists argue there are some expected benefits from climate change. It may open new opportunities for tourism and economic development, such as ship travel to the Arctic Circle. It may increase food production in areas that will shift from cold to warmer average temperatures. Bjorn Lomborg (2007, 16–17) argues, for example, that warming will reduce the number of people who die as a result from cold weather, a number currently much greater than the number of deaths associated with heat waves. Another organization, the Competitive Enterprise Institute, lobbies against climate change science; the real threat, it suggests, is not environmental disruptions but rather a dramatic increase in government regulation that would stifle free enterprise and, ultimately, human freedom (Yeatman 2008). The CEI is one of several groups that support climate skeptics by drawing attention to any possible contradictory evidence, but it is primarily concerned that global warming will provoke governments to impose stifling new regulations. Far better, they argue, is for free markets to allow people to adapt to whatever problems and challenges occur.

Because there are great uncertainties about the rapidity and impacts of climate change, the scientific debate is far from over. But the policy debate cannot wait until the scientific debate ends. The nonatmospheric scientists, who must decide whether to engage in policy making in response to the threat of climate change, might draw either of two conclusions. It is possible that more than 90 percent of the atmospheric scientists are wrong and the few dissenters are right. However, that is not a reasonable way to bet when the stakes are so high. Peer-reviewed science is the best, albeit imperfect, way we have to produce the most persuasive analyses and conclusions we can. It is striking that the arguments made in the early years of climate science have largely been reaffirmed by subsequent research. The trends continue to point to the seriousness of the threat; little evidence has surfaced over the past twenty years that conflicts with the early climate science (Collins et al. 2006).

Second, uncertainty cuts both ways: changes may be more disruptive and damaging than anticipated rather than less. Given the magnitude of the possible impacts of climate change and its consequences for current and future generations of humankind, a cautious, precautionary approach is compelling. This is all the more reasonable because, as discussed in the chapters that follow, most of the measures we can take to reduce the threat of climate change will produce other important benefits that are desirable even if climate change becomes less of a threat. The uncertainties pose daunting challenges—uncertainties about how much warming will occur for any increase in GHG concentrations, what the impacts of warming will be around the world, and how well we will be able to adapt. Investing in insurance against these uncertainties seems to be the safest, most prudent approach to take (Schelling 2006).

Climate models predict that changes in the coming century and beyond will be much larger than we have already experienced. Part of the changes will occur as a result of the inertia of the climate system and the long lifetime of GHGs; CO_2 emitted today, for example, is expected to remain in the atmosphere for a hundred years. Furthermore, as the planet warms, feedback mechanisms are expected to stimulate further warming. The process by which CO_2 is removed from the atmosphere on land and in the oceans is expected to slow down as temperatures rise, although the processes by which vegetation and soils take up carbon are not well understood and quite difficult to predict. One group of scientists emphasized that we and our descendants, as well as all other forms of life, will be living with the consequences of climate change "for at least the next thousand years," and summarized our plight this way:

> We are now living in an era in which both humans and nature affect the future evolution of the earth and its inhabitants. Unfortunately, the crystal ball provided by our climate models is cloudier for predictions out beyond a century or so. Our limited knowledge of that response of both natural systems and human society to the growing impacts of climate change compounds our uncertainty. (Collins et al. 2006, 71)

Energy, as Thomas Homer-Dixon has argued (2006), is the "master" resource, ubiquitous and essential for everything we do. As the price of energy increases and the environmental impacts of climate change escalate, largely driven by energy use, societies will be forced to confront the impossibility of continual economic growth. The tremendous volatility of oil prices in recent years has made the debate over the future of energy complicated. Warnings that the global supply of oil has peaked and, as a result, prices will steadily rise clash with the fact that prices were lower in 2009 than in 2008. Yet rather than simply watching the price of oil fluctuate, policy debate can be guided by monitoring and comparing the amount of energy required to produce a particular form of energy. Much like evaluating the rate of return on other investments, the "energy return on investment" (EROI) measures the efficiency of energy production by dividing the quantity of energy produced by the total amount of energy needed to produce it. For example, the EROI of coal is a ratio of the usable energy in coal to the energy used to mine coal, transport it, crush and prepare it for use in power plants or other devices, and to build and maintain the required equipment. As fossil fuels become more scarce or more difficult to extract, the ratio falls; as it approaches 1:1, economies must invest more and more of their wealth to pay for energy generation. One study of U.S. oil and gas development found that between the early 1970s and today, the EROI fell from about 25:1 to 15:1. That trend has occurred around the world as well, as the cheapest places to develop oil and gas fields and hydroelectric sites have already been exploited. As we shift to nuclear power, tar sands, and some other "new" sources, the energy inputs required are greater. The EROI for Alberta, Canada, tar sands, for example, is about 4:1 because of the large amounts of natural gas used in processing. Unfortunately, in terms of climate change, the plentiful reserves of coal around the world entice countries to shift from natural gas to coal, the fossil fuel that produces the greatest emissions per unit of energy produced (Homer-Dixon 2006).

All this emphasizes the importance of ensuring that energy prices reflect all the costs of production and environmental impacts of its use. But market prices will not be enough to produce technological advances fast enough to prevent serious climate change risks. One of the clearest examples of this is the failure of market forces to prompt investments even in energy efficiencies that clearly pay for themselves in the three- to five-year medium term. This failure is due to inadequate resources to invest now for later reductions, a mismatch between owners and renters, lack of knowledge and information, inertia, and other factors. Many large companies that do not face cash flow problems have invested in energy efficiency and regularly report significant savings. In any event, energy efficiency must be dramatically diffused to reduce energy use and associated emissions. Technological innovations are desperately needed: despite a forty-year national goal of reducing energy imports, they continue to rise; despite a commitment in 1992 to stabilize greenhouse gas emissions, they have steadily increased. We still lack dramatic progress in the deployment of clean energy, sequestration of carbon dioxide emissions, and other advances that have been widely recognized as essential for our energy and climate security (Homer-Dixon 2006).

Globalization, Sustainability, and Global Environmental Threats

Globalization assumes that economic growth can continue indefinitely and can simply follow historical trends. One study, for example, projected that trade-driven economic growth would produce by 2030 an additional 2 billion new middle-class consumers—defined as having a per capita income ranging from $6,000 to $30,000 a year (Samuelson 2008). But as more and more people move into middle-class consumption, the pollution produced and resources consumed is unsustainable. Studies of the ecological footprint of modern economic activity demonstrate that consumption is not only depleting nonrenewable resources, but it is also outstripping sustainable taking of renewable resources. Consumption is often confused with population growth—the more people there are, the more resources are consumed—but population growth is only a relatively small part of the problem of unsustainable consumption. Environmental impacts are a function of population, affluence, and technology; impacts are a function of consumer values; the kinds of technologies involved in producing, consuming, and disposing of goods; and a host of other factors (Princen, Maniates, and Conca 2002, 4–7).

Jared Diamond (2008) explains how consumption is the key to understanding the unsustainability of economic growth: "the average rates at which people consume resources like oil and metals, and produce wastes like plastics and greenhouse gases, are about 32 times higher in North America, Western Europe, Japan, and Australia than they are in the developing world." In other words, the billion richest residents of the planet have a "relative per capita consumption rate" of 32, while the other 5.5 billion people have rates below 32, mostly closer to 1. The 30 million residents of Kenya, for example, have a relative per capita rate of 1 (meaning that their impact on the planet per person is quite low). Thus, even if their population growth rate is high, their impact on the planet remains small. The United States has 10 times the population of Kenya and consumes 320 times more resources and produces 320 times more pollution and waste. For people in the developing world, the promise of globalization is increased consumption, with an American or Western European lifestyle as the goal. Take, for example, a 100-year supply of a fixed resource such as a pool of oil. If consumption rates remain current, the oil supply will last for 100 years. But if consumption grows at 5 percent annually, the oil will last about 36 years. If the pool is actually much larger, like a 1,000-year supply, it will only last 79 years. If it is a 10,000-

year supply at current rates, a 5 percent growth rate means it will be drained in 125 years (Princen, Maniates, and Conca, 2002, 10).

China provides the most sobering example of the unsustainability of economic growth. Per capita consumption in that country is about eleven times below that of the United States, but it has the world's fastest growing economy, and its leaders are committed to propelling the nation into the developed world as fast as possible. If China were to approach U.S. consumption levels, that would more than double the world's total consumption of resources. If India were to do so as well, total consumption would close to triple. If the entire world reached U.S. levels of resource use and waste production, it would be as if the world's population grew to 72 billion (at current consumption rates). But that is precisely the assumption of globalization: "we often promise developing countries that if they will only adopt good policies—for example, honest government and a free-market economy—they, too, will be able to enjoy a first-world lifestyle. This promise is impossible, a cruel hoax: we are having difficulty supporting a first-world lifestyle even now for only one billion people" (Diamond 2008).

Diamond argued that it is possible to envision a sustainable world with a stable population and consumption rates "considerably below the current highest levels." Residents of the wealthy world would see their consumption fall, not because political leaders will inspire them to sacrifice for the well-being of others but because current rates are simply unsustainable. This does not necessarily mean that their standard of living will dramatically decline, because so much consumption is wasteful and contributes little to quality of life. "It is certain," Diamond wrote, "that within most of our lifetimes we'll be consuming less than we do now," and, conversely, consumption in developing countries "will one day be more nearly equal to ours." Stopping growth or even cutting it to a negative growth rate is essential in stabilizing the earth's ecosystem and securing a sustainable future, but it is hard to imagine a more daunting political task than to challenge the expectation of economic growth and ever-increasing consumption (Diamond 2008).

Although ethical arguments appeal to many people, the argument that global environmental problems threaten our self-interest is much more potent. As Diamond and others demonstrate, our economic self-interest requires we begin now to take more ambitious climate and environmental protection actions. The survival of all, including those in the wealthy world, is dependent on how the emerging economies of Asia and South America seek to grow economically as well as how the richest countries deal with pressures to continue to increase consumption. Why countries have not taken more ambitious and effective actions to protect their interest in a healthy planet is the subject of the next chapter.

Chapter Two
UNDERSTANDING GLOBAL ENVIRONMENTAL POLITICS
Theories of International Relations and Political Science

There is broad and deep agreement among environmental scientists that climate change, water shortages, and loss of biodiversity combine with other global environmental problems to threaten the future of humankind. They point out that droughts and other extreme weather events, declining fisheries, emerging diseases, and inadequate food production are some of the results of these crises. The evidence of environmental harms is clear, and there is widespread consensus among ecologists that risks are increasing. Yet that scientific knowledge has not resulted in thorough policy responses. This chapter examines the political and behavioral factors that have kept us from developing effective responses to global environmental threats. This means asking why we have been so unwilling to address threats to our well-being, especially as taking timely action seems so clearly in our self-interest.

One way to think about these challenges is to lay them out on a continuum. At one end are environmental consequences that can be managed under existing institutions of government; the task at this end is to continue with existing efforts and expand these efforts incrementally to meet new problems. International relations (IR) theories are best suited to address these kinds of consequences, but unfortunately, there is little agreement that consequences will be so limited. At the midpoint in the continuum are consequences that require major changes in the policy-making capacity. These involve creating the ability to bring about needed changes in the way people in the wealthy world consume resources and to foster a type of development in poor countries that dramatically increases their peoples' well-being without also increasing their environmental impacts. At the other end of the continuum, environmental changes are likely to be chaotic, unpredictable, and catastrophic. IR theory is not well suited to suggesting how far-reaching changes in policy capacity can be fostered, and it has few resources for understanding human behavior in the face of catastrophic environmental change.

The goal of this chapter is to explore how these individual environmental problems and the policy-making efforts surrounding them can be understood and explained as part of a pattern of global politics. This pattern results from activities at multiple levels. Thus, so all theorists of international relations pay attention to different levels of analysis, ranging from the individual to the nation-state to world systems (Sterling-Folker 2005). Different theories of international relations provide alternative analytic frameworks through which the multilevel activity that is environmental policy making can be explained and understood. Much like how different lenses of a camera—such as telephoto and wide angle—can be used to illuminate different aspects of a scene, different theories of international relations can be used to identify various patterns and key elements.

Realism, International Relations, and the Global Environment

Realism, still the dominant theory in international relations, focuses on nation-states as the primary actors in international affairs (Keohane 1986). Each state is analyzed as a unitary actor, pursuing its own interests in competition with other states and making decisions in light of how they affect its relative power and prerogatives. Because there is no global government to compel action, states' interests collide in an anarchic system in which conflict is endemic. Although armed conflict is not omnipresent, the threat of violent clashes is always looming.

Realism also emphasizes that power is distributed unequally across the world, and the great powers are constantly vying for power and influence (Mearsheimer 2001). During the Cold War the distribution of power was biopolar, as the United States and the Soviet Union competed to dominate international affairs. The current global distribution of power, however, is now more fragmented or multipowered, as many nations compete to dominate their neighboring states and beyond. International relations are characterized by balance-of-power politics that is unstable and fraught with the possibilities of conflict due to strong competitive forces. In the past, world wars have occurred when once-powerful states lost their power and others sought to take their place.

From the perspective of realism, China and the United States are in the middle of a classic shift in the balance of power. China's growing economic, military, and political power threatens to eclipse American hegemony. As realists see it, the expansion of China's power and influence means the two countries are destined to collide (Terrill 2003). In fact, conflicts between the two nation's navies have already occurred in the South China Sea as China seeks to expand its military presence and influence. Furthermore, China has aggressively pursued arrangements with African and South American countries to supply key natural resources to fuel China's growing industries, thereby fueling fears of future resource wars as shortages occur. Conflicts over Taiwan add to the tension. Because of their relatively large size, many realists believe that China and the United States are destined to expand their rivalry to military action or at least to a new Cold War in which each nation will seek to contain the other through the threat of military action rather than cooperation (Hyer 2009).

Neoliberalism and Global Institutions

Neoliberal theorists agree with realists that states seek to protect their sovereignty and power. Realists, however, view commitment to sovereignty as a broad barrier to cooperation and effective global policy making. Neoliberals, in contrast, suggest that if global environmental protection can be framed as a matter of self-interest and global policies sufficiently respect the centrality of sovereignty, then effective collective action is possible in the area of environmental and many other policy areas (Jackson and Sorensen 2003; Vig 1999). Neoliberals and realists alike assume that nation-states are rational, self-interest-seeking entities. Yet unlike realists, who regard security and military power as the state's primary concern, neoliberals argue that it is in the interest of the state to promote democracy, free trade, economic development, and globalization because these practices promise benefits to all parties. In neoliberals' conception of international relations, military conflict is not inevitable;

rather, common interests can be identified and pursued, and cooperation can be encouraged through economic ties. International trade thus plays a critical role in linking the material interests of nations and causing nations to conclude that their interests lie in pursuing common causes rather than unilateral actions. Free trade, environmental protection, public health collaboration, the sharing of technology, and national security can all be pursued more effectively through cooperation rather than conflict (Keohane and Nye 2001).

As countries become more economically intertwined, then, the threat of conflict or military action recedes. The spread of democracy reduces the differences in the domestic political systems of would-be adversaries. Similarly, the globalization of markets reduces economic differences. Military and political competition is replaced by economic competition, which is best pursued in a relatively stable geopolitical environment. The dominance of national power is thus replaced by a more complex system of national sovereignty and global institutions. Multinational corporations then spread across the world, thereby increasing ties between nations, sharing ideas and norms, and working with governments to facilitate trade and interconnectedness. Nongovernmental organizations increase scientific, educational, and cultural exchanges, all of which increase interdependence in other areas of life. Transnational NGOs work together to lobby countries to take on common environmental, health, economic, human rights, and other obligations. Scientific research, telecommunications, and other developments also encourage global cooperation and the creation of extensive networks that link countries and their citizens together (Keck and Sikkink 1998).

Thus, neoliberals see some hopeful signs in U.S.-China relations in addition to the threats that realists perceive. For instance, trade between the two countries has dramatically increased, growing by 400 percent during the past decade. China owns US$800 billion in U.S. government debt, enough to inextricably link the two national economies ("China and America—The odd couple" 2009). So as the economies of these two countries continue to grow together and business, educational, scientific, and other relationships expand, neoliberal theory suggests that the likelihood of military clashes decreases. Many observers are optimistic that the growing economic and cultural connectedness between the two nations will make them both stakeholders in peacefully managing their international relations. As the two become the dominant economic, political, and military poles of power, optimists hope their influence will spread elsewhere in order to reduce conflicts and promote international cooperation (Friedberg 2005).

There are, in fact, many examples of states giving up some sovereignty to secure the benefits of participating in collective action, such as arms control, trade, banking and commerce, human rights, and environmental protection. International environmental law scholars have catalogued close to 200 international environmental agreements addressing environmental problems on a wide range of issues. Major treaties focus on reducing the pollution of the atmosphere, controlling imports and exports of hazardous substances, and protecting marine resources, species, habitat, and biodiversity. Moreover, the provisions contained in these treaties vary considerably. Many of these agreements are in the form of framework conventions that have been supplemented with protocols that establish specific goals and requirements. Some treaties take the form of "soft" law—guiding principles and rules to be tested through practice before they become binding or "hard" law." (Hunter, Salzman, and Zaelke 2002, 349). These treaties, however, are typically characterized by problems such as inadequate resources, insufficient monitoring, and a lack of effective enforcement. As realists suggest, nation-states may be willing to accede to treaties, but they still guard their sovereignty jealously and remain hesitant to relinquish it to international bodies. Thus, the key issue remains how to get states to give up some of their sovereignty in order to deal with collective problems (Litfin 1998; Jasanoff and Martello 2004; Clapp and Dauvergne 2005).

Proponents of developing international law implicitly adopt the neoliberal assumption that agreements are means of pursuing national interests, reinforcing the legitimacy of the state, and underpinning the notion that international agreements are the primary political/legal institution in addressing common problems and concerns (Weiss 1999, 98). Although realism emphasizes sovereignty, autonomy, power, and independence, neoliberalism emphasizes cooperation through institutions that help countries pursue their self-interest. Advocates of neoliberalism argue that the level of international agreements and cooperation suggests that states are quite interdependent and have many common interests that lead them to take collective action. Not only do international laws and institutions allow nation-states to pursue their shared interests, but they also create further incentives for cooperative efforts. Contrary to realists, neoliberals argue that these international efforts actually influence and shape the preferences and behaviors of states. Whereas realists focus on relative benefits and advantages, neoliberals look for absolute benefits that accrue to all who participate in collective efforts (Vig 1999, 3–4).

Other Theories of International Relations and Global Environmental Politics

Constructivist theories of international relations emphasize the role of normative values in encouraging global cooperation. Constructivism suggests that nations will submit to the authority of global laws and institutions because they are committed to norms and values that go beyond the calculations of economic self-interest that characterize neoliberalism and realism (Finnemore 1996; Ruggie 1998; Keck and Sikkink 1998). Constructivists thus pay attention to the processes through which ideas and beliefs are generated and disseminated. In analyzing global environmental politics, constructivists are particularly concerned with the ways in which scientific knowledge about the environment is taken up in the policy process. One prominent constructivist conception emphasizes the role of epistemic communities—networks of experts formed around addressing a specific global problem—that help first produce shared understandings of the causes of problems and then propose solutions to address those problems. With environmental threats such as stratospheric ozone depletion, the loss of biodiversity, and climate change, the most relevant epistemic communities consist of scientists. As scientists develop a coherent and compelling body of understanding of ecological processes, that information then becomes part of the case for collective action (Haas 1992). The status of scientists as deeply knowledgeable persons who base their conclusions on observable evidence rather than ideology gives them a claim to authority that allows them to construct knowledge out of uncertainty. If they have political influence in nation-states concerned with environmental issues, they are then able to encourage an international convergence of action around a solution (Harrison and Bryner 2004, 8).

This is not to argue that science drives policy making in an orderly process of moving from problem definition to identification of alternatives to selection of optimal policy options. The policy process is much messier, as policy breakthroughs often occur almost accidentally when windows of opportunity are opened by the confluence of independent streams of problems, policies, and politics (Kingdon 1984). The theory of epistemic communities does not explain how scientists and nonscientists both share the policy-making process or why scientific consensus in some areas leads to action whereas scientific consensus in others does not.

Not all scholars agree that realism, liberalism, and constructivism fit so neatly together. Some scholars center on methodological debates between scientific or positivist approaches that assume the world can be understood and explained through observation and experience, which will then be followed by generating and then testing hypotheses and ultimately producing verifiable, objective conclusions. Conversely, post-positive approaches reject the possibility of producing objective, generalizeable conclusions on the basis of a belief that all knowledge is socially constructed. For post-positivists, scientific discourses are mixtures of facts and values located in broad "sets of linguistic practices embedded in networks of social relations and tied to narratives about the construction of the world" that constitute a form of political power because they determine "not only what can be said, but what can be thought" (Litfin 1994, 8). Critical theorists reject the idea of immutable laws, arguing instead that world politics are constructed by powerful states rather than discovered by objective researchers. Post-modern theorists reject the possibility of discovering objective truths because the social science itself used to uncover these truths is historical, political, and, therefore, biased. Finally, feminist IR theorists believe that the most significant of these biases are rooted in gender differences. Natural science as it has developed since the Renaissance has been a male-dominated activity, and analyses rooted in the perspectives of women are essential in understanding nature and environment fully. Ideas of women as care givers and nurturers and men as conquerors of nature have profound impacts on how global environmental politics is understood (Jackson and Sorensen 2003; Merchant 1992, 1995).

The interaction of science, politics, knowledge, and policy complicates environmental policy making. As is true of ecology, everything is connected to everything else in the realm of environmental policy; thus, there is no singular, unidirectional relationship between science and politics. Although science may first identify an issue, it is the interaction of science and politics that frames policy choices. Science and politics develop together, often in parallel, and they interact recursively. Furthermore, science and politics are shaped by individuals and their personal preferences, groups and their values, the processes and institutions in which individuals and groups interact, accidental events, and changes in collective expectations. They are also shaped by context, as the science and politics of each environmental issue is different. Actors, issues, values, interests, challenges, and knowledge vary widely. Even though environmental science is an international activity with standardized rules of conduct and involving participation by scientists from a wide range of nations, cultural differences are what shape the level of trust given to scientific research; as a result, countries differ in their reliance on specific scientific data when making public policies (Harrison and Bryner 2004, 11).

Political ideology further complicates efforts to articulate national self-interest on environmental issues. Conservatism suggests caution in the face of serious threats and seems inconsistent with the continuation of consumption and pollution patterns that many scientists consider to be a reckless experiment with the biosphere. However, many conservatives appear to fear a dramatic growth in the size and power of government more than they fear climatic cataclysms. For this reason, they reject mainstream climate science because they fear that its logical implication in the policy realm is to expand the power of the state. There may also be a broader sense of skepticism about science among conservatives, particularly among the social conservatives who reject the scientific consensus on other issues, such as evolution, and who mistrust scientists who don't embrace traditional values and ideas rooted in conservative religious belief.

At first look, liberals appear to provide a much less complex case. Their support of climate policy is consistent with long-standing environmental protection commitments. Despite their ideologically based fear of the accumulation of state authority, they long ago accepted governmental power as a necessary element in promoting equality. However, liberalism's emphasis on individual rights and freedom seems to be a weak base on which to build environmentalism, which seems better grounded by claims of community preservation and shared responsibility. Environmentalists are quite illiberal in their willingness to constrain individual freedom in consumption choices so that future generations can enjoy abundant natural resources and healthy ecological services. This willingness to limit current choices and consumption to benefit future generations is one of the most fundamental and admirable of human traits.

Beyond the Realism/Liberalism Debate

Realism and liberalism can be used descriptively to explain differences in the world and also to predict or suggest how countries will respond to future challenges. They can also be used prescriptively to suggest how countries could act in order to address global environmental threats. Both realists and neoliberals agree that countries act in their self-interest, but their conceptions of what constitutes that interest differ widely. Pursuing a realist mode of foreign policy making seems destined to lead countries eventually to conflict, as growing environmental problems cause economic disruption as well as create environmental refugees and increased competition for increasingly scarce resources. The more countries act along the lines of neoliberal theory, the more likely they are to come together cooperatively to address common problems. The more environmental problems seem manageable, the more feasible is the neoliberal approach. Conversely, the more these problems become unmanageable crises, the more countries will likely be encouraged to hunker down in isolation and seek to insulate and protect their populations from the turmoil engulfing the rest of the world.

Political science, as I have already argued, does not have a lot to say about how to make policy in the face of crises, and nor do the other social sciences. Economics, the most influential of the three, centers on incremental adjustments made through market forces. When crises strike, shortages occur, the prices of goods skyrocket, or markets collapse, economic analysis relies on the assumption that supply and demand will eventually reach a new equilibrium. However, it has little to say about either the interim before the new equilibrium is established or that the new equilibrium, when it is reached, may be at price levels that exclude a significant share of the population.

In pursuing the neoliberal hope of global cooperation to address environmental threats, we should not lose sight of the limits to cooperation in the contemporary world system. The scope and depth of ecological problems can become so great that incremental changes are no longer possible, and coping with crisis then has to replace the neoliberal mode of incremental adjustment. However, anticipating when this will happen is difficult, and premature abandonment of adjustment can mean missing opportunities to develop effective policy change. The discussion that follows in this and subsequent chapters focuses on what might be required to pursue the neoliberal approach to global cooperation. In this, the formation of international regimes emphasizes the importance of institutionalizing policy responses, so the remainder of this chapter examines the idea of international regimes. The next three chapters then look at the three issues that help form the agenda for the evolving environmental

regime: making markets work, fostering ecologically sustainable development, and ensuring fairness and justice in the distribution of environmental harms and risks.

The complexity of the interaction between environmental science
and politics means that no single theory about politics, science, or their
interaction is likely to explain satisfactorily the full range of environmental policies in place or those that appear to be feasible. The political challenge of producing the profound shift in climate policy that is required
to address the climate change threat is daunting. Promoting economic
growth and consumption while also reducing energy prices are universal political imperatives. People are skeptical of calls for national sacrifice
and fear that tight energy supplies will mean a diminution of quality of
life. From this perspective, the vested interests in the status quo are too
strong, and the breadth and depth of changes that are required overwhelms the capacity of the political system. All this may be true. If so, the
policy debate is fruitless. But we should not be so quick to conclude that
policy changes are not possible. Keeping in mind the limitations posed
by a global political system firmly dedicated to recognizing national sovereignty and providing only limited support for the idea of global governance, creating and developing international environmental and natural resource regimes is a very significant development. To fully appreciate
the prospects for policy change, we need to know how effective these
efforts to remedy global environmental problems have been.

Global Environmental Regimes[1]

The idea of global environmental regimes entered scholarly and practi-
tioner parlance as an important way of conceptualizing the nature of the
global environmental and natural resource challenges that confront
humankind as well as the adequacy of the responses devised to cope with
these threats. Scholars such as Oran Young defined regimes as "social
institutions that consist of agreed upon principles, norms, rules, decision-
making procedures, and programs that govern the interaction of actors in
specific issue areas" (Young 1997, 5–6; Young 1998; Young et al. 2002).
Much of the focus on environmental regimes is on global institutions
such as the United Nations and its many agencies, which include the UN
Environmental Program, the World Bank and the International Monetary Fund, and the Global Environmental Facility. The administrative

bodies created expressly to manage the implementation of some major environmental treaties are also sometimes described as the center of a regime. Nongovernmental organizations, including the large, globally active environmental groups as well as regional and even national and subnational advocacy groups, are also essential elements of environmental regimes (Wapner 1996; Keck and Sikkink 1998).

As discussed earlier, international environmental law scholars have catalogued close to 200 international environmental agreements addressing environmental problems on a wide range of issues. Major treaties focus on pollution of the atmosphere, protection of marine resources, imports and exports of hazardous substances, and protection of species, habitat, and biodiversity. The policy provisions contained in these treaties vary considerably. Many of these agreements are in the form of framework conventions that have been supplemented with protocols that establish specific goals and requirements. Some treaties take the form of "soft" law (Hunter, Salzman, and Zaelke 2002).

Treaties typically either include the creation of secretariats or give authority to existing organizations to administer treaties, formulate additional requirements, monitor implementation, provide for resolving disputes, and perform other functions. The United Nations in general and the UN Environmental Programme as well as special units of the United Nations in particular have been given responsibility for many global accords, but creating a new body to manage the implementation of a treaty is more typical.

Unlike international trade, where there is one overarching global regime managed by the World Trade Organization, and regional organizations that fit within this broader regime, such as the North American Free Trade Agreement and its implementing bodies, there is no one global environmental regime. The regimes surrounding each major environmental treaty vary widely in terms of their development of specific, binding rules; the resources given to the managing secretariat; the number of signatories; and other characteristics that help determine the effectiveness with which states implement the agreement and then remedy the environmental problem the regime is designed to address.

There is no agreement over how many global environmental regimes have been created, but a useful beginning point is the Fridtjof Nansen Institute's description of major international environmental agreements (Bergesen, Parmann, and Thommessen 1998). That compilation lists four agreements dealing with the atmosphere and seven on hazardous substances; eight global, five regional, and nine conventions within the UNEP regional seas program; three agreements on marine living resources; nine agreements on natural conservation and terrestrial living resources; four on nuclear safety; and one agreement on freshwater resources. These regimes vary tremendously across a wide set of variables and are difficult to compare and contrast: some have received major attention whereas others are largely unknown; some have been divisive whereas others have been the product of near consensus; and some have major resources committed to them whereas others are marginal undertakings. Porter, Brown, and Chasek (2000, ch. 3), in their study of global environmental politics, focus on nine major regimes:

- Acid rain—the Convention on Long-Range Transboundary Air Pollution, 1979
- Ozone depletion—the Vienna Convention for the Protection of the Ozone Layer, 1985, including the Montreal Protocol on Substances that Deplete the Ozone Layer
- Whaling—International Convention for the Regulation of Whaling, 1946
- African ivory trade—Convention on International Trade in Endangered Species, 1973
- International toxic trade—Convention on the Control of Transboundary Movements of Hazardous Wastes and their Disposal, 1989
- Antarctic—The Antarctic Treaty of 1959
- Climate change—the United Nations Framework Convention on Climate Change, 1992, including the Kyoto Protocol
- Biodiversity loss—Convention on Biological Diversity, 1992
- Desertification—Convention to Combat Desertification, 1994

There is a vast literature revealing the tremendous variety in environmental regimes. Rather than examine and compare specific regimes in detail, the sections that follow examine general features of the accomplishments that have resulted from forming international environmental regimes, identify the obstacles that have been recognized and overcome, and explore future choices, challenges, and opportunities. An analysis of the effectiveness of a regime in achieving its goals and the appropriateness of the goals themselves in remedying environmental problems is largely a subjective undertaking. The relevant variables at each level are difficult to measure or limited in their explanatory power. Regimes are comprised of a number of elements, and it is difficult to know which ones to examine. Effectiveness is largely a comparative enterprise: regimes are compared in terms of each other, but the components are complex political phenomena that are difficult to compare precisely.

Even if the impacts are clear and positive, it is difficult to know whether these benefits outweigh the costs of designing and implementing the regime and the actions taken by others to comply with its mandates. Assessing effectiveness is difficult because it requires determining what has been achieved versus what would have happened had no regime been formed as well as identifying what the maximum impacts might have been—both of which are difficult to estimate. The effectiveness of a regime is susceptible to so many influences and affected by so many factors that it can be difficult to assess which influences or factors are responsible, but the question of what determines the effectiveness of a regime is nonetheless a question of great importance (Miles et al. 2002, ch. 1). In addition, regime rules and institutions may produce compliance with the regime's mandates but not necessarily improve environmental conditions. Assessing environmental improvement raises questions of what environmental indicators to use, how to measure them, and how to assess those measurements in order to judge whether a regime is actually improving environmental quality and protecting natural resources. As Oran Young concluded in his book on the formation of regimes to protect the Arctic, although the Arctic Environmental Protection Strategy and the Barents Euro-Arctic Region program are "well into the stage of day-to-day operation," the "extent to which each of these regimes has contributed to solving the problems that motivated its members to create it in the first place is a complex issue beyond the scope of this study" (Young 1998, 198–99).

These difficulties notwithstanding, research in policy implementation for environmental, natural resource, and many other kinds of public policies indicates that assessments of regimes focus on the extent to which (1) treaties are implemented, (2) compliance with the provisions implemented is achieved, (3) the regime achieves the objectives laid out in the treaty, and (4) the achievement of those objectives actually improves environmental quality and natural resource protection (Jacobson and Weiss 2000, 5). Although implementation, compliance, and effectiveness are distinct phenomena, they are still closely related, with their successes and shortcomings intertwined. Researchers applying this analytical framework have made substantial progress in identifying the conditions under which regime effectiveness is more or less likely to occur. Four sets of factors have been identified as especially noteworthy: variations in regime characteristics, pressures from civic society, extent of free-rider problems, and capacity in developing nations.

The Importance of Regime Characteristics

Stephen D. Krasner's (1983, 1) formulation of international regimes as "principles, norms, rules, and decision-making procedures around which actor expectations converge in a given issue-area" is widely cited as identifying the core elements of regimes. Similarly, Marvin Soroos (1998, 28) defines international environmental regimes as "the combination of international institutions, customary norms and principles, and formal treaty commitments that guide the behavior of states related to a specific subject, project, or region." Research on the formation and functioning of environmental regimes typically conclude that they have made a difference in activities affecting environmental quality and natural resource protection (Keohane and Levy 1996; Haas, Keohane, and Levy 1993; Young 1999, 249). David G. Victor and Eugene B. Skolnikoff's (1999, 18) study of the implementation and effectiveness of international environmental agreements found that although there has been a high degree of compliance with these agreements, that is largely due to the modest requirements they have imposed on participating nations.

Edward L. Miles and his colleagues (2002, 456–57) concluded their study of the effectiveness of environmental regimes with several optimistic findings:

- Most environmental regimes succeed in changing actor behavior in the direction intended.
- Processes of regime formation and implementation can have a significant impact even if they do not produce collective decisions, and this is because governments as well as societies quite often make unilateral adjustments in response to new ideas and information or in anticipation of new regulations.
- Even strongly malignant problems can be solved effectively; the exceptions do not detract from the fact that the overall progress

made in coping with politically malignant problems is higher than
we expected.

- Most regimes tend to grow and become more effective as they
  develop beyond their initial stages.
- Knowledge can be improved through investment in research and
  more effectively transformed into decision processes through the
  design of institutions and processes for dissemination and consen-
  sual interpretation.

They also offer several negative assessments:

- The solutions achieved by and large leave substantial room for
  improvement.
- Some of the overall improvement observed seems to be due to
  fortunate circumstances rather than any feature of the regime
  itself.
- The most fundamental factor intervening is a general growth in
  public demand for and governmental supply of policies for environmental protection, so the success may be very hard to sustain
  in periods with declining public concern.
- Before rejoicing at instances of declining problem malignancy, we
  should realize that the shift is sometimes a consequence of the fact
  that the situation has deteriorated to the point where there is not
  much left to fight over (see whaling).
- In brief, this study provides ample evidence to suggest that we still
  have a long way to go and formidable obstacles to pass before we
  can claim that problems are effectively solved (Miles et al. 2000,
  457–58).

The global environmental regimes that have been successful in promoting implementation and compliance typically share the following
characteristics: (1) norms, rules, principles, and shared commitments to
the preservation of natural resources, the protection of ecosystem health,
and sustainability; (2) a broad cross section of governmental and nongovernmental actors and institutions that come together for collective
action; (3) binding obligations codified in formal agreements that specify
what actions are prohibited and required; and (4) administrative and
other mechanisms to monitor implementation, make available technical

and financial support where needed, enforce obligations, and provide a forum for revisions to the agreements. These four elements seem to capture the essential elements of what is required for regimes to address global environmental challenges effectively. The more developed each of these characteristics is, the more likely the regime will have the capacity to engage with nation-states and other actors to encourage their implementation of and compliance with treaty provisions.

Other scholars studying the effectiveness of regimes have emphasized the importance of shared expectations and common understanding of the causes of problems and their remedies (Low and Gleeson 1998; Orr 1992). Other scholars do not expressly analyze international regimes but emphasize the importance of shared understanding (MacNeill, Winsenium, and Yakushiji 1991; Milbrath 1989; Clark 1989). Forming and maintaining regimes play a fundamentally important role in defining problems, identifying possible solutions, and articulating compelling rationales and reasons that can provoke action. The importance of scientific knowledge and expertise has been the focus of important scholarship that emphasizes the role of epistemic communities—experts whose work comes to the attention of influential policy makers and to the general public and generates demands for actions to remedy the problems identified.

The Critical Role of Civic Society

Characteristics of the actors forming and implementing regimes are also critical to regime effectiveness. The continuing primacy of the principle of national sovereignty in global affairs means that several variables associated with nation-states have significant impact on regime effectiveness. As Karen T. Litfin (1998) and others have indicated, sovereignty is a complex concept, sometimes operating in ways that foster efforts to protect the global environment and sometimes in ways that hinder them. Nation-states, after all, largely retain responsibility for the implementation of international law within their borders. Prior research suggests that the extent to which states enact implementing legislation and effectively enforce provisions is a function of domestic political support for the international effort, the commitment of the government in power and their interest in global leadership, and the capacity of government regulatory agencies to monitor and enforce compliance and enforcement. Implementation includes the actions of a government to put in place regulatory requirements and the efforts of key actors to comply with those requirements.

Many assessments of the effectiveness of regimes focus on the role of environmental NGOs. They argue that many of the issues on the international environmental agenda are there because of the efforts of NGOs and that NGOs have played an indispensable role in designing and implementing effective environmental agreements. Victor and Skolnikoff (1999, 18) concluded that "the most successful efforts to engage stakeholders have been those that have altered the incentives for them to participate— for example, by making useful environmental data available so that public interest groups could participate on an equal footing with private firms and governments." The strength of nongovernmental actors is a critical variable in the prospects for effective regimes. National governments that are hesitant to impose strict requirements on domestic industries and other powerful interests may be compelled to act if there is sufficient demand from environmental advocates. Environmental NGOs play a critical role in developing support for global agreements, for generating commitments from political leaders, and for generating domestic pressure to keep global commitments (Weiss and Jacobson 1998). NGOs that operate on a global scale are particularly important in helping to develop nascent movements in developing countries that can, in turn, pressure their governments to take action. For-profit firms engaged in renewable energy, environmental remediation, conservation, and other "green" enterprises can also play key roles in generating support for implementing global agreements.

Victor and Skolnikoff (1999; also see Victor, Raustiala, and Skolnikoff 1998) also warn that NGOs are rarely in a position to perform independent oversight of compliance efforts because they usually lack the resources to obtain the information required. However, as regulatory regimes begin to embrace market-based approaches to regulation, such as emissions trading, monitoring and enforcement are critical in ensuring that these innovations produce real reductions in emissions and protection for resources. Governments need to have realistic expectations of what NGOs can and cannot do in contributing to the enforcement and, ultimately, effectiveness of global environmental accords. Fostering NGO participation must be combined with strong incentives, such as financial assistance, and sanctions, such as trade penalties for noncompliance.

The great diversity of environmental NGOs and the energy and dedication they bring to international negotiations, global consciousness raising, and monitoring compliance with treaties and agreements are impressive. Their participation in international negotiations has had a major impact on the direction of talks and the agreements fashioned. They have provided strong voices to hold international institutions accountable for the environmental impacts of the projects they fund. They have played a critical role in putting a number of issues on the agenda, such as persistent organic pollutants. They foster sharing information and empowering citizens worldwide. They supply the political pressure necessary to link global obligations with domestic laws and programs. But they are fragmented. There are major divisions between NGOs in the North and South that parallel the differences between the two regions: they have different priorities, they struggle with different problems, and they have greatly uneven resources. Some coalitions have formed, and some groups have broadened their vision to recognize that the interests of the rich and poor are closely intertwined, but as Philip Shabecoff (1996, 73) wrote, "it would take a great leap of faith to speak of a coherent global movement."

The Free-Rider Problem

The problem of free-riders pervade international relations: there are clear advantages for nations to not sign agreements—or sign but not implement them—and then benefit from the international efforts while not bearing the costs. International bodies charged with overseeing the implementation of environmental regimes agencies need to be able to compel the production of reports, possess the technical capacity to assess the data and identify problems, and create effective incentives and sanctions that promote compliance. They also need to be able to assess progress in remedying the problems the regime was created to address and to provide a forum for signatory states to revise agreements as circumstances require (Victor, Raustiala, and Skolnikoff 1998).

A complex of global environmental institutions already exists, including the traditional UN bodies, the UNEP and other agencies, the Global Environment Facility, UN regional economic commissions, regional development banks, regional offices of major UN agencies, and other regional organizations that are part of the UN structure for sustainable development and environmental protection, as well as the World Bank and regional multilateral lending institutions (World Resources

Institute 1994, 225). Yet there is little coordination among these some-times competing organizations, and there is no overarching body to ensure that environmental concerns are given priority at the highest lev-els of policy making. There is, in short, no environmental equivalent to the International Atomic Energy Agency or the World Trade Organiza-tion. Despite the success of the 1992 Earth Summit in drawing attention to environmental and developmental issues, environmental concerns still lack a central place in international relations.

A UN Environment Programme (1997, 2) report argued that "sig-nificant progress" has been made during the past decade "in the realm of institutional developments, international cooperation, public participa-tion, and the emergence of private-sector action." The report highlighted the spread of environmental laws, environmental impact assessments, eco-nomic incentives, and other policy efforts among states as well as the development of cleaner, less-polluting production processes and tech-nologies in the private sector. These innovations, it argued, resulted in several countries reporting "marked progress in curbing environmental pollution and slowing the rate of resource degradation as well as reduc-ing the intensity of resource use." However, the report also concluded that "from a global perspective, the environment has continued to degrade during the past decade, and significant environmental problems remain deeply embedded in the socio-economic fabric of nations in all regions. Progress towards a global sustainable future is just too slow." The report found that a "sense of urgency is lacking" as are the financial resources and the "political will" to reduce environmental degradation and protect natural resources. There is a "general lack of sustained inter-est in global and long-term environmental issues," global "governance structures and environmental solidarity remain too weak to make progress a world-wide reality," and, consequently, the "gap between what has been done thus far and what is realistically needed is widening" (UNEP 1997, 3).

Yet innovative and important examples of progress in regime gover-nance exist. One very promising institutional development has been the establishment of the Global Environment Fund (GEF), created to chan-nel funds to the developing countries in order to help them implement programs to reduce pressure on global ecosystems (Global Environment Facility n.d.). As part of the 1990 London amendments to the Montreal Protocol on reducing ozone-depleting emissions, the industrialized countries agreed to pay developing countries' "incremental" costs of compliance with the Protocol. These costs are defined as the expenses for developing alternatives to ozone-depleting substances beyond what these countries would otherwise spend to modernize their economies (French 1997, 162–65). A US$240 million Interim Multilateral Fund was created on the basis of early estimates for these costs. The World Bank administers the trust fund; UNEP, relying on an international Scientific and Technical Advisory Panel, provides technical and scientific assistance in identifying and selecting projects; and the UN Development Program (UNDP) coordinates the financing and manages technical assistance and pre-project preparations. In 1992 the states' parties to the ozone regime agreed to make the Multilateral Fund permanent. Between 1990 and 1996 the Fund disbursed US$540 million to ninety-nine countries for some 1,300 projects (French 1997, 162–63). In December 1999 the parties to the Montreal Protocol agreed to spend US$440 million between 2000 and 2002 for a new round of projects to convert refrigerators, air conditioners, and other consumer goods and industrial processes in developing nations from halons and CFCs. By 2000 the multilateral fund had provided some US$1 billion in aid to 110 countries since 1991 (International Environment 1999, 978). Grants typically go to private sector parties for projects like recycling CFCs, monitoring greenhouse gas emissions, and protecting biodiversity (Global Environment Facility n.d.).

This is not to suggest, however, that the GEF has not had problems of its own. Both the Climate Change and Biodiversity Conventions require that funding mechanisms be accountable to all parties and include an equitable and balanced system of representation and governance. Unfortunately, these features have not been enough to ensure that the projects being funded address the environment and development priorities of the developing world (World Resources Institute 1995). One study of the GEF argued that the Fund initially enjoyed widespread support because there was a strong commitment to the general idea of assisting the developing countries, but consensus collapsed into conflict when GEF officials made specific decisions regarding implementation. As a result, during the pilot phase, the GEF failed to have an impact on the environmental policies of the developing countries (Fairman 1996). The Montreal Protocol Multilateral Fund has operated more smoothly, but project implementation has been slow, as has been progress in reducing emissions in the developing countries (DeSombre and Kauffman 1996). The GEF projects play a key role in ecologically sustainable development, but its funding is miniscule in light of other spending, such as private investments in the developing countries.

Capacity Limitations in the Developing World

Effective governing institutions in nation-states, particularly in the developing world, are just as important as global institutions in building effective regimes. The World Bank's investments in building the institutional capacity of governments promise to have long-term benefits because they give those countries the tools to design and implement programs effectively that will help them meet international obligations and ensure economic activity is environmentally sustainable. Unfortunately, these efforts face tremendous barriers (Bryner 1997). Many developing countries lack the government organizational infrastructure to develop effective regulatory programs, traditions, and cultures of compliance with regulatory requirements, or the scientific infrastructure needed to examine the problems they confront. Developing nations must address a whole range of obstacles to effective national governance, including rapid population growth, extreme disparities of income and wealth, public- and private-sector corruption, and inadequate technical and managerial standards of competence (Miller 1991, 46.).

The World Bank and GEF projects aimed at reinforcing institutional capacity for environmental protection projects are important responses to these problems in the South, but the level of funding provided is not sufficient to help build effective governing institutions. Furthermore, even if spending increases, the political instability that has engulfed so many areas prevents progress in environmental protection and development. Interstate wars, internal conflicts, and other forms of military activity also pose tremendous environmental challenges. Natural disasters further hinder effective programs (Perlez 1991).

Agenda 21, one of the agreements to come out of the 1992 Earth Summit in Rio de Janeiro, created an expectation that the North-South partnership that is critical to building effective regimes would develop. A key question for both the North and South, then, is whether that partnership has been firmly established. The first high-level opportunity to assess developments came in June 1997, when the UN General Assembly convened its Special Session to Review Implementation of Agenda

21 (UNGASS). It heard assessments of the progress made toward Agenda 21 by 197 heads of states or government, cabinet-level ministers, and UN Representatives. The Programme for the Further Implementation of Agenda 21 that was adopted at the end of the Special Session painted a pessimistic picture of the lack of progress in achieving the Agenda's goals. It noted that globalization has accelerated, but its impact has been uneven because foreign direct investment and world trade have increased in only a limited number of developing countries, whereas many countries continue to be plagued by foreign debt and receive little assistance. It also indicated that poverty has prevented developing countries from participating in and benefiting from the global economy and that they require assistance to help them meet basic needs. The total number of poor people in the world has increased since the Rio meeting, and the gap between the wealthy and poor countries "has grown rapidly in recent years" (UN General Assembly 1997a).

Furthermore, whereas some countries have reduced emissions of pollutants and resource use, and population growth rates have declined in most areas; overall, global environmental conditions have worsened and "significant environmental problems remain deeply embedded in the socio-economic fabric of countries in all regions." Persistent poverty continues to contribute to ecological decline and threats to fragile ecosystems, and in many developing countries foreign debt remains "a major constraint on achieving sustainable development" (UN General Assembly 1997a, paragraphs 17–20). In sum, the state of the global environment "has continued to deteriorate . . . and significant problems remain deeply embedded in the socio-economic fabric of countries in all regions. . . . Overall trends remain unsustainable. As a result, increasing levels of pollution threaten to exceed the capacity of the global environment to absorb them, increasing the potential obstacles to economic and social development in developing countries" (UN General Assembly 1997a, paragraphs 17–20).

The UNGASS identified a number of issues requiring urgent attention and pressed for the "invigoration of a genuine new global partnership, taking into account the special needs and priorities of developing countries" (UN General Assembly 1997b). The list of issues to be addressed is daunting: integrate economic, social, and environmental objectives in national policies; promote a dynamic global economy "favourable to all countries"; eradicate poverty; expand access to social services; change unsustainable consumption and production patterns;

make trade and the environment "mutually supportive"; further promote the decline in population growth rates; enable all people to "achieve a higher level of health and well-being"; and improve living conditions throughout the world (UN General Assembly 1997b, 23–32). It reaffirmed the long-standing UN goal that industrial states should devote 7 percent of their gross domestic product to Official Development Assistance to poor countries, encourage increased private investment and foreign debt reduction in developing countries, and call for more transparency regarding subsidies, increased transfer of environmentally sound technologies to developing countries, and continued efforts to build their capacity for effective policy making (UN General Assembly 1997b, paragraphs 76–115). UNGASS agreed to again review progress in the implementation of Agenda 21 in the year 2002 (UN General Assembly 1997b, paragraph 137).

Comparing the 1997 UNGASS with the 1992 Earth Summit provides one indicator of the very limited success of Agenda 21 in reshaping discourses of economic growth and environmental preservation. The problems confronting the delegates to the 1992 Rio conference largely resurfaced in the 1997 meeting. In 1997 there was still little discussion of regulating private capital flows, corporate behavior, or the impact of trade on environmental quality. On the positive side, there was more discussion and monitoring of concrete indicators of reproductive health care as well as consumption and production patterns. The 1997 meeting was a frank assessment of the lack of progress rather than an attempt to "paper over the cracks in the celebrated 'global partnership' for sustainable development and pretend that things are better than they are" (IISD 1997). Nevertheless, the question of funding the implementation of Agenda 21 in the developing countries seemed as vexing in 1997 as it was five years earlier. The UN meeting reminded global leaders of the idea of sustainable development, but it seemed to lack any ability to identify strategic plans or generate commitments to specific actions. UN documents dutifully catalogued the myriad of global environmental challenges but failed to take on the international trade and private investment decisions—the dominant forces in economic activity and development—and was unable to focus attention on a limited set of actions that deserve priority or even provide some direction to and coordination of the activities that are undertaken under the auspices of the United Nations. Most troubling was the lack of direction for the future: the "question dominating debate at UNGASS," according to one observer, was "where to go from here?" (IISD 1997).

Yet creating and implementing international environmental and natural resource (ENR) regimes *have* made a difference in fostering the capacity of governments and nongovernmental actors to devise solutions to global environmental threats. When international ENR regimes are assessed in terms of how much progress has been made in global environmental institutional building over the past three decades, a quite positive picture emerges, which bodes cautious optimism about the future. Yet when these regimes are assessed from the more important perspective of their contributions to establishing sustainable patterns of economic activity, a decidedly different picture emerges. Their capacity to help preserve for future generations at least the same level of natural resources and environmental quality required for them to meet their needs as enjoyed by current generations is still unproven. Hence, the future development and performance of international regime management will be driven and conditioned by the extent to which "ecological sustainability" becomes the conceptual basis for a new round of global environmental accords and regimes. This will depend, in turn, on the extent to which a sense of community develops at the national and international levels, an ethic that has proven elusive thus far.

Sovereignty poses a perplexing paradox. We need to strengthen sovereignty as well as limit it. That is, we need to strengthen the governing capacity of nation-states but also create incentives for them to use their sovereignty in the service of collective goals. For now, at least, there is no substitute for sovereignty, and strong, effective governments are needed. But sovereignty is also used by national leaders to insulate themselves from global responsibilities. New institutions are needed that can develop and carry out programs that help bring about changes in human behavior and to coordinate efforts to deal with cross-cutting problems. International institutions tend to focus on single problems, but solutions to those problems intersect. Increasing the production of biofuels to reduce energy from fossil fuels, for example, may threaten the food security of poor nations. Planting forest plantations to sequester carbon dioxide from energy emissions may clash with efforts to protect biodiversity (Walker et al. 2009, 1345).

Institutions are needed that create incentives to cooperate and that can impose effective sanctions for noncompliance. Countries need to see that they are better off cooperating than not. The most prominent example of global cooperation is the World Trade Organization. Most countries have decided that the benefits of reduced trade barriers are worth the cost of submitting to WTO authority. Even when a country faces restrictions in response to unfair trade practices, they typically remain in the WTO because the benefits of continued participation outweigh those of withdrawal (Walker et al. 2009, 1346).

Beyond Self-Interest

Despite the creation of international environmental regimes, only a very modest set of environmental policies are in effect and being implemented. Why is there so little global action to combat these clear global environmental threats? It is primarily, I believe, because the evidence of environmental crises is largely invisible in the wealthy world. Some environmental conditions, such as urban air pollution, have improved. There are extensive statutes, regulations, and agencies in place that may give the appearance to many that environmental problems are under control. But for the most part, the wealthy world is insulated from global environmental stresses. As long as that remains true—that people in the United States and other developed nations believe that their lives are sustainable and, implicitly, that technological advances will ensure they are able to maintain their standard of living in the future—then there will be insufficient support for global environmental action. The threats of environmental crises simply don't appear to be immediate threats in developed countries, and uncertainty about the timing, scope, and distribution of environmental consequences makes accurately identifying the threats all the more complicated.

As a result, it is not clear what is in the self-interest of nations. Is it to be a free-rider, letting other countries take the expensive actions that benefit everyone? Is it to be a global leader in taking on global environmental threats? Is it to focus on border or regional issues that address immediate, identifiable threats but leave longer-term problems for the next administration? Political leadership, massive educational and media campaigns, and environmental activism may make marginal changes in raising awareness about the global environmental predicament and provoke modest actions, but we will not likely see a dramatic policy response until global problems actually threaten those in the wealthy world. Once that occurs, predicting what will happen is difficult because such a crisis of resources and environmental quality has never occurred in recorded history. Perhaps the mobilization of the Allies during World War II provides a model: countries will unite to fight a common enemy. But it may be more likely that scarce resources will cause them to compete for those resources, seeking to get as much as they can individually rather than cooperate to share shortages. Does all this mean that the only rational response is to abandon efforts and cooperation? Given the magnitude of the threats, small, incremental steps that may be able to delay or soften some of the greatest impacts are important and lay the foundation for a new generation of more effective institutions that may be formed in the midst of crisis.

As rational actors, nation-states are primarily oriented toward self-preservation, the protection of autonomy, and securing national well-being. Being actively engaged in international environmental protection agreements is certainly within the scope of self-interest. The more evidence that accumulates about global environmental threats and the more national leaders come to understand the nature of these threats, the more they will come to see that it is in their interest to join collective efforts. The more those efforts move forward, the greater the pressure on recalcitrant states to join. The problem with a reliance on self-interest, however, is that it is typically a short-term calculation: immediate costs and benefits dominate over those in the future. So even enlightened self-interest has not been—nor will likely be—enough to prompt preventative or precautionary action. The political debate over international environmental policy making can begin with an appeal to self-interest, but more is needed. Because self-interest is such a powerful, dominant force, recognizing that it is not enough to ensure collective action suggests that we are locked into a future of environmental decline. That is certainly the trajectory we are on, and there is little to suggest that we are going to alter course. But there is hope that, at least at the margins, we can reduce the magnitude of adverse environmental impacts.

While presuming the primacy of self-interest, it is also reasonable to believe that ideas matter because the way in which we frame environmental issues can have an impact on definitions of self-interest and on political action. The balance of this book is dedicated to that proposition. There are ideas that have already prompted considerable global activity and can serve as the basis for continued progress toward the goal of global environmental protection. Three propositions are particularly important and are the subject of succeeding chapters. First, many environmental problems can be effectively remedied through public policies in pursuit of true cost prices. Although many blame capitalism for global environmental problems, numerous effective actions to reduce these threats can be pursued in ways that take into account capitalism's strengths. Markets are widely viewed as central to the economic well-being of nations, but they require effective government intervention to make sure they work well, especially when ensuring that all of the costs of producing and distributing goods and services are included in the prices charged so producers and consumers can make ecologically sound choices.

Second, the principles of equality, justice, and fairness that are at the heart of Western political culture compel those nations to consider that ecological decline around the world is not just a threat to their self-interest but also to their most important commitments. If Western societies are interested in perpetuating their way of life and their fundamental values, they will necessarily have to confront and decide how to respond to the environmental injustices produced by the global economy.

These two concerns—making markets work in ways that ensure they produce the benefits they promise and the importance of a commitment to justice and fairness—suggest the third key idea to be debated: how to integrate developing countries into global markets. Integrating developing countries more fully into global markets is in the interest of the wealthy countries, but there are different ways in which that can take place—with different environmental consequences—and the future well-being of the planet requires a strong commitment to ecologically sustainable development.

Chapter Three
CAPITALISM AND THE CHALLENGE OF MAKING MARKETS WORK

Capitalism is at the root of global environmental crises in two ways. First, its emphasis on fostering economic growth driven by ever-increasing consumption encourages whole societies to adopt unsustainable lifestyles, and second, its emphasis on minimizing costs tempts firms and households to externalize the costs of pollution and resource depletion rather than including them in the prices of goods and services. Poorly regulated markets in natural resources as well as production based on the untamed exploitation of degradable ecosystems have damaged forests, wetlands, grasslands, water bodies, and airsheds around the world. Greenhouse gases accumulate because emitters are not required to include the cost of reducing them or the costs of adapting to their consequences in prices of the goods and services that generate them. The environmental consequences of producing and using energy are simply ignored in an effort to keep energy prices as low as possible. Supplying water in dry areas is almost always subsidized for political reasons and in ways that mask the true cost of supplying water. Biodiversity is lost because it is largely not valued in decisions about developing resources or expanding human developments.

Yet harnessing competitive markets to the task of protecting the ecosystems on which life depends is essential. Decisions about protecting specific regions and ecosystem functions require trade-offs, and markets are widely recognized as providing a very effective and efficient mechanism for making trade-offs between competing allocations of resources and effort. However, effective environmental protection requires that prices charged for goods reflect the true costs of producing, using, and disposing of them so that the real costs of alternatives can be compared. But individual economic actors have strong incentives to lower their own costs by externalizing those costs. And others onto whom those costs are passed may not be able to prevent the absorption of those costs individually. Thus, making markets contribute to environmental sustainability requires very effective government to limit cost externalization and make sure comparisons reflect real costs. Making markets work through regulatory programs that make consumption of goods reflect true costs will not solve all environmental problems, but it would make a dramatic difference in environmental quality.

This is an area where liberals and conservatives should be able to find some common ground, but many advocates of markets believe that markets function best when government regulation is minimized. The collapse of financial markets in 2007 and 2008, however, and the recession of 2008–2009 generated a major debate about the role that governments need to play in regulating markets. This chapter makes the case that effective and efficient markets have always required public policies to ensure those benefits. It then discusses the political opposition to government regulation and how overcoming this opposition is central to developing broader support for government regulation to protect environmental quality through markets that reflect true costs. Capitalism as practiced today drives global environmental problems, but it also contains at least a partial solution to them if cost externalities are internalized.

The economic policies governments have traditionally pursued are essential elements of a political economy of markets, and they illustrate how capitalism is inextricably intertwined with government. Rather than a politics-markets or government-business dichotomy, in a long historical or functional sense, markets are best understood as an organic part of the state. When markets are treated institutionally and historically, we realize that we are not looking at an economy but at the *economic expression of a government*. It is no paradox or mystery that "liberal democracy has arisen only in nations that are market-oriented" (Lindblom 1977, 5). Although the discussion below focuses primarily on politics and markets in the United States—because it is the leading capitalist nation—comparative examples will also be used to help broaden the analysis.

Making Markets Work: Policy Preconditions for Markets

Economies depend on a variety of public policies to ensure that markets actually produce the important and valuable benefits they promise, such as securing the stability and public order required for economic activity to flourish and guaranteeing the health of the natural environment on which economic activity depends. Capitalism, therefore, is inescapably dependent on institutions of government to provide these functional prerequisites of markets. Many of these functions are so taken for granted today that they are not recognized as the results of public policies or the exercise of political authority. Theodore Lowi (1999) identified the key functions of government in a capitalist economy:

- Securing law and order so that the marketing, production, and distribution of goods and services can occur in a stable environment
- Creating and enforcing private property rights by providing courts and other mechanisms to define and vindicate rights
- Enforcing contracts to create an expectation that contracts will be protected
- Ensuring fair competition by enforcing antitrust policies
- Establishing currency and credit for the efficient conduct of commerce
- Providing for the conveyance of the public domain to private ownership
- Providing public goods such as communications and transportation infrastructure and national defense
- Allocating responsibility for injury and dependency and indemnifying injuries
- Preventing externalities that harm third parties or those that are not part of market transactions
- Regulating production and distribution so that prices include true costs
- Facilitating economic activity through licensing of professions and corporations
- Developing basic workplace skills through compulsory education
- Reducing risk by indemnifying producers and sellers of products against responsibility for at least some of the products they produce and sell

Several of these governmental foundations of the economy deserve more emphasis in order to understand how an economy *is* government. First and most obvious is the provision of law and order, a prerequisite for commerce as well as every other aspect of life. In this, provisions for contract enforcement are critical. If there is a dispute over the terms of a contract and a court decides who wins, the prevailing party can appeal to the powers of government to enforce decisions (Lowi n.d., 8).

Property represents all the things the state does to permit individuals to call something their own and enforce those claims. Two kinds of property regulation make clear its public character. First, eminent domain is the right of government to take property for a public use. We regulate eminent domain through constitutional procedures, but the right of the state to take property is widely accepted. Second, bankruptcy is another example of how capitalism depends on public policy for its regulation. Just as there are legal procedures for acquiring and exchanging property, there are procedures for liquidating it. Property used in economic enterprise is private as long as the enterprise is successful. As soon as it fails, the property becomes public, either permanently or temporarily, through the process of receivership.

Other examples of property regulation include licensing, which is permission from the government to undertake a particular type of activity. Corporations are themselves licensees. A corporate charter is a public document granting privileges such as limited liability and the right to sue and be sued. The corporate charter was once used as a mechanism for regulating corporations, and this practice could be revived if lawmakers so chose. Furthermore, much of what is considered property is based on licenses or other forms of governmentally granted privileges. Although much of the value of economic goods is attributable to exchange in the marketplace, the artificial restrictions of governmentally granted privileges that raise the value and price of certain goods and services is also a significant source of exchange value (Lowi n.d., 11).

Providing "social overhead capital," such as currency, transportation infrastructure, and communication systems, is another precondition for markets. Not all of it is provided by government policy, but most is because these are widely viewed as "public goods." Providing for human capital is another policy precondition for markets. Because this is now largely seen in the United States as a responsibility of schools, governments here and elsewhere have enacted laws protecting and encouraging apprenticeship and other forms of on-the-job training (Lowi n.d., 12).

A final example of the role of public policy preconditions for markets is provisions for regulating the consequences of risk. No rational person would sell a good or render a service if he or she had to be personally responsible for all its uses and consequences. Modern capitalism seems impossible without tort law and a system for determining who is responsible when things go wrong. Means have to be devised to determine who shall be responsible. Shall it be the seller or the victim? Shall responsibility be apportioned or absolute? How do we deal with negligence and contributory negligence? Doctrines such as contributory negligence have often put the government on the side of business rather than employees or consumers, but this favoritism has been limited by court rulings and statutes, thus giving more protection to consumers and employees. The shift from attributing blame proportionate to the contribution to indemnifying injury rather than determining blame or cause led to replacing tort law in many areas with insurance. An increasing share of risk indemnification over the past half century has been provided by Social Security, disability, and related state and federal policies (Lowi n.d., 13). Lowi argues that the socialization of risk

> is a bundle of government policies that combine all three of the approaches that we have taken historically to the problem of risk: (1) policies providing for the allocation of responsibility for injury; (2) policies providing for indemnification of injury, with or without attribution of fault; and (3) policies whose goal is the relative and absolute reduction of risk. All three of them are vital preconditions for the conduct of a market economy (Lowi n.d., 14).

The notion of the socialization of risk ties together some fundamental preconditions of our contemporary economic system. It also provides an insight into the changes in the uses of the state that are bringing the United States and other countries of the West into an entirely new system, without revolution—indeed, without notice.

In sum, there is no such thing as an economy; there is only *political economy.* The functional prerequisites of the market economy are provided by laws, policies, programs, and other institutionalized governmental activity. In the United States, the constitutionally mandated scheme of federalism meant that states were responsible for enacting laws that provided the prerequisites for a market economy, and the existence of few national policies caused many Americans to mistakenly believe that, in the past, business was free from governmental regulation and interference. Even today states in the United States continue to provide most of the legal prerequisites of capitalism, despite the tremendous growth of

federal power since the 1930s. In the other advanced democratic industrialized nations, governments play the same role in providing for capitalism and markets.

Although much economic theory is based firmly on a political
economy of unfettered markets, some economists have recognized the
importance of government in making markets work. In his study of the
historical evolution of markets, John McMillan made a strong case for
them, arguing that "people are ingenious at finding ways to make
exchanges that bring mutual gains." However, he also contended that
markets accomplish their goals "only if they are well structured. Any successful economy has an array of devices and procedures to enable markets to work smoothly." McMillan identified five characteristics of good
markets:

- Information flows smoothly,
- Property rights are protected,
- People can be trusted to live up to their promises,
- Side effects on third parties are curtailed, and
- Competition is fostered (McMillan 2002, ix–x).

The design of markets is shared between two actors: the market participants themselves, who, through trial and error, find better ways to trans-
act their business and pursue their interests, and government, which provides common regulations through public policies (McMillan 2002,
11–12). Though innovations rise from the bottom up, which means that
"spontaneous evolution is the main driver of markets," markets need the
help of government "to reach their full potential" (McMillan 2002, x).

Markets involve voluntary exchange in which either party can veto
the agreement by which goods and services are bought and sold. Yet even
in a market economy country, most transactions do not occur within a
market. Three areas of economic activity together dwarf market exchanges:
unpaid work inside households, government spending, and transactions
within corporations. But all this activity takes place within the context of
a market economy and is affected by its norms (McMillan 2002, 6–7).
Although markets are decentralized and no one is really in charge of them,
the design of markets is critical in providing the context in which free
decision making, which is at the heart of markets, takes place. McMillan
described the task this way:

Market design consists of the mechanisms that organize buying and selling; channels for the flow of information; state-set laws and regulations that define property rights and sustain contracting; and the market's culture, its self-regulating norms, codes, and conventions governing behavior. While the design does not control what happens in the market—as already noted, free decision making is key—it shapes and supports the process of transacting (McMillan 2002, 9).

For McMillan, the key questions are how much of the economy should be left to markets and what should be the role of the state in the economy? "The collapse of central planning is sometimes held up as proof that the government should stay right out of the economy," he wrote. "This is a non sequitur. Observing that something is not black, we are not impelled to infer it must be white. That governments often fail does not prove the ideal state is the minimal state. To frame the choice as planning versus completely free markets is oversimple" (McMillan 2002, 166).

The importance of state regulation to the effective functioning of markets was demonstrated during the 2007–2008 financial crisis and ensuing recession. The financial crisis stemmed from the inability of markets to avoid or contain speculative bubbles. Pursuit of high profits through investments in subprime mortgages, complex forms of credit-default swaps, and other financial derivatives meant that financial markets failed to perform their basic functions of managing risk, allocating capital, and keeping the economy as a whole from racking up excessive debt (Stiglitz 2009). Some of these activities occurred outside the reach of prevailing banking regulations, whereas others reemerged as financial and banking regulations that were adopted to avoid bubbles after the Great Depression of the 1930s were repealed by a new generation of policy makers. Enticed by the ideology of laissez-faire economics, political elites—particularly in Britain and the United States—ignored both historical experience and others' practical criticisms of laissez-faire in order to pursue their vision, which also had the effect of further reinforcing the position of conservative political leaders and corporate executives (Cassidy 2009).

The experience of China and Russia during the past two decades is instructive for understanding the roles of markets and public policy in the economy. Russia moved rapidly to markets and democracy, including privatizing companies before the necessary market structure was in place, and the result was economic decline. Many of these companies were large, an artifact of the Soviet belief that bigger firms were better, so these companies were still monopolies after privatization, operating without checks or competitive pressures from other firms. As McMillan noted, "Russia's shock therapy created an institutional vacuum. Private owner-ship matters, but not enough to produce efficient firms. Also needed are functioning product and financial markets. Shock therapy privatized the firms before the market support they needed had time to develop. It demolished the old institutions and it took years to build the new ones" (McMillan 2002, 203).

China, in contrast, instituted reforms gradually, without major dem-ocratic reforms and with major government involvement in the econ-omy. China's economy is expected to become the world's largest by 2030:

> Rather than privatizing its state-owned firms, China left them under state control, doing little privatization until the late 1990s. . . . Initially highly inefficient, the state firms significantly improved their produc-tivity in response to a range of incentives. The government allowed firms to retain some of their profits, which were used to fund worker bonuses, benefits such as housing and health care, and investment in new plant and equipment. Managers' pay came to be based on their firm's performance. . . . By the end of the 1980s the state firms were much less inefficient than they used to be, and they contributed to China's growth. . . . Instead of privatization, China fostered the forma-tion of new firms. (McMillan 2002, 205)

The intersection of politics and markets is illuminated through empirical inquiry. The role of government in successful economies is apparent, and the lack of effective governance in unsuccessful economies is also clear: "The best way to understand the interaction of state and market is not to debate it in the abstract but to examine how real economies with varying degrees of government intervention actually work. Whether intervention is warranted, and by how much, is best decided case by case. It requires looking into the details of the specific market, while taking into account any distortions the government's actions would bring." Both liberal and conservative assumptions and val-ues seem relevant. "Economic growth is good for the poor," Macmillan wrote, going on to state that "the incomes of the poor usually rise when incomes rise overall. . . . On the other hand, the growth studies show that equality is good for growth; countries with a more equal distribution of income tend to grow faster than less equal countries." (McMillan 2002, 226–27). In sum, "when markets are well designed—but only then—we can rely on Adam Smith's invisible hand to work, harnessing dispersed information, coordinating the economy, and creating gains from trade" (McMillan 2002, 228).

Another economist, Ha-Joon Chang, concluded from his analysis that, in every case studied, wealthy countries attained prosperity, through protectionist policies and other governmental interventions in the economy. For example, in the 1950s South Korea was widely considered to be a basket case. A USAID report even called it a bottomless pit. By 1961 the per capital annual income in South Korea was US$82, half that of the average citizen of Ghana and similar to that of the average citizen of Mozambique. Forty years later, however, it was one of the wealthiest countries in the world and a leading center of technological innovation. South Korea was a successful exporter of simple garments and cheap electronics not because it was committed to free trade but because it knew that it had to earn hard currencies to pay for the foreign technologies and machinery it needed to develop more sophisticated industries. The Korean government, therefore, mandated tariff protection and subsidies, and did so not to protect Korean firms from international competition forever "but to give them time to prepare to compete in world markets. As Chang pointed out, "Practically *all* of today's developed countries, including Britain and the United States, the supposed homes of the free market and free trade, have become rich on the basis of policy recipes that go against the orthodoxy of neo-liberal economics" (Chang 2008, 15). The four emerging Asian economies—China, Indonesia, South Korea, and Singapore—continued to benefit from effective policies that shaped their participation in global markets during the 2008–2009 recession. During the first part of 2009 their economies grew by an average annualized rate of more than 10 percent, whereas the G-7 countries' economies were contracting at an annualized rate of 3.5 percent ("Asia—An astonishing rebound" 2009).

Chang traces the evolution of liberal economics from the eighteenth-century views of Adam Smith and his followers to the neoclassical economics that emerged in the 1960s and within two decades became economic orthodoxy. For Adam Smith and his generation, competition in the free market unconstrained by government is the best way to produce wealth because in their experience government intervention generally worked to restrict new entrants into a market and, hence, reduce the economy. The neoclassical propositions then went further in removing government from the economy. Chang noted that

> The core neo-liberal agenda of deregulation, privatization, and the opening up of international trade and investment has remained the same since the 1980s. . . . The neo-liberal agenda has been pushed by an alliance of rich country governments led by the U.S. and mediated by the 'Unholy Trinity' of international economic organizations that they largely control—the International Monetary Fund, the World Bank, and the World Trade Organization. (Chang 2008, 13)

Chang argued that free trade "is *not* the best path to economic development. Trade helps economic development only when the country employs a mixture of protection and open trade, constantly adjusting it according to its changing needs and capabilities" (Chang 2008, 83). Thus, the most successful economies are pragmatically managed. State-owned enterprises, for example, may work very well in situations of natural monopolies or are useful in jump-starting companies' participation in markets (Chang 2008, 113). During the 1960s and 1970s, when developing countries were pursuing protectionist policies and governments intervened in their economies, their per capita incomes grew by an average of 3.0 percent a year. In contrast, since the neoliberal policies were instituted in the 1980s, growth has been 1.7 percent a year (per capita income in the rich countries also fell during these years, but not as far because the decline moved from 3.2 percent to 2.1 percent a year). The gap, however, is actually wider because the developing country figures include China and India, which have largely refused to embrace neoliberal policies. In 1980 those two countries generated only 12 percent of the total developing country income, but their share had grown to 30 percent by 2000. Excluding India and China means the average growth rate of developing countries was even lower since the 1980s (Chang 2008, 27).

Why do wealthy countries deny their own history of governmental intervention in capitalism? In 1841 a German economist criticized Great Britain for preaching free trade to others, despite its history of protectionism: "It is a very common clever device that when anyone has attained the summit of greatness, he kicks away the ladder by which he has climbed up, in order to capture larger shares of the latter's markets and to pre-empt the emergence of possible competitors" (quoted in Chang 2008, 16). The wealthy countries have "rewritten their own histories to make them more consistent with how they see themselves today, rather than as they really were." The result is that many Bad Samaritans, as he calls them, are recommending to poor countries free trade and free-market policies in the honest but mistaken belief that those are the routes their own countries took in the past to become rich. In recounting the economic history and contemporary experience of the United States, the United Kingdom, South Korea, and other economic powerhouses, however, Chang concluded that, "free trade reduces freedom of choice for poor counties." He also argued, against neoliberal tenets of privatization and uncontrolled capital flows, that "keeping foreign companies out may be good for [poor countries] in the long run" and that "some of the world's best firms are owned and run by the state" (Chang 2008, 16–18).

Corruption is a serious problem in many developing countries, but it is used by free marketers to explain why neoliberal policies have failed and to reject a role for government in regulating markets. But, Chang argued, corruption and patronage flourished during periods of great economic growth in Britain, France, and America. Electoral fraud and vote buying characterized American elections well into the twentieth century. If a bribe was given and that money was then spent on another project that was at least as productive as how it might otherwise have been spent, then the corruption redistributed wealth but did not reduce growth. Corrupt government officials may even be more crafty investors than some unskilled capitalists, and corruption can actually result in higher economic growth. However, corruption is a problem whenever the diverted funds are siphoned off to foreign private bank accounts, as often happens. In those instances, corruption means a flow of money out of the country, with adverse consequences for growth. Thus, the impact of corruption on growth depends on what kind of corruption is taking place. Chang stated, "That is why we observe such vast differences across countries in terms of the relationship between corruption and economic performance" (Chang, 2008, 166). He went on to argue that

> Markets are political constructs in so far as all property rights and other rights that underpin them have political origin. . . . The political origins of economic rights can be seen in the fact that many of them that are seen as natural today were hotly contested politically in the past—

examples include the right to own ideas (not accepted by many before the introduction of intellectual property rights in the 19th century) and the right not to have to work when young (denied to many poor children). When these rights were still politically contested, there were plenty of "economic" arguments as to why honouring them was incompatible with the free market. (Chang 2008, 175–76)

The Politics of Antiregulatory Policies

Anyone advocating a better balance between markets and government faces an uphill struggle in countries where neoclassical economic prescriptions are well entrenched. The strength of antiregulatory sentiment is particularly intense in the United States, where decades of antigovernment rhetoric have distorted public understanding about the central role of government in making markets work well. Government regulation has become a wedge issue, used by Republicans to generate campaign contributions from business owners and investors who seek to maximize profits by minimizing policies aimed at making markets work. Rather than befriending markets and seeking to find ways for public policies to contribute to well-functioning markets, conservatives have usually tried to undermine the very policies on which markets depend. Such individual undermining is rational and expected, as those with political and economic resources seek to insulate themselves from the competitive pressures and from the demands for the true-cost accounting that characterizes efficient markets. For individual firms, maximizing profits means reducing competition, externalizing as many costs as possible, and escaping the discipline that comes from well-functioning markets.

Free-market ideology undermines government regulation of markets by arguing that government decisions are dominated by inefficient, rent-seeking behavior. For decades, strategies of stigmatization have included advocating deregulation so as to reduce government licensing and control of economic activity; promoting privatizing provisions of services that have traditionally been seen as governmental functions, such as producing energy and operating prisons; and seeking devolution of regulatory power to local governments (Lowi 1998, 6–7). Each of these strategies plays a distinct role in undermining government regulation of markets; together they amount to a rejection of all government participation in the economy.

Deregulation

In the United States the conservative backlash against regulation that began during the Ford administration and took a firm grip in the Reagan years was rooted in two distinct arguments about markets. Some deregulation advocates did not care about well-functioning markets; they simply regarded government regulation as an obstacle to increasing their own profits. A second group believed that regulations were usually so flawed that the economy was better off with less regulation. Conservatives found several ways to slow down regulatory activity without directly amending environmental or other laws. They did so by imposing generic requirements on the regulatory agencies, such as cost-benefit analysis and paperwork reduction requirements. Recent presidents have issued a series of executive orders aimed at specifying when and how agencies are to take into account and balance the costs and benefits of the actions they propose.[1] Although these efforts have been motivated by a variety of goals, such as reducing the cost of compliance with regulations in order to foster economic growth, increasing the cost-effectiveness of regulations so that benefits are maximized, and ensuring that agency actions are consistent with administration policy objectives, the net effect is to slow down the process.

The regulatory process was further politicized in January 2007 when the George W. Bush administration issued an executive order that required each federal agency to establish a regulatory policy office headed by a political appointee to oversee the rule-making process. The purpose of the change was to strengthen the power of the White House to assess the costs and benefits of proposed rules and to ensure that these rules are consistent with the president's policy priorities. The order ensured that political appointees, rather than career civil servants, served as regulatory gatekeepers. The order also required agencies to identify the "specific market failure" that required a regulatory response and required agencies to give the White House an opportunity to review "any significant guidance documents" before they are issued. The Office of Management and Budget's general counsel described the order as a "classic good-government measure that will make federal agencies more open and accountable." Business groups lauded it as having the potential to reduce the burden of federal regulations; consumer, labor, and environmental groups said it gave too much control to the White House and would reduce the ability of agencies to protect the public (Pear 2007).

Privatization

Privatization is a different policy principle, but it serves the same purposes as deregulation in a globalizing era. There is definitely a genuine
commitment to privatization of many hitherto publicly owned or mixed
public/private enterprises that undertake to produce goods and services
for consumers. Of equal importance is the more ideological use of privatization rhetoric to stigmatize government itself. Both of these goals
are quite real, and the latter can be fulfilled even as the former moves
along slowly.

Throughout Europe and industrialized Asia, state-centered economic policies led the impressively successful economic growth of the
1960s, 1970s, and 1980s. But beginning in the latter part of the 1980s
there was a significant switch to privatization, albeit in varying degrees
from country to country. The United Kingdom, led by Margaret
Thatcher, led the way, but policy makers all over the world followed her
lead. Socialist French President François Mitterand reversed many of his
socialist or social democratic policies. Liberal Tony Blair continued privatization through the "Third Way," which was likewise embraced by
U.S. President Bill Clinton, who declared the era of big government over.
All this marked an important transformation in Europe and North
America toward privatization, thereby weakening governmental power
over markets (Dionne 1998).

American conservatives refined the pattern of profiteers who come
to Washington to fight the battle against government and make money in
the process. But the Clinton administration also enthusiastically embraced
the practice of outsourcing. Defenders of privatization and contracting
argue that the benefits of creating jobs for local residents and encouraging "innovation, flexibility, and efficiency" are significant, despite the problems of accountability and fraud (Stanger and Omnivore 2007). Examples
of Bush-era profiteering through privatizing government activities are
stunning. Between 2001 and 2007 one hundred private office buildings
were built or redeveloped in downtown Washington, DC to house the
tremendous increase in outsourcing government activities. Some 4.4 million square feet of new office space for federal agencies have been added
in Washington since 2000; 3.4 million square feet are located in private
buildings. The Securities and Exchange Commission alone pays US$3.8
million a month to rent space for its headquarters. The Department of
Transportation is also housed in a privately owned building (Brook 2007).

Total spending on contractors doubled during the Bush years; half of the contracts have been issued without competitive bids. There are now more private employees who work on federal contracts than actual federal employees. In 2005 the Department of Energy spent 94 percent of its budget on private contracts (Brook 2007). Throughout the world, contractors have replaced government employees for services such as diplomacy, development and assistance, intelligence collection, and security (Stanger and Omnivore 2007).

Naomi Klein's examination of "disaster capitalism" presents a sobering set of examples of how extreme free-market ideology undercuts the viability of markets through privatization. She noted that "Politicians have been free to cut taxes and rail against big government even as their constituents drove on, studied in, and drank from the huge public works projects of the 1930 and 1940s." Time has now run out on that scam. The August 2007 collapse of the I-35 bridge in Minneapolis during rush hour, which plunged dozens of cars and their occupants into the Mississippi River, resulting in thirteen deaths and many more injuries, became a symbol for the consequences of cutting taxes and privatizing public services. Yet despite the public outcry over the collapse, Congress failed to respond quickly to the disaster. One year after the tragedy, increased funding for bridge safety still had not been approved (Schaper 2008). The American Society of Civil Engineers warned that maintenance of public infrastructure—dams, bridges, road, and schools—had been so seriously neglected by governments over the last several decades that it would require spending US$1.5 trillion over five years to bring the structures up to current standards (Klein 2007, 48).

The failure of the levee system during Hurricane Katrina that resulted in the inundation of New Orleans resulted partly from design mistakes but primarily from inadequate funding. A study commissioned by the Army Corps of Engineers and released in 2007 found that constructing the flood wall system was delayed because of problems with the design and the environmental impacts, and during the delay, cost estimates rose tenfold, from US$80 to US$800 million. In the meantime, hurricane scientists concluded that the chance of a more powerful storm than anticipated was greater and that the levees as designed would be too low. Not only did Corps officials ignore the new research and maintain their approach, but they also sought to save money by changing their own design criteria, thereby building with shorter support pilings, which increased the instability of the walls (Whoriskey 2007).

Klein reiterated the importance of infrastructure by comparing orderly life in the "Green Zone" created by the U.S. occupying forces in Baghdad, with its own electrical grid, water and sanitation, hospital, and other facilities, and that in the "Red Zone," constituting the rest of the city, which lacks adequate infrastructure and is mired in chaos, floods of sewage, filth, and danger. Although this disparity was one result of the war, she found a similar pattern of infrastructure collapse in disaster zones such as post–Hurricane Katrina and post-tsunami Sri Lanka. In those places public infrastructure was "demolished by ideology, the war on 'big government,' the religion of tax cuts, the fetish for privatization."

Though public outcry does arise after disasters, Klein suggested why political elites fail to respond: "After each new disaster, it's tempting to imagine that the loss of life and productivity will finally serve as a wake-up call, provoking the political class to launch some kind of 'new New Deal.' In fact, the opposite is taking place: disasters have become the pre-ferred moments for advancing a vision of a ruthlessly divided world, one in which the very idea of a public sphere has no place at all." Klein labeled this "disaster capitalism," and she argued that "every time a new crisis hits—even when the crisis itself is the direct by-product of free-market ideology—the fear and disorientation that follow are harnessed for radi-cal social and economic re-engineering. Each new shock is midwife to a new course of economic shock therapy" (Klein 2007, 49). Within a few weeks of Hurricane Katrina, the Gulf Coast "became a domestic labora-tory for the same kind of government run by contractors that was pio-neered in Iraq. The companies that snatched up the biggest contracts were the familiar Baghdad gang: Halliburton's KBR unit received a US$60 mil-lion contract to reconstruct military bases along the coast. Blackwater was hired to protect FEMA operations, with the company billing an average of US$950 a day per guard. . . . Their contracts ended up totaling US$3.4 billion, no open bidding required" (Klein 2007, 50).

Similarly, after the Minnesota bridge collapse, the *Wall Street Journal* called for private investors to construct and operate public roadways and bridges. After the New York subway was flooded because of unusually heavy rains, a *New York Sun* headline called for the four subway lines to be sold to private companies who would compete with each other. "It's not hard to imagine what this free market in subways would look like," lamented Klein (2007, 49): "high-speed lines ferrying commuters from the Upper West Side to Wall Street, while the trains serving the South Bronx wouldn't just continue their long delay—they would simply drown. Problems at London's Heathrow airport provoked a similar remedy from *The Economist*: allow the different terminals to compete with each other. That is, "different firms could provide different forms of security checks, some faster and dearer than others" (Klein 2007, 49).

In Klein's view, privatization has undermined the benefits that came to communities in the past: "Not so long ago, disasters were periods of social leveling, rare moments when atomized communities put divisions aside and pulled together." Instead of generating unity, however, disasters have become moments that reinforce inequality, moments "when we are hurled further apart, when we lurch into a radically segregated future where some of us will fall off the map and others ascend to a parallel privatized state, one equipped with well-paved highways and skyways, safe bridges, boutique charter schools, fast-lane airport terminals, and deluxe subways" (Klein 2007, 50).

Klein warns that the military-industrial complex famously described by Dwight D. Eisenhower in 1961 "has morphed into what is best understood as a disaster-capitalism complex, in which all conflict- and disaster-related functions (waging war, securing borders, spying on citizens, rebuilding cities, treating traumatized soldiers) can be performed by corporations at a profit." The ultimate goal here is not simply to "feed off the state, the way traditional military contractors do: it aims, ultimately, to replace core functions of government with its own profitable enterprises" (Klein 2007, 50). Furthermore, the consequences extend well beyond disasters:

> The implications of the decision by the current crop of politicians to systematically outsource their elected responsibilities will reach far beyond a single administration. Once a market has been created, it needs to be protected. The companies at the heart of the disaster-capitalism complex increasingly regard both the state and nonprofits as competitors; from the corporate perspective, whenever governments or charities fulfill their traditional roles, they are denying contractors work that could be done at a profit. . . .

When the disaster bubble bursts, firms such as Bechtel, Fluor, and Blackwater will lose much of their primary revenue streams. They will still have all the high-tech equipment bought at taxpayer expense, but they will need to find a new business model, a new way to cover their high costs. The next phase of the disaster-capitalism complex is all too clear; with emergencies on the rise, government no longer able to foot the bill, and citizens stranded by their hollow state, the parallel corporate state will rent back its disaster infrastructure to whoever can afford it, at whatever price the market will bear (Klein 2007, 52, 54).

Klein discussed the way in which spectacular profit making from disasters has prompted some people to believe that large corporations and their political partners are actually causing disasters to occur, such as the one-third of Americans who said in a 2006 public opinion poll that they believed the U.S. government was involved in the 9–11 attacks or failed to prevent them "because they wanted the United States to go to war in the Middle East" or those who believe the New Orleans levees were secretly blown up in order to flood low-income neighborhoods:

> The truth is at once less sinister and more dangerous. An economic system that requires constant growth while bucking almost all serious attempts at environmental regulation generates a steady stream of disasters all on its own, whether military, ecological, or financial. . . . Our common addiction to dirty, non-renewable energy sources keeps other kinds of emergencies coming: natural disasters (up 560 percent since 1975) and wars waged for control over scarce resources (not just Iraq and Afghanistan but lower-intensity conflicts such as those in Columbia, Nigeria, and Sudan), which in turn spawn terrorist blowback. . . . Given the boiling temperatures, both climatic and political, future disasters need not be cooked up in dark conspiracies. All indications are that if we simply stay the current course, they will keep coming with ever more ferocious intensity. Disaster generation can therefore be left to the market's invisible hand. (Klein 2007, 58)

Devolution

Devolution is the most rightward of the three rightward efforts to stigmatize government because of the nature of politics at different levels of government. Debates about devolution are concerned with the scope of government, the size of its sphere, and its jurisdiction. The principle of devolution seeks to ensure that government is close to the people so they can hold it accountable, and ensure there is sufficient knowledge of local conditions to make good policy and guide its implementation. In principle, then, devolution is neither rightward nor leftward in orientation. However the U.S. experience with devolution is instructive for understanding how devolution can acquire ideological coloring. The Framers of the U.S. Constitution limited the powers of the national government to the husbandry of commerce—patronage policies aimed at fostering economic activity. State governments exercised the police power as well as the power to control health, safety, and morals. State governments regulate property, corporate formation, marriage and divorce, compulsory education, and professional licensing. As a result, the national government became the home of liberalism, and state governments the home of conservatism. National policies have traditionally been primarily liberal, instrumental, and free from moral imperatives. State policies have typically been imbued with moral purpose, regulating conduct that is either deemed inherently harmful or becomes harmful because of negative impacts. Hence, most state laws are conservative and aimed at preserving law and order and sexual morality.

The political consequences of devolution in the United States is to strengthen conservatism because local governments are inherently conservative, focused on maintaining social order, keeping classes and groups in their place, keeping the poor invisible through segregation or, more acceptably, community. National grants to cities gave them the resources to continue segregating groups through urban development and redevelopment. Cities use their discretionary power and resources to contain people in their places and to maintain social relationships.

This pattern is not unique to the United States. Cities throughout the world are segregated along class, ethnic, and religious lines and are designed and organized for social control. All politics is local; all social control is local. As cities become more tied to their local tax base because of the reduction of national-level funding, they become more oriented toward the interests of property owners and those with wealth. The devolution that may be most important is the police power and increases in the number of police officers. Although the response to globalization is national, social control policies are expressed and implemented locally. Economics may drive globalization, but politics must pick up the pieces (Lowi 1998, 5).

Challenges in Making Markets Work

Markets rest on two key assumptions. First, only actions that involve the exchange of money—that is, for which there is a cash nexus—are to be counted in the official economic statistics that guide policy making. That may make sense because it is easy to do, but it simply ignores all the work done and benefits produced from actions where there are no prices to be used as a measure of value. Second, participants in the market are materialistic, egoistic, selfish, and motivated by the pursuit of self-interest. For Adam Smith these constitute the essence of human nature, and markets turn those traits to common advantage because market players pursuing their self-interest produce things we need. However, recent neuropyschological studies have shown that there are significant motivational and behavioral differences between males and females. Susan Pinker (2008), for example, argued that women are more consensus oriented and committed to teamwork, better at reading and interpreting visual cues, and stronger in developing and maintaining social networks and relationships than are males. Such research provides additional reasons to believe that the conventional image of economic actors does not correspond to human reality.

Contrary to free-market ideology, markets are inescapably located in and constrained by the natural world. Natural resources are exhaustible, and natural systems are irreplaceable. Attaining ecological sustainability requires taking a long view. In contrast, market ideology requires discounting and devaluing costs and benefits that extend very far into the future. Conventional cost-benefit analysis is rooted in the well-recognized idea that people prefer income and consumption sooner rather than later. People naturally prefer receiving $100 now more than receiving $100 in the future (Cline 2007). Market ideology extends that idea to the natural world and suggests that environmental benefits in the future should be given very little value compared to current consumption. But present consumption benefits the current generation, whereas the environmental harms are imposed on future generations who get none of the benefits of current consumption but only the costs of unsustainable economic activity. If the benefits and burdens affect the same people, then discounting future value may make sense, but it seems profoundly unjust when the benefits are enjoyed by one set of people and the burdens are experienced by another. As a result, as Ophuls and Boyan put it, "critical ecological resources that will be essential for our well-being even 30 years from now not only have no value to rational economic decision makers, but scarcely enter their calculations at all" (Ophuls and Boyan 1992, 219–20).

Correcting this time horizon bias requires revising economic indicators such as the gross national product to include measures of sustainability, such as the depletion of natural resources and the costs of cleaning up pollution and treating environmentally induced illness. One study of electric power generation in the United States estimates that its annual environmental cost, the money that would be needed to abate pollution, avoid or correct contamination of wells and surface water near coal-fired generators by fly ash, and deal with impacts of fuel extraction for fossil fuel–using generators, to be at US$420 billion in 2007—US$143 billion more than the whole industry's reported annual income. Covering the environmental costs of fossil fuel plants would require raising the price of electricity by 13 cents per kilowatt hour, which would more than double its price in many parts of the country (International Energy Agency 2008).

Correcting time horizons also requires using broader measures of human well-being to guide economic policy. One promising effort is the World Bank's proposal to measure a country's wealth by estimating not only how much it produces but also its investments in natural and human resources. The new system breaks down national wealth into three major attributes: (1) natural capital—the economic value of timber, mineral deposits, land, water, and other environmental assets, (2) produced capital—the value of a nation's machinery, factories, roads, and other human-made assets, and (3) human resources—such as the educational level and skills of a population. National wealth is ultimately viewed as the value of produced goods minus consumption, depreciation of produced assets, and use of natural resources. Such indicators can focus attention on the value of investments that increase human capital, identify changes in a country's development so adjustments can be made, and help identify the long-term consequences of selling off natural resources in the short term; thus, although rapid harvesting of resources might appear as a gain in the production-oriented economic figures like gross domestic product, they will appear in this scheme as a loss to the nation's natural resource wealth (World Bank 1995; Serageldin 1995).

Economic accounting systems based on GDP and associated measures also ignore unpaid household labor and care giving, which are performed primarily by women (Loh 2008). The role of human reproduction, without which the whole economic system would collapse, is similarly valued at zero. Marilyn Waring (1988) provided examples after examples: the work of African women from 4 a.m. to 9 p.m. each day to find water, grow and prepare food, and care for children, the ill, and the infirm counts for nothing, whereas a male engaged in drugs and prostitution adds to the GDP. Similarly, ecological services performed by nature that provide clean air and water and other benefits essential for life are not counted in a country's wealth, but work to clean up a chemical spill or toxic waste dump adds value to economic indicators. Economic analysis provides no tools for valuing these essential services that lie outside of market exchanges, but ignoring them means we are likely to make giant mistakes.

The globalization of markets is intertwined with growing global environmental threats because global capitalism is entirely dependent on the resources of the natural world and its ability to process wastes. Furthermore, poor people are most vulnerable to the consequences of environmental decline. Poverty in developing countries is often a reflection of inadequate natural resources such as good soil and water. Short-term economic pressures cause poor farmers and others to engage in practices that produce immediate but unsustainable benefits. Yet only economic activity that is consistent with ecological conditions and limits is sustainable in the long term. However, the ideological emphasis on the need for unfettered markets among some advocates of globalization blinds them to the threats posed by market-based prices that fail to reflect the true costs of production and therefore cannot provide the signals essential for making efficient decisions about the use of resources.

Effective governance is required in order to rescue globalization from unsustainable environmental and economic trends, but part of the contradiction of globalist market ideology is its commitment to weakening government. More broadly, globalist market ideology fails to reflect the larger community of land, resources, biomes, languages and cultures, and institutions in which economic activity is embedded and on which it depends (Daly and Cobb 1994). The inherent dynamic of markets has produced a global environmental deficit stemming from a "collective and mostly unanticipated impact of humankind's alteration of the earth's atmosphere, water, soil, biota, ecological systems, and landscapes" and exists, Herbert Borman and Stephen Kellert maintained, because "the longer-term ecological, social, and economic costs to human welfare are greater than the shorter-term benefits flowing from these alterations" (Borman and Kellert 1991, xii). Environmental deficits rob future generations by permitting profligate consumption by current generations who pursue their own interests rather than ensure that the needs of future generations can be met.

Toward More Effective Markets

In a world primarily organized around markets, well-functioning markets at all levels, from local to global, are essential for ecologically sustainable economic activity. The continued decentralization of world politics means that national, regional, and local governments play an essential role in making markets work well; a key question, then, is what are the critical policies governments need to design and implement? Given relatively weak support for government intervention in the global economy and the lack of effective global institutions, how can we develop the political support for more effective public policies aimed at making markets work? In the United States that task is daunting, rooted in strong ideological commitments among conservatives for unfettered markets. These commitments trigger an almost automatic opposition to any proposal for strengthening regulation and contribute to widespread public misunderstanding and ignorance about how government works. The first problem was evident throughout the debate over the rescue of the financial markets in 2008, when conservative commentators insisted that the problems were caused by too much regulation and that more regulation could not be a solution. A classic example of the latter occurred in a letter President Barack Obama received during the debate over health care reform in 2009 from a woman who was very motivated to lobby for her interests but had little comprehension of how health policy works. She wrote: "I don't want government-run health care. I don't want socialized medicine, and don't touch my Medicare" (Armquist 2009).

Yet there are ways forward through better incorporating the value of natural resources and ecosystem services into economic calculations, changes in tax policy, and measures to promote internalization of environmental as well as other costs of production or activity.

Though ecosystem services are priceless because life is not possible without them, developing some rough measures of the value of natural resources and ecosystem services is essential in order to move toward the goal of establishing true costs. One approach to estimating ecosystem services involves calculating the cost of restoring damaged systems to a more pristine, undisturbed, and functional state. Another is based on estimating the cost of constructing a particular ecosystem. Less useful methods rely on surveys of people's willingness to pay for broad ecosystem services such as aesthetics, although more concrete inquiries about how much people value recreational opportunities can help shed light on values that could be incorporated into prices. Comparing property values of land near natural amenities and protected areas with those near developed sites can provide rough estimates of ecosystem worth.

Estimating the cost of ecosystem services is difficult and inspires opposition from those who believe that attempts to put price tags on services that are, in reality, priceless diminishes their value. Estimating costs is also associated with standard economic cost-benefit analysis. Critics of cost-benefit analysis argue that such analysis is inevitably biased in favor of values that can be unambiguously quantified, such as the cost of complying with environmental regulations by installing new control equipment. Estimating the value of the benefits stemming from such installations, such as protecting ecosystem services, is much more difficult, so they are likely to be seriously underestimated during cost-benefit analysis.

In all policy areas there are a number of challenges to using cost-benefit analysis. These include how to quantify nonmarket values, how to identify costs and benefits, what impacts are to be included in assessing costs and benefits (what should be the duration of the chain of possible impacts arising from an economic actor's or regulatory agency's actions included in the analysis), how to address distributional issues—particularly when the costs are borne by one set of people and the benefits largely accrue to another—and how to determine the present value of future costs and benefits. Newer variations, such as cost-effective analysis, can be used to identify options that produce the greatest benefits per unit of costs or greatest total benefits, given the resources available, or some other measure. The difficulties cannot be allowed to stymie analysis because some kind of assessment of the costs and benefits of damaging (or restoring) ecosystems or converting natural resources into manufactured goods or other forms is unavoidable. If ecosystem services are not estimated, the debate will be dominated by narrow, economic-based assessments.

Tax policy can be a powerful means of promoting sustainability by integrating economic and environmental policy. Shifting taxes away from desirable actions, such as earning profits and paying salaries, and directing them toward undesirable actions, such as producing pollution and harvesting scarce resources, can strengthen economies and make them more ecologically sustainable at the same time. Taxing pollution ensures that producers of pollution take some responsibility for the harms they create. It also ensures that those who benefit economically from industrial production also pay the costs and do not impose them on others who do not enjoy the benefits. It creates clear incentives for people to reduce harmful activities without the heavy government hand and inherent loss of flexibility and freedom that comes with command and control regulation. It thus encourages pollution reduction to be efficient (Roodman 1995, 10–19). The primary goal of green taxes should be to ensure that prices communicate accurate information about the environmental costs of production. Imposing taxes on excess profits from natural resources would still allow producers to earn profits and also give them an incentive to produce, but society would gain the windfall when resources become increasingly scarce and the producers' prices are forced upward (Roodman 1995, 13).

Pollution taxes are often regressive; they raise the price of energy, transportation, manufactured goods, and other essentials, so they take a larger bite out of the total income of poor households than middle-class or wealthy ones. To be equitable, pollution taxes must be combined with reducing income taxes levied on low-income families, rebates for energy taxes, or other adjustments. Taxes must also be integrated with other laws and policies. The benefits of increased gasoline taxes, for example, are countered by land use decisions that encourage urban sprawl and more driving. Increasing taxes may not solve problems of how pollution sources are distributed and their tendency to be concentrated in low-income communities. Taxes alone will not protect biodiversity. Some severely endangered species will require absolute protection and a ban on killing them (Roodman 1995).

Formulating tax policy that secures the desired environmental gains can be challenging because in many sectors of the economy it has to encourage large, long-term investments. The renewable production tax credit applied to encourage a shift to wind-, water-, and solar-powered electric generation in the United States was only partly effective. It was first adopted for tax years 1992–1999 and then readopted for 2001, 2003, 2005–2007, and 2008. Although eliciting greater reliance on renewable sources during the years it was available, production from renewable sources fell; the credit was not enough to elicit significant investments in renewable sources.

Other policy measures or changes in private practices can promote the internalization of the environmental costs of production and marketing. One of the most effective is to prevent pollution from occurring. Another innovative possibility is for manufacturers to retain ownership and responsibility for their products, leasing them to consumers rather than selling them, and then take back the used product for recycling and reuse of parts. Sustainability can also be pursued through regulations such as emission standards that go beyond the separate media (water, air, and land) to involve a much more integrated and effective program of reducing emissions. Property rights in resources can be allocated in ways that ensure that if depletion of a resource occurs, that it is then reflected in higher prices and that the most efficient reductions in pollution are made through trading emission rights. Liability rules and the cost of insurance can contribute to conservation. Another critical step in generating true cost prices is ending public policies that subsidize environmentally destructive activities. Logging, mining, pesticide and fertilizer use, and energy development are subsidized rather than taxed, thereby encouraging inefficient production and consumption. The Group of 20 governments took an important step in this direction in September 2009 when they agreed to phase out some US$300 billion in subsidies on fossil fuel use (Group of 20 2009)

Making Markets Work: The Case of Water

Like oil, water lubricates modern economies. It is not just farms and households that use water; energy development, the production of electronic components and equipment, and most every other economic activity involves using water. Analysts have been warning about the water crisis that many countries face, as demand outstrips supply and resources are drained at unsustainable rates. Scarcity has been an enduring condition of water in the western United States, but the traditional solutions—building more dams, drilling more wells, and diverting more water—are no longer options because groundwater levels have fallen, few good dam sites remain, and diverting redistributes but does not affect the total water supply. Extreme engineering solutions such as towing icebergs from the Arctic or building continent-spanning pipelines are infeasible, whereas widespread desalination of sea water is expensive, consumes vast amounts of energy, and produces briny waste streams that pose difficult disposal problems (Glennon 2009).

Improving the efficiency of water use and promoting conservation are essential, and markets can be used to promote conservation. Robert Glennon (2009) has proposed a water market system that would rely on market forces to drive conservation. It begins with ensuring that all residents have access to enough water to meet basic needs, then increasing the price of additional water use through block rates that rise with consumption levels. New users entering a water district would be required to offset their new water use by paying other users to use less, just as new entrants into an airshed suffering from air pollution must offset their emissions by paying established users to reduce their emissions by a corresponding amount. One of the biggest uses of water, about one-third of domestic water use in the United States, is to dispose of human wastes, and alternative technologies are needed to avoid treating water that is then simply flushed down the drain.

As populations increase and economies develop, water use will necessarily shift from agricultural to residential and commercial use. That has already happened in the western United States, where water transfers have shifted water from farming without reducing farm income. Farmers have been inspired to invest in more efficient irrigation systems, take marginal lands out of production, and shift to less water-intensive crops; many have then sold their "excess" water (portions of water use rights they do not use on the farm) to other users.

In many areas of the world, water scarcity is an increasingly vexing problem as demand for water grows inexorably with population growth and economic development while supplies shrink because of pollution and climate change. In the western United States, for example, where population growth has been steady, domestic water use has more than doubled since 1960 and per capita water consumption has steadily increased despite decades of warning about scarcity and calls for improved efficiency. The water shortages that are occurring around the world will continue to worsen as global climate change unfolds. Temperature increases will affect the timing, location, and volume of rain and snowfall. Different levels of precipitation will disrupt agricultural irrigation patterns. Warming will affect evaporation rates and the moisture content of soils as well as stream flows and groundwater levels. Water managers can no longer count on historic hydrological data and trends when planning for future needs and estimating available supplies, but instead they need to be able to develop plans in the face of great uncertainties. They need to develop institutions that are resilient and adaptable, nimble enough to quickly adjust to changes in supply as well as develop effective ways immediately to increase water efficiency and conservation (Adler 2008, 14–15).

Advocates of water markets argue that markets are the best way to provide for the resiliency, adaptability, and flexibility that climate change is likely to require. Water markets have emerged around the world as a way to encourage conservation by allowing water rights holders to sell or lease their unneeded water and to facilitate the allocation of water to its highest-valued uses. Well-designed water markets greatly reduce the amount of information that water managers would otherwise need to gather about supply and demand and the relative value of different uses. Furthermore, water markets are relatively simply to create. They require defining property rights in water as use rights (usufructary rights) rather than as ownership of the water. The use rights must be well defined, enforceable, and transferable. Other necessary policy reforms include eliminating government subsidies for artificially low water prices and reducing regulatory barriers to water transfers such as prohibitions against interbasin and interstate water transfers. As Jonathan Adler (2008, 16) noted, "Prices are an essential component of any well-functioning market, and water markets are no exception. Price signals provide powerful incentives for conservation while simultaneously communicating information about collective judgments about the relative scarcity of resources across time and space."

The most effective opposition to water markets comes from those who support government subsidies for water. Politicians can claim credit for providing cheap water. In the United States and many other places, water is subsidized for agriculture uses, which reflects the political power of farmers. However, subsidies provide no incentive to conserve; in fact, inefficient water uses are a rational response to low water prices (Anderson and Snyder 1997). Water markets will raise the price of water in most areas, thus necessitating programs to help poor residents pay the increased cost. But improving efficiency and conservation are absolutely essential in adapting to climate change and its consequences for water as well as the shortages that are projected to occur independent of climate disruptions as a result of population growth and water pollution.

Other actions can also help avert water shortages. A major challenge is to overcome the conflicts in water management that come from overlapping political jurisdictions wherever watersheds cross jurisdictional lines. More data are needed to supply decision makers with the information they need to manage limited resources in creative ways that respect existing laws and agreements but also allow them to fashion solutions that minimize conflict and contention (Limbaugh 2009). Cleaning up contaminated groundwater basins, capturing rainwater through new infrastructures, expanding groundwater storage, and reducing the discharge of pollutants into water bodies will also contribute to increasing supplies (Stoner 2009).

The Limits of Markets

Making markets work through true-cost pricing is critical, but it is not sufficient to produce ecological sustainability. Although the market price mechanism handles incremental change with relative ease, it tends to break down when confronted with absolute scarcity or other serious discrepancies between supply and demand. In such situations (for example, in famines), markets collapse or degenerate into uncontrolled inflation because the increased price cannot trigger an equivalent increase in supply within the relevant timeframe of need. Markets also fail to respond to the problems of ecological scarcity because scarcity tends to inspire competitive bidding and preemptive buying. Scrambles to buy can lead to extreme price fluctuations, market disruption, and inequitable or inappropriate distribution of resources, as those with ready cash crowd out other would-be buyers.

Avoiding dire resource scarcities would reduce the likelihood of catastrophic market failure and the social disruptions it entails. This provides another reason to shift toward sustainable patterns of economic activity, particularly sustainable development of the poorer countries. Sustainable development is the subject of the next chapter.

Chapter Four
SUSTAINABLE DEVELOPMENT

Adopting public policies that produce well-functioning markets that reflect the true costs of activity and resource use are an essential first step toward reducing global environmental problems. However, they are not enough to reverse the currently unsustainable trajectory of the global political economy because they do not provide a sufficiently broad normative framework for guiding decisions about the whole range of human activities affecting the environment. Some broader orienting concept is needed. The idea of sustainable development—famously defined by the World Commission on Environment and Development (also known as the Brundtland Commission) as development that "meets the needs of the present without compromising the ability of future generations to meet their own needs" (1987, 43) has become the dominant normative discourse in discussing the future of the global economy. It permeates the academic literature and the policy agendas of nongovernmental organizations, international development agencies, and national governments alike.

Part of its attractiveness is that it is such a broad and vaguely defined concept. Because there are dozens and dozens of competing definitions, anyone can likely find a suitable one to embrace, which surely contributes to its popularity. Critics argue that it is popular precisely because it is so weak and undemanding, and thus it is capable of being stretched to justify continued commitment to the status quo without challenging the fundamental elements of the economic system that clash with ecological realities (Carter 2007, 207–40). But it also appeals to basic principles of equality and fairness that are attractive to many even as they struggle with defining sustainable development's core concepts and policy implications.

Competing Definitions of Sustainability

The notion of sustainability has deep roots in the natural sciences and, through interest in sustainable harvests and yields, in resource economics. The carrying capacity of an ecosystem determines the level of renewable resources that can be harvested over time. The idea of "natural capital" reflects similar concerns. The idea of the "triple bottom line" of planet, people, and profit adopted by advocates of corporate social responsibility calls for paying as much attention to environmental and social goals as to monetary ones. Though many companies have adopted the concept, there is little agreement on what environmental and social indicators should be used or how to measure them, leaving those lines less clear than the economic bottom line, with its well-established metrics (Toffel and Lifset 2007).

The idea of sustainability is viewed as compelling for several reasons. Its breadth provides the potential to aggregate a wide range of interests under its umbrella, but proponents also find enough specificity to give some direction to policy choices. Some argue that the idea of sustainability is most useful in narrow settings, where parties can agree that certain practices are not sustainable and should be changed, but it is too vague to illuminate broader issues (Jamieson 1996). Others argue that sustainability, like other transformative ideas, promises to inspire a remaking of the world through comprehensive redirecting of human reflection and choice. Sustainability is a powerful concept, Hempel (1999, 44) noted, because it is "sufficiently ambiguous to be embraced by diverse interests, yet coherent enough to inspire movement in a particular direction." Sustainability has the potential to become one of the ideas—like justice, equality, and freedom—that create fundamental expectations for public and private behavior.

Like those other broad concepts, the definition of ecologically sustainable development is contested. Some see sustainability as satisfied by continuing to pursue economic growth while minimizing environmental damage and resource use whenever doing so is not too expensive or disruptive of economic goals. Others define it as requiring industry to reinvent itself in ways that promote pollution prevention, energy efficiency, and technological innovation. For others, it means economic and environmental goals are given roughly equivalent status, requiring that they be pursued in tandem and in innovative ways that promote a much wider range of values than are incorporated in market prices. The most demanding definition centers on preserving the biosphere as the most important objective because it is a prerequisite for every other human endeavor, so it takes priority over any economic goal. Thus, the notion of sustainable development can either be a call to continue with current practices and priorities as long as we are careful to give more attention to ecological protection and conservation of resources, or it can be a radical goal, a new way of defining problems and devising responses to them.

Thick and Thin Notions of Sustainability

These divergences can be understood more readily by distinguishing between visions of sustainability that offer modest, weak, or thin agendas for change and visions that offer a deeper, more radical, or thick prescription. Thin forms of sustainable development hold that economic and environmental concerns can and must be balanced. Their advocates acknowledge that economic growth has been given priority and seen as paramount in the past; they agree that economic growth must now be refined and balanced with environmental sensitivity. But fundamental changes are not required: current technologies and patterns of production and consumption are acceptable as long as they are tempered by environmental/resource considerations. We can largely continue to do what we have done in the past as long as we are more "sensitive" to environmental conditions. Similarly, the overall value of the natural and economic capital for future generations should be undiminished by the current generation. The goal, then, is to ensure the same level of resources while also permitting some substitution of natural resources for an equivalent amount of capital.

Addressing environmental problems through geoengineering is more compatible with thin notions of sustainability. Geoengineering proposals take many forms. Some geoengineers have proposed reducing atmospheric warming by increasing the albedo effect that sends sunlight radiating back into space. This could be done close to the earth's surface by artificially increasing cloud cover, at the stratospheric level by increasing aerosols, or in the upper atmosphere by deploying large sunshades. Others have proposed reducing carbon dioxide through carbon sequestration or adding carbonates to the oceans to increase their absorptive capacity (Lenton and Vaughn 2009). However, even proponents of a thin notion of sustainability would ask more pointedly than geoengineering enthusiasts whether the proposed solutions would cause other environmental problems severe enough to make them inadvisable.

A thick form of sustainable development, what might be called ecological sustainability, holds that environmental preservation is the paramount value. It places a major constraint on economic considerations; only those economic activities consistent with the fundamental criterion of ecological sustainability are acceptable. The current distribution of critical natural capital must be maintained in some form so that the ecosystem services it provides are maintained. It cannot simply be harvested to generate economic wealth that is to be passed down to subsequent generations. Industrial activities, energy production, transportation, and consumption must be fundamentally transformed to avoid ecological disruptions and protect regenerative processes. Ecological survival simply outweighs economic growth as the primary public priority (Sandler 1997; Pirages 1996). Because ecological conditions make possible all life, including economic activities, preserving those conditions must be given priority. Balancing environment and economics is not enough; ecological values must come first, and they must define and limit what kinds and levels of economic activity are acceptable. Policy goals such as free trade and economic efficiency are subordinated to preserving biodiversity, protecting wild lands, and reclaiming damaged areas.

Thick visions of sustainability underlie much of the critique of urban sprawl that has been an increasingly prominent feature of land use discussions in the United States. Here, far more than in other industrial countries, public policies encouraged highway construction by funding highways through earmarked revenues or trust funds rather than from a general pool of money for financing all transportation, promoted automobile ownership through zoning and tax policies that kept the costs of owning and running motor vehicles relatively low, created tax policies encouraging ownership of detached single-family homes, and implemented zoning that increasingly separated residential from commercial and light industry areas (Nivola 1999). Though some attempts have been made to control sprawl, these have tended to be overwhelmed by personal desires to live "the American dream" of a home and yard of one's own, by the desires of those already in a house to avoid the increased density of building where they are, and by an increasingly vocal property rights movement challenging federal, state, and local efforts to limit sprawl (Orski and Shaw 2005; Flint 2006). Advocates of "new urbanism," "smart growth," and decentralizing food production all present visions of more sustainable communities designed for compactness, minimal motor vehicle use, and close connections between farms and dinner tables. One of the more elaborate visions, developed with global implementation as a goal, is provided by NewVistas in their vision of sustainable communities built one at a time but scalable into clusters inhabited by up to a million people (see www.newvistas.com).

Achieving ecologically sustainable development requires a high degree of policy integration. Advocates of sustainable green cities, for example, have developed comprehensive models for integrating economic, environmental, and social goals into specific plans for a new form of urban development that is focused on creating smaller-scale communities where neighbors can know each other and interact face-to-face. They seek to integrate all aspects of human settlements—housing, agriculture, industry, commerce, recreation, and community services—through comprehensive metropolitan planning.

Another important feature of this thick notion of sustainability is its integration of social equity and political empowerment with ecological protection and economic activity. In thick visions of sustainability, sustainable development prioritizes reducing poverty and helping the poor gain some measure of self-sufficiency through a more equitable distribution of resources rather than economic growth in general. Political participation is a key ingredient in ensuring that decisions affecting economic and environmental conditions be made more inclusive (Lafferty 1996). Consequently, sustainability is not an ecological concept alone, but also one of social justice, inclusion, fairness, community well-being, and political engagement. These social and political values are important and valued in their own right as well as because of their contributions to ecological protection. Thus, proponents of thick conceptions of sustainable development directly face the problem of economic inequality in the contemporary world.

Addressing Inequality

Both the stark differences between the life chances and quality of life of the wealthy and the poor and the tremendous human suffering associated with extreme poverty inspire claims that equality should be a global public policy priority. Yet even among those who prioritize equality there is considerable disagreement about what it means. Economists, political scientists, and other social scientists have long debated how to measure and assess levels of economic equality and inequality. Philosophers and others have offered competing justifications and descriptions of equality, rooted in such fundamental normative conceptions as human dignity and worth, freedom and individual autonomy, and collective obligations to and responsibilities for those who are most vulnerable.

Proponents of equality rest their arguments for making a public commitment to promote equality on various foundations. Providing for an equal distribution of resources, or at least some level of redistribution from the wealthy to the poor, reflects a recognition of the profound and equal worth of each person. A redistribution of resources toward the poor can also be justified by the value of ensuring everyone has at least some of the resources necessary to become authors of their own lives and to make and pursue basic life choices. Because inequality often results from the actions of others, such as colonial-like exploitation of natural resources or corrupt governments or civil wars, there is a moral obligation to remedy past injustices. Equality is intertwined with democracy and empowering individuals to participate in political, as well as economic and social activities.

Egalitarianism takes many other forms, as its proponents grapple with issues such as when should all people be treated the same, when should people in like circumstances be treated alike, and what distinctions are legitimate ones for basing differences in treatment. Libertarian egalitarians believe that every person should be left alone as much as possible to pursue those life choices; for them the role of public policy is to provide essential public goods, enforce private contracts, and then get out of the way so people can make of their lives what they can. People should enjoy equal freedom and be as free as possible from collective efforts that may actually increase inequalities, such as public policies that reward the politically well connected at the expense of everyone else. Though basing their conclusions on an individualistic conception of human nature, liberal egalitarians accept public intervention to ensure that every person enjoys at least some level of the prerequisites for a self-directed life because they believe that many people lack the genetic endowment, nurturing childhood, or physical health or are subject to a host of other factors beyond their control that nevertheless shape their life chances. Conversely, communitarian egalitarians justify egalitarianism by its effects on communities rather than individuals; they regard equality as more conducive to the spirits of solidarity and sharing needed to maintain the communities that sustain human life and provide the infrastructure necessary to individual self-realization. In all, there are enough variants of equality to satisfy adherents of a tremendously wide range of political and economic ideologies.

Yet advocates using public policy to foster equality face a host of challenges in making their case. They must be able to define and measure equality clearly enough so we know when policies are promoting equality and when they are not. They must also be able to show that the benefits of egalitarian policies outweigh the costs to other values such as economic efficiency. Thus, the burden on them is to explain exactly what equality requires in terms of public policies and actions and what kinds of efforts will promote equality.

In particular, they face the challenge of addressing the widespread allure of efficiency, because proponents claim that increasing efficiency promises greater wealth and productivity than a system focused primarily on redistribution and equity. In a classic essay on equality published more than thirty years ago, economist Arthur Okun argued that the idea of equality that champions equal justice, equal political rights, and one vote for each person must be balanced with economic inequalities intended to encourage the hard work, the productivity, and efficiency that comes from market capitalism. In his view, society faces a trade-off between equality and efficiency. However, Okun did caution that often the result of market capitalism is a society that "allow[s] the big winners to feed their pets better than the losers can feed their children" (Okun 1975, 1).

In many countries efficiency seems to have largely won the war of ideas. The practice of international politics is dominated by rationalism and the idea that states are self-interested actors, primarily oriented toward maximizing their economic interest. States rationally and objectively calculate their utility, including the expectations they believe they will result from cooperative behavior. Rational decisions will result from the operation of free markets, and the role of the state is to defer to market decisions as much as possible and, when it must intervene in markets, to do so guided by cost-benefit analysis that seeks the most efficient interventions and using marketlike mechanisms, incentives, and policy instruments. Equality takes a back seat to the pursuit of efficiency.

The idea of market-guided globalization reinforces the dominance of rational theory. Its proponents champion notions of "the end of ideology," claiming that the end of the Cold War proved there is only one way to pursue prosperity and freedom, which is to promote an uncritical embrace of markets, "free" trade, powerful multinational corporations largely unregulated by public authority, and unrestrained technological innovation. In this conception of the contemporary world, nations are no longer divided into distinct first, second, third, and fourth worlds; instead, they are seen as forming a continuum of countries ranging from developing to developed. Globalization advocates suggest that consensus has replaced debate over the nature and distribution of economic and political power. For Francis Fukuyama (1993), the end of ideology meant total victory for liberal democracy, markets, consumerism, technological progress, and limited government regulation. Ideological debate over global politics was now replaced by universal values of the pursuit of rational self-interest.

The end of ideology is not a new claim, though it has taken different forms. For Daniel Bell (1960), the end of ideology meant the rise of a rational, moderate, pragmatic synthesis of capitalism and socialism. Nor has this hybrid approach won universal adherence. By the late 1990s protesters contested the elite consensus surrounding economic rationality because they believed global markets, shaped by trade agreements, favor the interests of wealthy nations and multinational corporations. They challenged notions that globalization is an objective and inevitable result of evolutionary forces beyond human control, and they deconstructed it as the consequence of the exercise of political power. Constructivists countered notions of an inevitable convergence on rationalist ideas by arguing that identities and meanings are created within a social context and, therefore, not inevitably shaped by economic self-interest. Furthermore, environmentalists criticized market-based globalization as inconsistent with the ecological constraints that necessarily shape and limit economic activity.

Most critics of market-based globalization agree that the well-being generated by global markets is selective and asymmetrical. The benefits of globalization have largely been concentrated in the wealthy countries, where it has helped widen the gap not only between rich and poor countries but also rich and poor persons. Globalization's benefits come at a high price, as it profoundly disrupts traditional societies and cultures. For environmentalists its most troubling feature is a type and level of economic activity that is not ecologically sustainable and poses profound risks to the future of the planet.

Advocates of efficiency are not likely to cede the ground to advocates of equality; rather, they argue that growth is the best way to promote greater equality. Economic growth helps the poorest increase their standard of living, as a rising tide lifts all boats. Some go further and maintain that economic growth is essential for reducing inequality because it reduces the conflict and tension that would occur if equality was pursued only through redistributive policies. Economic growth, Benjamin M. Friedman argued, "more often than not fosters greater opportunity, tolerance of diversity, social mobility, commitment to fairness, and dedication to democracy" (Friedman 2005, 4).

If economic growth, stimulated by the rewards tailored to individual effort and enterprise, can produce a host of societal benefits and reduce inequality, the problem is solved. In theory, economic efficiency and certain inequalities work together to promote growth and, ultimately, economic equality—or at least reduced economic inequality—along with improved life chances for the poor. However, that logical possibility does not answer the question of what has happened in practice. Has the consensus surrounding economic efficiency, markets, and growth in reality reduced inequality?

The Persistence of Global Inequality

Recent books by Branko Milanovic and Frederic S. Mishkin make significant contributions to our understanding of the persistent problem of inequality. Milanovic's study of global inequality is particularly valuable because it provides a wealth of details about the extent and evolution of inequality. Both offer thoughtful and competing remedies for promoting global equality that nicely frame much of the contemporary debate over how to reduce inequality.

Milanovic (2005, 8–11) argued that there are three fundamentally different concepts of inequality that need to be distinguished:

- Unweighted international inequality, which compares the income or per capita Gross Domestic Product (GDP) of nations. This is a measure of international inequality because it compares countries and is unweighted because it does not take population size into account and is not a measure of inequality among persons.
- Population-weighted international inequality, which uses the average income in a country to make cross-nation comparisons but takes into account the number of people in each nation. It is

also a measure of international inequality because it does include the distribution of wealth among persons within each nation.

- World income distribution, which ranks all six billion people on the earth from poorest to richest. This is a measure of inequality among persons without regard to countries.

These different measures of equality allow us to determine whether nations are converging in terms of their income levels as well as what is happening to the distribution of individual wealth. But they must be combined with other measures, such as Purchasing Power Parity exchange rates, which converts national incomes into similar bundles of available consumption so they can be more accurately compared in terms of actual purchasing power. There are also questions about whether analysts should compare individual and household income or expenditures in order to best understand life situations. There is also a debate about how to compare per capita figures in countries with many versus few children in households, as large households do not need as much per capita income to be as well off as small ones (Milanovic 2005, 12–19).

Milanovic assessed the degree of inequality with the Gini coefficient. It measures the difference between perfect equality and the percentage of total income received by the cumulative percentage of persons when the persons are ranked from lowest to highest income. The lower the score, the greater the equality in the distribution of wealth: a coefficient of 0 means all persons have the same income; a coefficient of 1 (more typically given as 100) represents maximum inequality. He found that intercountry inequality increased significantly in the late twentieth century. The intercountry Gini coefficient hardly changed between 1965 and 1982, going from 46.9 to 47.3. Inequality increased sharply between 1982 and 1994, grew more slowly afterward, and at the end of the 1990s the intercountry Gini coefficient was 54.5. He argued that inequality did not change much during the 1960s and 1970s because slow economic growth in Africa was offset by higher growth in Latin America, Eastern Europe, and the wealthy nations; whereas stagnating growth in Latin America and Eastern Europe produced the increase in inequality seen in the 1980s and 1990s (Milanovic 2005, 111–13).

Western nations have increased their wealth in comparison with the rest of the world, and in only a few, exceptional cases, have non-Western countries been able to catch up. The gap in incomes between the 20 percent of the richest and the poorest countries has grown from 30 to 1 in

1960 to 82 to 1 in 1995 (World Bank 2003a.). Milanovic placed countries into one of four categories: the rich, the contenders within striking
distance of catching the rich, the third world countries whose GDP per
capita is between one- and two-thirds of the least wealthy of the wealthy
nations, and the fourth world countries whose GDP per capita is less
than one-third of the least wealthy of the wealthy. In 1960 twenty-two
countries appeared to be contenders with the potential to move into the
rich country category, but only two (Singapore and Hong Kong) did so
while the others not only did not move forward but actually fell into a
lower category of countries. Two-thirds of the countries in the third
world category in 1978 had slipped into the fourth world category by
2000, as an emptying out of the middle-income countries has occurred.
In sum, the proportion of rich countries and contenders declined, while
the proportion of third and fourth world countries increased. Looking at
individuals rather than countries and comparing individual incomes to
the world mean income of US$3,526, Milanovic found that 77 percent
of the world's population is poor (having incomes less than the world
mean), 7 percent is in the middle class (having income between 75–125
percent of the world mean), and 16 percent is rich (having income more
than 125 percent of the world mean) (2005, 128–35).

   Milanovic placed much of the blame for the woes of the developing
world on the wealthy world and the United States in particular. The key
point was the 1979–1980 transition when the United States shifted from
being a major capital exporter to an importer in order to finance its growing deficits, a trend that continued during the 1980s as deficits grew to
fund the Cold War and tax cuts. Poor countries found themselves having
to compete with the United States for capital in world financial markets,
and capital flows to these countries fell. Buffeted by higher oil prices, countries, particularly in Africa, that lacked plentiful cheap labor, entrepreneur-
ial talent, a strong state, and access to global markets fell further behind. In
sum, contrary to the claims of its advocates, globalization and the remarkable economic growth during the late twentieth century has only had a
modest impact on reducing inequality (Milanovic 2005, 79–80).

Causes of Persistent Poverty and Inequality

Frederic S. Mishkin is interested in explaining why countries have moved
or failed to move from developing to developed or near-developed status

and have made the transition from being a poor to a wealthy country. He concluded that the key is their ability to devise strong and effective institutions that secure private property rights, reduce corruption, and ensure that financial investments are made in productive enterprises. He maintained that the countries that have prospered since 1960 have vibrant, effective public institutions that perform the essential functions on which healthy markets depend. These critical functions include securing the stability and public order required for economic activity to flourish, creating and enforcing private property rights, enforcing contracts so that commerce can occur, ensuring fair competition through enforcing antitrust/ competition policies, and providing public goods such as communications, transportation infrastructure, and national defense. Nations are poor, he argued, because they have weak public institutions. The poorest countries, for example, typically lack the basic establishment and enforcement of property rights and are plagued by rapacious governments. In contrast, the emerging countries now regarded as contenders are developing private property rights and other essential institutions. "Nations are poor," he argued, "because their institutions are weak; they are 'institutionally challenged'" (Mishkin 2006, 12).

Excessive risk taking by banks, large budget deficits, high interest rates from mishandled finances, currency crises triggered by financial imbalances, and the spread of crises from one country to another all contribute to the financial problems that have plagued developing countries and hobbled their progress. Mishkin focused on the financial crises in the emerging market economies of Mexico, South Korea, and Argentina to draw lessons about how governments should develop the public institutions needed to produce strong financial systems, ensure the flow of information essential for well-functioning markets, and open their financial markets to global capital flows in ways that help integrate them into growing global markets. He offered a number of policy prescriptions that countries should follow to avoid crises and to promote economic growth, and these primarily center on effective regulation of banking and financial services, opening the financial sector to foreign investors to lower the cost of capital, preventing excessive budget deficits, stabilizing prices, and expanding international trade.

Mishkin argued that wealthy countries can contribute more to developing countries' progress through expanded trade than through increased aid. Aid, he argued, does not provide the right incentives to ensure its productive investment, and wealthy countries opening their markets to goods and services from developing countries creates precisely the kinds of incentives for more effective use of financial capital. Such market opening would benefit the developed nations as well, and the wealthy world need only overcome their domestic political pressures to protect inefficient industries for global economic growth and prosperity to occur.

Milanovic also expected that economic growth will reach more of the world's poor and, thus, poverty will be decreased. However, he relied less on markets than on information flows and political changes for this to occur. Political pressures for redistribution will only increase, he argued, as the globalization of communication and ideas makes inequality more visible. The ever-increasing flow of information and migration will generate increasing pressure to reduce gross disparities, as people learn more and more about the conditions of those around the world. The inexorable movement toward greater democracy between and within states plus the development of global governing institutions during the past century will produce increasing pressures to reduce inequality, thereby making the issue as hot internationally as it is within the more equity-minded states today (Milanovic 2005, 157–62).

Yet directing increased capital flows to developing countries and ensuring that the capital is put to productive uses are not likely to reach the poorest of the poor, who lack the human and financial capital to participate in markets. As Jeffrey R. Sachs argued, the poorest of the poor are "too poor to save for the future and thereby accumulate the capital per person that could pull them out of their current misery" (2005, 57). Thus, there is compelling reason to believe that specific efforts must be made to assist the poorest of the poor. The commitment to reduce inequality needs to go beyond a general commitment to help poor countries and became a focused commitment to help those who live in the most abject poverty.

Development projects, such as microcredit, microenterprise, and other programs, aimed at empowering families and communities to increase their income hold promise to help the poorest of the poor directly now rather than waiting for economic growth to trickle down to the poor. As Milanovic persuasively argued, the gap between rich and poor is growing, and the middle class is shrinking. Grassroots-level development promises to reach the poor directly, thereby increasing their freedom to participate in economic, political, and social life (Sen 1999; Daubon 2002).

Grassroots development empowers communities not only to increase their income but also to develop social capital and networks that can help them address the host of problems that threaten poor and marginalized people around the world. Grassroots development alone, however, is not enough to reduce poverty significantly. Public health measures, infrastructure provision, and the kinds of governmental reforms discussed by Mishkin also have to occur. But programs aimed *directly* at the poorest to engage and empower them need to be a central part of efforts to promote equality.

Sustainability and the Ideal of Equality

The growing evidence of global environmental threats means that it is irresponsible to discuss options for promoting equality and economic activity without framing those options in terms of ecological sustainability. The scientific consensus surrounding the causes, dimensions, and effects of climate change and other global environmental threats indicates that the widely accepted view that economic growth as currently practiced is possible, inevitable, and politically desirable is itself not sustainable. But political leaders, economists, and others have been slow to understand that if the climate is seriously disrupted, conventional expectations of economic growth will be shattered. Although it is true that some environmental indicators show dramatic improvement over the past decades—air and water pollution in many areas, particularly in the wealthy world, are improving—other indicators suggest that the global economy is not ecologically sustainable. Growth in greenhouse gas emissions and toxic wastes, the decline of biodiversity and habitat, the loss of topsoil, and the depletion of aquifers are examples of environmental threats that inexorably expand with global economic growth (American Association for the Advancement of Science 2000; Kennedy 2006). Sometimes efforts to mitigate one environmental harm worsens another, as in the effort to protect the stratospheric ozone layer by substituting hydrofluorocarbons (HFCs) for chlorofluorocarbons (CFCs), even though HFCs are potent greenhouse gasses that worsen atmospheric warming (Velders et al. 2009). Thus, efforts to assist and empower the poorest of the poor must be broadened to give increased attention to doing so in ways that ensure an ecologically sustainable future.

Thick definitions of sustainable development integrate ecological protection and economic activity with social equity and political empowerment. These prioritize reducing poverty through helping the poor gain some measure of self-sufficiency through a more equitable distribution of resources. They also identify broadened political participation as a key ingredient in ensuring that decisions affecting economic and environmental conditions become more inclusive. Sustainability is not an ecological concept alone; it is also one of social justice, inclusion, fairness, community well-being, and political engagement. Sustainability extends these values to include intergenerational equity and justice so that future generations have the resources to pursue their life choices even as the benefits of current activity are extended to all in the current generation.

In the thick conceptions, then, ecological sustainability requires a radical set of changes in order to ensure fairness in the distribution of benefits and burdens, the preservation of a perpetual resource base and basic ecological services, and a social system that helps the most vulnerable secure at least a minimum level of resources necessary to help them overcome the high infant mortality, low life expectancy, poor health, and inadequate nutrition that plague so many of our planet's inhabitants.

Because it is defined in such broad terms, sustainable development requires a clear set of principles that can be translated into an effective guide for policy making. Reducing global poverty and meeting the demands of poor countries for economic growth and development can clash with the environmental protection agenda of the wealthy world. However, the cooperation of both North and South are required to effectively address climate change, biodiversity preservation, and other issues, and securing the South's cooperation requires the North's commitment to development. The South's possession of natural resources and ecological services that the North seeks gives the South an opening for making their development more visible. Furthermore, the prospects for cooperation are in some ways quite promising because the developing countries also have an interest in ensuring that their own development occurs in ways that are consistent with global ecological constraints. Taking advantage of these overlaps of interest and formulating guidance for effective action also raises questions of institutional design, including issues of how to ensure that aid from developed countries addresses both the immediate challenges, such as improving their people's quality of life and remedying visible environmental problems like water and air pollution, as well as the longer-term challenges, such as addressing climate stabilization and preserving biodiversity (Milbrath 1989; Panayotou 1993; Kirkby, O'Keefe, and Timberlake 1995; Daly 1996; Prugh, Costanza, and

Daly 2000; Lafferty and Meadowbrook 2000; Harris et al. 2001; Lafferty and Hovden 2003; Lafferty 2004; Hossay 2006).

The globalization of commerce, culture, and communication has occurred during a period of unprecedented economic growth, the spread of new technologies, the expansion of individual freedom and recognition of human rights, increased flow of information, and an upsurge in democratic politics and government. Most comprehensively defined, globalization is the process of integrating more and more of the world's population into one vast network of economic, information, and cultural exchange. Globalization involves expanding trade, economic connections, investment, and commerce, but it also includes expanding a wider set of connections ranging from the global flow of information to entertainment and culture.

So far the benefits of globalization have been quite selective and asymmetrical, largely concentrated in the wealthy countries. In general, regions blessed with an educated workforce, effective transportation and communications infrastructure, and already-established high levels of income do much better than other areas. The average per capita income in the wealthiest twenty countries in 2002 was 37 times that in the poorest twenty countries—twice the ratio that existed in 1970. The middle strata of developing countries, namely those with per capita incomes of between 40 and 80 percent of the average in the advanced countries, are thinner now than they were in the 1970s (World Bank 2003a; United Nations Conference on Trade and Development 2002). Economic conditions worsened considerably in some twenty-five countries during the 1990s. Proponents of unregulated markets argue that inequality is an inevitable outcome of globalization and a desirable one insofar as it creates competitive pressures that drive costs down. But the abject poverty that accompanies globalization reflects a profound indifference to human dignity, a squandering of human potential, and a violation of basic human rights (Sen 1999).

Sustainability and Poverty

Sustainability offers a breathtakingly ambitious program for recasting globalization by calling for a comprehensive, integrated approach that includes securing social justice and improving the life chances of the poor, transforming economic practices, and supporting participatory democracy and empowerment of citizens. It links the wealthy and poor countries, as they all share the challenge of making their economies eco-logically sustainable and reflective of the needs of the poor within their own boundaries as well as the needs of future generations. It promises to find a path to reconciling the stubborn conflicts between environmental protection and economic growth, equality and efficiency, and the differ-ent agendas of the North and the South.

However, despite the global appeals to sustainability, the concept seems to be intertwined with the idea of local community. The most thriving examples of sustainability seem to be in that context. Sustain-ability is also bound up with notions of strong democracy, participation, and community, and these social characteristics are fostered through per-sonal interaction. So too is a commitment to a land ethic. As Aldo Leopold defined the land ethic, sounding much like a proponent of sus-tainable communities, "An ethic, ecologically, is a limitation on freedom of action in the struggle for existence. . . . All ethics so far evolved rest upon a single premise: that the individual is a member of a community of interdependent parts. . . . The land ethic simply enlarges the bound-aries of the community to include soils, water, plants, and animals, or col-lectively: the land" (Leopold 1966).

Furthermore, Garrett Hardin's 1968 essay, "The Tragedy of the Commons," was a critical exposition of the ideas that eventually matured into the idea of ecological sustainability. Hardin suggested that an open access commons would be lost unless government regulation intervened to protect it. However, some have argued that there is a third alternative: developing a shared set of values and sense of responsibility that encour-age the users of a commons to act in concert to conserve the resource on which they all depend.

People act in pursuit of their own best interest; the key is to figure out how to help them see that collective solutions are in their interest and that depleting the commons can be avoided if they limit their con-sumption and resist the temptation to get all they can out of a resource before it is gone (Burger and Gochfeld 1998). Other theorists have sug-gested that users may make individual decisions that produce bad collec-tive outcomes for multiple reasons. They may lack information about what others whose actions affect their interests will do, lack a means of coordinating their responses, or lack ways to prevent some parties (free-riders) from enjoying the benefits of others' restraint while exercising none themselves. A combination of education—inculcation of shared values and sense of responsibility—and effective regulation seems to work better than either alone. As users come to see the connection between their use of resources and the consequences that follow, they will come to see that it is in their interest to preserve the common resources.

The Problem of Environmental Decline and the False Promise of Economic Growth

Advocates of free market–based globalization suggest that environmental conditions will improve as countries modernize. Some analysts argue that there is a simple relationship between wealth and environmental quality. Though pollution levels rise as countries move from extreme poverty to medium income level, pollution levels decline as wealth continues to grow past that medium income point, and this is for two reasons. First, developing countries can achieve economic growth as well as a better environment through buying progressively cheaper, cleaner technology from the industrialized nations. When this occurs, growth and environmental quality are not opposites but are mutually reinforcing. Second, as governments decide to pursue an improved quality of life for the population, they adopt political measures that make pollution more expensive through regulations and taxes: "There are no decisive reasons to assume that the same development will not happen in the Third World which today faces serious environmental problems equivalent to those we faced 50–80 years ago" (Lomborg 2001, 176).

However, extrapolating from the history of economic and environmental development in the North to predict the emergence of a similar pattern in the South is problematic. The presumption underlying globalization of trade and markets is that there is one model of development and modernization—the high-consumption, high-pollution model embraced by the West. As globalization continues and population grows, pressures on natural resources and ecosystems will only increase. Unless there are revolutionary changes in technologies that go well beyond the incremental, steady improvements in efficiency that have characterized the past few decades, it seems inevitable that resource shortages and rising pollution will eventually overwhelm any effort to expand consumption. Developed nations do not share their cleanest, most efficient technologies with their competitors in the developing world, who already enjoy considerable comparative advantages due to cheaper labor, typically resulting in more pollution per unit of economic output in the South than in the North.

As globalization continues, pressures on natural resources and ecosystems will only increase. Ecologists warn that it is quite unlikely that everyone in the world can come to enjoy the same standard of material living that people in the United States and other wealthy countries now enjoy; resource shortages and pollution will likely overwhelm such efforts. The ability of the atmosphere to absorb wastes from growing industrialization does not appear to be as great now as it has been in the past. Competitive pressures create powerful incentives for corporations to externalize environmental impacts resulting from production and to avoid including the true costs of production in the prices they charge. Those pressures also discourage governments from imposing regulations aimed at reducing these externalities. These problems are likely to worsen over time. World population, which doubled between 1960 and 2000, will increase by a further 50 percent to nine billion over the next fifty years. However, the rate of population growth has decreased considerably in recent years because fertility rates are falling rapidly in most parts of the world. The fertility rate gives the average number of children a woman of childbearing age will have during her lifetime. Because of deaths of children, the replacement rate is 2.1 in rich countries and 3.0 in poor countries. Today the fertility rate in half the world is 2.2, and some demographers expect it to fall below replacement rate sometime between 2020 and 2050. It took 130 years for the fertility rate in Britain to fall from 5 to 2; a similar transition occurred in South Korea in the twenty years between 1965 and 1985; and in Iran the rate fell from 7 to 1.9 between 1984 and 2009 (Go Forth 2009). Economic growth, urbanization, education of women and girls, and increased access to family planning have brought about a situation in which the "population bomb" has been defused. However, environmental strain will continue to rise. One study projects that humanity's use of biological resources will increase from 20 percent above the earth's biological capacity in 2000 to between 80 and 120 percent above biocapacity in 2050 (World Wildlife Fund 2002b, 20).

Approximately one-quarter of the earth's surface, about 11.4 billion hectares, is productive land and sea space; the rest is unproductive areas of icecaps, desert, and open ocean. Divided among the global population of six billion people, this total equates to just 1.9 hectares per person.

Although the Ecological Footprint (a measure of the consumption of renewable natural resources) of the average African or Asian consumer was less than 1.4 hectares per person in 1999, the average Western European's footprint was about 5.0 hectares, and the average North American's was about 9.6 hectares (World Wildlife Foundation 2002b). According to another set of calculations, if every person on earth consumed like the most affluent 15 percent do, it would require an additional two-and-one-half earths to provide the required resources (UNEP 2002).

According to a World Resources Institute report, "the kind of resource-intensive production that is commonplace in developed countries probably cannot be replicated in a large number of other countries without causing serious environmental harm" (World Resources Institute 1998). Between 1970 and 1995, the value of total consumption in industrialized countries increased from $8.3 trillion to $16.5 trillion, and developing countries from $1.9 trillion to $5.2 trillion (UNFPA 2001). The inexorable pressure resulting from exponentially increasing rates of consumption make the global situation today much different than that in which the wealthy world industrialized. The economic development of the poorer countries of the world cannot simply follow the pattern set by the wealthy world; because of the pressures inherent in the exponential growth of consumption, it is simply not possible for consumption, pollution, and waste to expand until each person lives like those in the wealthy world do. As discussed earlier, consider once again a pool of oil that will last 100 years at current rates of consumption. At a 5 percent annual growth rate in consumption, it will only last 36 years. If the pool turns out to be larger and can provide a supply at current rates for 1,000 years, the 5 percent annual growth rate would exhaust it in 79 years. Thus, the presumption of ever-increasing consumption rates bumps up against the reality of limited resources, whether they be oil, clean water, topsoil, or other resources essential for life (Princen, Maniates, and Conca 2002, 6–10).

The differences in consumption between the wealthy and poor nations are enormous. One-fifth of the world's population in the industrial countries is responsible for close to 90 percent of the total personal consumption. Despite two decades of globalization and aggregate growth, the number of people earning US$1 a day or less has remained static at 1.2 billion, whereas the number earning less than US$2 a day has increased from 2.55 billion to 2.8 billion people (United Nations Development Program 2007). Some 5,500 children die each day from diseases linked to polluted food, air, and water. About one-seventh of the world's population, 1.02 billion people, lack enough food (FAO 2009). Consumers in high-income countries—about 16 percent of the world's population—spent about 80 percent of the money devoted to private consumption, whereas purchases by consumers in low-income nations—the poorest 35 percent of the world's population—engaged in less than 2 percent of all private consumption. On average, a person living in a developed nation consumes twice as much grain, twice as much fish, three times as much meat, nine times as much paper, and eleven times as much gasoline as a person living in a developing nation. A child born in the developed world consumes thirty to fifty times as much water resources as one in the developing world. Fossil fuel consumption and carbon dioxide emissions, on a per capita basis, are ten times higher in North America than in the developing regions. The world's billion poorest people use only 0.2 tons of oil-equivalent energy per capita annually, whereas the billion richest—those earning on average over US$20,000 a year—use nearly twenty-five times as much (World Bank 2003b).

Ecology, Economy, and Equity

A primary feature of sustainability is the commitment to give priority to ecological preservation rather than economic growth and the recognition that the economy is part of the global ecosystem and completely dependent on it. Economic production is fundamentally "the process of converting the natural world (renewable and nonrenewable resources and the ecosystems they constitute) to the manufactured world (houses, cars, computers, roads, books, plastic toys, etc., and non-natural ecosystems such as parks and fields)" (Prugh, Costanza, and Daly 2000, 19). The economy grows at the expense of the environment, but it cannot outgrow its host; hence, economic growth is finite. As the amount of manufactured goods increases and the amount of natural resources dwindles, eventually more is lost by reducing natural capital further than is gained by expanding manufactured capital, and then economic growth will actually make people worse off (Prugh, Costanza, and Daly 2000, 21). Underlying efforts to balance ecological and economic considerations is the importance of equity and fairness. Any effort to protect and conserve resources must, therefore, recognize the great inequality in the distribution of resources and the importance of alleviating poverty and suffering in the current generation.

Ecological Integrity, Ecosystem Services, and Natural Capital

Ecosystems can be understood and valued in terms of the services they provide to humankind. Sustaining those ecosystem services is of fundamental importance to our survival. A primary function of ecosystems is to produce food; the primary concern here is the degradation of soil. In the past, soil degradation has been offset by increased use of pesticides and fertilizers, but it is not clear how long that can continue. Water quantity is threatened by growing diversion of water for human use, which leaves less for environmental values. Water quality has improved in some wealthy countries but not in developing ones, and pollution threatens water systems throughout the world. Increased food production has reduced the capacity for carbon storage, as forests have been converted to agricultural lands. Biodiversity is threatened by pollution, invasive species, and loss of habitat. Demand for ecosystem goods and services continues to grow; thus, sustainability requires a major commitment to ecosystem management to secure these services for current and future generations.

Concern for sustainability is rooted in the need to protect against unintended consequences, possible synergistic effects when ecological conditions interact, cascading effects and feedback loops that exacerbate ecological threats, cascading events that run out of control, cliffs and turning points that belie the belief that ecological change is incremental and predictable, as well as the sheer power of exponential growth (Brown et al. 2000, esp. ch. 2). At the heart of the commitment to maintaining ecological services and preserving natural capital is the precautionary principle. Given the uncertainty surrounding the consequences of resource use and pollution, we should err on the side of caution and preserve ecosystems and minimize pollution and resource use because the stakes are so high and some consequences are irreversible.

Box 4.1 summarizes the core elements of ecological sustainability. The greater the level of commitment to these values and the more they are embraced, the closer a society comes to the goal of ecological sustainability. As their implications for action are defined more specifically, we can develop a clearer picture of how to achieve sustainability and the magnitude of the change in behavior that it requires.

In 1996 Costa Rica enacted a forest law that included a program for the payment of ecosystem services that pays the owners of forests to preserve and protect their forests. A 5 percent tax on gasoline, the sale of carbon emissions credits called Certifiable Tradeable Offsets, and private

Box 4.1
The Elements of Sustainability

Ecological integrity, ecosystem services, and natural capital
- Ensure economic activity is within ecological limits
- Maintain ecological integrity, protect key ecosystem services
- Meet needs of present without compromising those of future
- Ensure sustainable yield of renewable resources
- Preserve and regenerate natural capital base
- Protect the ecosystem in light of uncertainty—the precautionary principle
- Use adaptive management to respond to the dynamic nature of the environment

True-cost prices and ecologically sensitive economic indicators
- Internalize environmental costs in market exchanges
- Prevent pollution to reduce wastes and externalities most efficiently
- Regulate emissions to reduce externalities
- Use emissions trading, pollution taxes, and other market-based regulatory approaches
- Reduce subsidies that have harmful environmental consequences—water, energy
- Create incentives for reduced pollution through legal liability and liability insurance
- Require economic valuation of ecosystem functions
- Develop economic indicators and measures that reflect depletion of natural resources
- Count pollution cleanup and treatment of illness as costs
- Devise broader measures of social and economic factors

Wealth, population, technology, and consumption
- Ensure intergenerational equity—non-declining per capital wealth
- Ensure intragenerational equity—current social, political, and economic equality
- Address interaction of poverty and environmental degradation
- Develop appropriate, efficient, conserving technologies
- Transfer and disseminate widely cleaner technologies

Democratic politics, community, and natural resource governance
- Foster strong democracy and participation
- Strengthen community, civil society, and social capital

donations produce between $16–20 million a year for the program. The program identified four ecosystem services of forests: protecting biodiversity, sequestering carbon, preventing erosion and purifying water, and providing scenic or aesthetic experiences; it then pays landowners to help achieve those goals. Landowners receive on average US$120/hectare for plantations, US$60/hectare for forests, and US$45/hectare for forest management and reforestation (Ferroukhi and Aguilar Schramm 2003).

Costa Rica is not alone. Malaysia enacted a National Forest Act to limit deforestation. The law specifies the length and age of trees that can be legally harvested, prohibits logging in reserves, and sets limits on total cuts. Satellite data are used to monitor compliance. As a result, the amount of forest area grew from about 59 percent of Malaysia's territory in 2000 to 64 percent in 2005 (Malaysia 2007).

Reducing Emissions from Deforestation and forest Degradation (REDD) is a proposal from developing countries to pay them to reduce carbon emissions by protecting forests. Funding would come from donations from developed countries, individuals, and organizations and from the sale of carbon credits. Carbon emission reductions would be verified through satellite monitoring.

The Oasis Project is aimed at protecting the Atlantic Rainforest in Brazil. Some 93 percent of the forest has already been lost to deforestation, but the balance is still a significant home for biodiversity and an important watershed. The project is managed by the Brazilian Fundação O Boticário, funded by the O Boticário cosmetics company and other corporate partners (for example, the Mitsubishi Corporation since 2006). The foundation operates two nature preserves near Curitiba, Brazil, and provides public education exhibits on the importance of protecting biodiversity. It also pays landowners to preserve their forests so that their ecosystem services continue. Forestry experts select possible areas to be protected, evaluates these sites in terms of their potential ecosystem services, contracts with landowners to protect their land, and monitors compliance. Areas are selected that provide the greatest watershed services for the São Paulo area and are in the most danger of deforestation. The average payment per landowner is $146/hectare/year, and these payments typically double or triple the annual earnings of landowners. São Paulo plans to create a one cent/liter tax on water users to expand funding for the project.

Toward Ecologically Sustainable Politics

The kinds of changes required to attain sustainability require levels of motivation and commitment that are more likely to come from people who feel a sense of responsibility and accountability for how their actions affect the quality of life of others. Maintaining the changes over time also requires engagement and empowerment, so that participants devise solutions with which they are then willing to comply. A strong sense of political efficacy encourages people to become involved in devising solutions to environmental problems. A robust commitment to community motivates people to reduce adverse impacts they impose on others and contribute to a shared quality of life. A spirited, vibrant civil society, composed of effective government and committed nongovernmental organizations, works together to ensure that the common interests of all are realized.

Given its broad sweep and integration of politics, economics, and environment, sustainability seems most promising as an idea for governing local communities. Indeed, the local is the only level of action at which such comprehensive efforts seem likely. However, a community may make itself sustainable by exporting its wastes or importing unsustainable levels of resources. Thus, a particular community may thrive while others live lives mired in poverty. How does sustainability guide us in these circumstances? Michael Sandel argued that a commitment to a more engaged local environmental politics can also contribute to greater sense of global politics, which is required in order to address problems affecting global commons such as protecting the oceans, stratospheric ozone layer, and climate. "A more promising basis for democratic politics that reaches beyond nations," Sandel stated, "is a revitalized civic life nourished in the more particular communities we inhabit. . . . People will not pledge allegiance to vast and distant entities, whatever their importance, unless those institutions are somehow connected to political arrangements that reflect the identity of the participants" (1996, 46). He argued that in the republican tradition of government, as articulated by Aristotle and subsequent theorists, self-government is understood as "an activity rooted in a particular place, carried out by citizens loyal to that place and the way of life it embodies." However, self-government now requires "a politics that plays itself out in a multiplicity of settings, from neighborhoods to nations to the world as a whole. . . . The civic virtue distinctive to our time is the capacity to negotiate our way among the sometimes overlapping, sometimes conflicting obligations that claim us, and to live with the tension to which multiple loyalties give rise." Participation and engagement in local political problem solving engenders a kind of commitment and sense of responsibility that might spread to broader and eventually global issues, in time becoming strong enough that national policy makers would find ignoring it increasingly difficult (Sandel 1996, 350).

Many advocates of sustainability appeal to virtues of self-abnegation and sacrifice to secure protection of ecosystems: they argue that humans must limit their consumption so that other species can survive. As global environmental problems such as climate change grow in severity, limiting consumption has been framed more and more as an issue of human well-being. The earth's capacity to absorb pollution and produce the goods and services on which human life depends is decreasing, thus prompting a reframing of the old idea of threat from a population bomb to the more complex concept of a consumption bomb in which the large ecological footprint of the wealthy minority and the much smaller but growing footprint of rapidly industrializing nations combine in unsustainable ways (Maniates 2005). So the conclusion seems inescapable that those in the North need to sacrifice current consumption so that those in the South can increase their consumption to levels needed to escape poverty and so that future generations will have the same resource base from which we draw to meet our needs and desires seems inescapable.

The notion of sacrifice has prompted a number of responses. One is to acknowledge its inevitability and to lament its political infeasibility. On this view people will never accept policies that limit their freedom to consume as much as they can; a crisis or a totalitarian revolution will be required to force fundamental changes in personal lifestyles. A second response is to suggest that technological innovation will rescue us from the need to make hard choices, that enough new energy sources and alternative materials will become available that consumption patterns need not change. But such faith in technological fixes seems unreasonably optimistic as the cost of innovations like clean energy make them affordable to the wealthy but not to the poor.

From a third perspective, sacrificing or limiting consumption does not require real sacrifice because human happiness does not depend on high levels of consumption. The New Economics Foundation (2006, 2010), a U.S. think tank, rather than using the conventional economic measures such as GNP, calculates a "Happy Planet Index" (HPI) based on a nation's ecological footprint (levels of consumption and the amount of land required to sustain a population at current levels of consumption and technological development), life expectancy (representing overall life span as well as other factors such as infant mortality that help shape well-being), and measures of happiness (asking people, to rate on a score of 1, being low, to 10, high, how satisfied they are overall with their lives). The formula is simple: HPI = life satisfaction x life expectancy/ecological footprint. In 2006 Vanuatu, a Pacific island country home to 209,000 people with a per capita income of US$2,900 was ranked number one, with mostly Central American countries filling in the top ten. In 2010 Costa Rica took first place with an HPI of 76.1 out of a possible 100, and the top ten were Central American, Caribbean, or Pacific Island states. In both years poor African countries comprise the bottom ten entries. Industrial countries ranked well down the list in both 2006 and 2010: the United States was ranked 150th/114th, the UK 105th/tied for 74th, Japan 95th/tied for 74th, and Germany 81st/51st.

Such rankings may not include all the variables one would want, but they do help make the case that long and happy lives are possible while living modestly with a much smaller ecological footprint. The authors of the index argue that, based on attainable levels of life expectancy and well-being, the target for the HPI should be 83.5. In 2010 they modified their approach, suggesting that by 2050 all countries should strive for a life satisfaction score of at least 8, a lifespan of 87 years, and an ecological footprint of no more than 1.7 "global hectares" per person. Costa Rica's HPI was only 76.1 mainly because its mean life expectancy is 78.8 years and its footprint is 2.3 global hectares per person. The primary point of the HPI and the targets is that all countries can do better to improve their quality of life and happiness while also reducing their ecological footprint. In this approach, pursuit of a smaller ecological footprint is not a sacrifice; it becomes consistent with life satisfaction and hence with individuals' self-interest.

A fourth response to the challenge posed by the idea of sacrifice is to embrace it willingly as part of an ethic of respect and caring for others and other forms of life. Sacrifice is regularly invoked in religious settings as a virtue: sacrifices produce spiritual blessings in return. The Oxford English Dictionary provides a more secular definition that also emphasizes sacrifice as consistent with the pursuit of one's self-interest: "The destruction or surrender of something valued or desired for the sake of something having, or regarded as having, a higher or more pressing claim." For example, parents happily limit their spending on themselves to create or expand opportunities for their children. Thus, self-interest can be understood differently by situating people in the relationships that give meaning to their lives rather than focusing solely on individual autonomy.

Overall, a strong commitment to future generations and to the well-being of the global community seems most likely to arise from people who have a political culture that encourages them to see their future as well as the future of their grandchildren as inextricably intertwined with those of their neighbors throughout the world. Many people find such a transformation inspiring, consistent with their personal commitment to a simpler, less selfish life that acknowledges the inherent value and sanctity of all forms of life. Theology and ecology are mutually reinforcing for some people, whereas for others sustainability is a secular enterprise. Some people argue that sustainability requires rejecting an anthropocentric worldview in favor of an ecocentric or biocentric paradigm in which humans are not the primary focus of attention; instead, all forms of life are valued equally. Yet commitment to sustainability can also arise within the existing paradigm of self-interested humans: it is simply in our interest to preserve all forms of life and help other species flourish because we are all elements of an intricate network of living things that stretches both backward and forward in time.

Attaining sustainability would also advance environmental justice. An ecologically sound economy would not generate the noxious emissions and hazardous or toxic wastes frequently concentrated in industrial areas and designated disposal sites. Many of these are located near places where poor and marginalized groups live, either because they lacked the political leverage needed to keep them from being located where they are or because nearby land was one of the few places where they could establish their shantytowns, hutments, favelas, or other informal neighborhoods. Chapter 5 takes up the problem of environmental justice.

Chapter Five
JUSTICE AND FAIRNESS IN
GLOBAL ENVIRONMENTAL POLITICS

Both chapters 3 and 4 discussed global environmental policy making in terms that can appeal to rational political actors. Making markets work clearly fits within conventional rational choice models. Making developing economies more sustainable can also be fit to such models depending on how the wealthy world perceives its self-interest: if the focus is on immediate results, the self-interest of the wealthy would likely favor continuing current policies at both national and global levels; if, however, the focus is extended to longer time periods, the self-interest of the wealthy could expand to include considerations of ecological sustainability and inspire far-reaching changes.

Justice and fairness should play a central role in debates over how to address global environmental threats. Although such considerations will never be able to compete on equal footing with appeals to self-interest, appeals to moral principles such as fairness and justice are pervasive and cannot be ignored. One way to think about these matters is that global environmental policy making will primarily need to be understood in terms of rational choices made by governments among alternative possibilities, but moral arguments can help strengthen the case for change and even shape at the margins decisions, such as providing assistance to those who are most vulnerable to environmental decline and its consequences.

Campaigns for environmental justice (EJ) bring together two of the most powerful social movements of the late twentieth and early twenty-first centuries: environmentalism and civil rights. They are particularly potent forces because of the compelling moral arguments they convey and because of the ways in which they complement each other. Although much progress has been made in reducing pollution and improving environmental quality in many areas, one of the most glaring shortcomings of those efforts is the limited progress in reducing race- and income-based disparities in environmental conditions, such as the levels of pollution to which individuals are exposed. Minority and low-income communities continue to bear a disproportionate share of environmental burdens. Civil rights and social justice advocates recognize the importance of addressing characteristics of the environments in which people of color and poor families live that contribute to poor health, reduced economic opportunity, and a diminished quality of life.

Expanding and fusing the agenda of these two movements is a compelling political goal, but it is also problematic in several ways. Environmental justice is rooted in claims of rights that represent powerful political obligations. In a democracy, asserting rights means invoking corresponding obligations and duties that outweigh majority interests; minority rights are to be vindicated even if the majority does not wish to pay the costs of vindication or have its options limited so that those rights may be exercised. But the power of these claims of rights may be diluted by their too frequent invocation; an inflation of rights claims might weaken the moral power that rights represent. There is also nothing to prevent the sum of rights claims from exceeding society's capacity to fulfill them. Hence, there is a need to set priorities, to allocate scarce financial and enforcement resources, and to ensure that the most serious problems are addressed first. A broadened agenda of environmental justice can and should generate support for more resources and expanded effort, but choices of allocating resources and efforts are inescapable, and trade-offs are inevitable. Conceptualizing environmental justice in ways that expand its reach while still preserving the power of its moral claims and its political potency is a daunting task.

Devising solutions to environmental injustices is similarly fraught with challenges. The inequitable distribution of the burdens and benefits of environmental protection reaches well beyond the site selection and pollution focus of the traditional environmental justice movement to include the management of natural resource extraction. Actions taken to improve environmental quality may not result in improved social equity and may even exacerbate inequities. Policies that promote justice and strengthen the political power and decision-making influence of the poor and other marginalized groups may not produce improvements in overall environmental conditions. Allowing indigenous groups to continue to hunt and fish on traditional lands, for example, may be a justice imperative, but it may also threaten the survival of endangered species or clash with plans for protecting wilderness. Pursuing the goal of environmental justice requires innovative remedies that balance and reinforce the goals of strengthening the power of politically disadvantaged communities as well as improving environmental quality.

A lively debate exists about the nature of the problem of environmental justice, the extent and seriousness of the risks, and the causes and underlying factors. But just as important and difficult is the question of what kinds of responses we should pursue. What are our options and how should we choose from among them? Natural resource laws and policies traditionally focus on encouraging development of resources, protecting natural systems, and ensuring the sustainability of resource development. These laws and policies are usually assessed in terms of how well they achieve these resource development and environmental protection goals and how they interact with economic goals of efficiency and growth. Environmental justice advocates argue equal importance should be accorded to the consequences of natural resource policy decisions for the societal goals of protecting individual rights, promoting justice and fairness, ensuring fair participation, and fostering social equity.

This chapter develops a framework for exploring alternative ways of defining injustices related to natural resources and the environment that are found in the relevant literature and public policies and also to suggest how environmental justice can be approached from different perspectives. The literature on EJ from U.S. scholars typically focuses on rights-based assertions of injustices in the distribution of environmental harms. More broadly, the EJ literature from the developing world centers on the lack of support for sustainable development for all humankind, particularly those in the poorest regions of the world. The chapter begins with a discussion of the alternative frameworks for defining EJ, which primarily come from the United States. It then takes up the question of EJ between nations. To broaden the analysis cross-nationally, it then turns to a brief case study on how the concept of environmental justice can help clarify some of the key issues surrounding climate change and the case of how the rights of indigenous peoples implicate environmental protection policy making.

Frameworks for Assessing Environmental Justice Issues

Defining Environmental Justice

The problems to be redressed through environmental justice might take one of two forms: (1) poor and minority communities are disproportionately exposed to environmental risks, or (2) these communities are less likely than others to benefit from natural resource access and development policies. Both cases are examples of injustices that arise from the lopsided ways in which benefits and burdens are distributed in society.

Hazardous waste treatment and storage sites, representative of the first kind of problem, are often located in low-income and marginalized minority communities because of low land prices and little political opposition. As a result, community members are exposed to greater levels of hazardous emissions, odors, water contamination, and other environmental risks than those who live in other communities. Or poor people may move into areas where these facilities already exist because housing prices there are cheaper. People of color may have fewer housing choices because of discrimination and have few options other than moving into areas with higher environmental risks. Poor and minority communities may be areas where there is less enforcement, prevention, mitigation, and other efforts to reduce environmental problems because the residents lack political influence.

Despite these barriers confronting minority communities, they have been increasingly successful in raising awareness of cases of disproportionate exposure to environmental hazards. African American children in Chicago chained themselves to dump trucks filled with hazardous wastes; a multiracial group in Los Angeles blocked the construction of an incinerator in their community. Tribes have protested threats to subsistence fishing and hunting by pollution from mining operations that have poisoned fish, game, and reservation lands. Cases brought forward in the 1990s continued to focus on toxic waste but also expanded to reach other issues. In Boston, community members protested plans to expand Logan Airport because of the impact of increased aircraft noise on working-class and poor communities. In Atlanta, environmental and community groups opposed highway projects that would increase air pollution in minority neighborhoods (Murray 2000). Despite these and other successes, tension exists between some elements of the environmental justice movement and the broader environmentalist movement. Many activists in the environmental justice movement believe the broader environmental movement has been unwilling to give sufficient priority to environmental injustices in the policy positions taken and even in their own organizational practices, policies, and hiring (Sandler and Pezzullo 2007).

Natural resources policy is another area in which environmental justice issues arise. The development of water and other natural resources in the arid western United States has been aimed primarily at politically well-connected communities. Subsidies and other policies typically benefit large, wealthy landowners more than small, low-income farmers and ranchers. The treaty rights of tribes have been regularly violated by states and private interests, who have ignored fishing, water, land, and other Indian rights so as to increase their own access to valuable natural resources. Environmental justice advocates have raised similar concerns about the impact of projects on minority and poor communities in other parts of the United States as well. The plan to restore the Everglades in Florida by redirecting fresh water into the area was criticized by some members of Congress for failing to give adequate attention to the impact of the loss of agricultural water on low-income and minority farmers. They urged the Army Corps of Engineers, the agency responsible for the Everglades project, to establish a monitoring panel to represent the interests of low-income and minority communities and to involve them in the implementation of the restoration project (Ferguson 2000).

Thus, a major challenge in environmental justice is deciding how to define the problem. Five options for framing the issue of environmental justice seem to capture most of the approaches taken by advocates and scholars. Furthermore, these frameworks are not mutually exclusive. They overlap considerably, and proponents of environmental justice favoring a particular framework may rely on elements of others as they frame individual issues.

The Civil Rights Framework

Environmental justice is typically viewed as a civil rights problem, with advocates suggesting remedies rooted in civil rights law and policy. In this view, minority communities are a target for siting hazardous sites because of their lack of political power. Similarly, politicians who make resource development decisions and policies that distribute benefits to politically powerful interests or violate treaty or statutory rights and agreements may do so because of the perception that there is little political cost and considerable political gain in ignoring these rights and commitments. Advocates of this framework typically recognize that the interactions of race, income, and political power are complex. The location of facilities may be driven by market factors, such as the price of land, access to transportation infrastructure, availability of labor, and the location of raw materials. However, choosing the location may be guided by appreciating which areas hold communities in which residents have less political power than in others—they may even be intentionally located in minority or low-income communities to escape the delays and added costs that organized NIMBY ("not in my backyard") opposition can impose. It is important to remember that site locations evolve over time: a site may have been located originally in an urban, working-class community, but over time residents in this community who could afford to move to more pleasant surroundings do so, leaving poorer residents and depressed land prices. In turn, low-income residents move in because of cheap housing prices (Ringquist 2000, 244–47). Market factors, discrimination, and the political powerlessness of marginalized communities that have little clout in policy-making decisions all contribute in complicated ways to environmental injustice (Foster 1998).

The civil rights framework is sometimes intertwined with broader notions of social justice. Robert D. Bullard, a distinguished environmental justice scholar, argued that several factors contribute to environmental injustice. One is inadequate concern for the process by which rules, regulations, and criteria are applied and the subsequent impact of procedural steps on participation in these processes by minority communities. The location of meetings to inform the public may be inaccessible to some, the publication of materials only in majority languages (say, English in the United States), and decision-making bodies with memberships that do not reflect the racial and ethnic makeup of the communities affected by those decisions may discourage wide participation. Another factor is the distribution of jobs and income from industrial activities. A third is the burdens caused by the disposal of industrial wastes; communities that house the waste sites typically receive fewer benefits than the areas where production occurs. Broader social inequity is another factor: environmental justice advocates in the United States are quick to point out the lingering racism in the United States and the extent to which communities of color are seen as sacrifice zones for pollution and hazardous waste. Bullard argued that race and class are "intricately linked in our society," but that race "continues to be a potent predictor of where

people live, which communities get dumped on, and which are spared"
(Bullard 1993, 11).

Two competing principles might guide decision making: nondiscrimination and race-based preference. The nondiscrimination standard
prohibits any consideration of race in the making of environmental, land
use, natural resource, and other policy decisions. That standard raises the
question of what constitutes a violation of the principle—how much difference constitutes a disparate impact? In environmental justice cases, the
question may be how does the environmental risk to health compare
across minority and nonminority communities, or how do the natural
resource benefits given to minority groups compare with those provided
to nonminority ones? However, the nondiscrimination principle may be
too conservative and acquiescent to the status quo. In embracing it, we
commit to no longer discriminate, but we do not directly address the
impacts already in place. Many argue that preferential treatment or a
race-conscious remedy is required in order to compensate for past discrimination. This may take the form of offering compensation to communities for the existing facilities in their community or the lack of
access to natural resources and perhaps preferential treatment to ensure
that the risks of environmental harms and the benefits of natural
resources are spread more evenly. These decisions turn on notions of distributive justice addressed more clearly in other frameworks. If preferential treatment is adopted, the thorny issues of when, if ever, it is no longer
justified and should be ended also arise.

The civil rights framework will likely continue to guide efforts to
pursue the goals of environmental justice. But problems with this framework must be addressed. For example, should environmental justice focus
only on people of color, or should impacts on low-income people also
be addressed? The civil rights solution may not work as well for income
as it does for race. Race and ethnicity are well established in U.S. constitutional law as suspect classifications, requiring heightened or strict
scrutiny by courts and a demonstration of a compelling government
interest when it serves as the basis for policy making. In contrast, federal
courts do not recognize class as a problematic distinction. Neither constitutional nor statutory provisions provide any basis for claims that class
or income status creates an actionable claim. Though some workers'
advocates have argued that affirmative action should be viewed as a remedy for income-based disadvantage, that view has yet to gain formal legal
or constitutional acceptance. If income or poverty is the ultimate root of

environmental and natural resource injustices, then we need solutions that go beyond the remedies available from civil rights law.

More broadly, should civil rights be at the center of the debate over the role of government in pursuing environmental protection policies at least for people of color? We rely on a discourse of civil rights to discuss the values and concerns that are most important to our political, collective lives. But a politics of rights makes trade-offs difficult because it emphasizes enforcing entitlements that claimants assert regardless of costs or competing concerns. A discourse of rights eschews the balancing that is inevitable when we have public demands that are contradictory or exceed the resources that are available. The controversies surrounding rights raise questions about their role in guiding public policy making. If rights are to play a transforming role in ensuring environmental justice, they will have to be thought of in different ways—not just as restraints on government but as ways of empowering individuals, reinforcing our responsibility for each other and for the kind of society in which we are a part, and asserting the moral and social responsibilities we have in common. Rights need not insulate individuals from each other; they can be part of defining membership in a political society and reinforcing shared commitments. Rights can help foster common concerns and encourage us to commit to ensuring that each person enjoys access to natural resources and environmental quality that are essential for realizing a meaningful life and enjoying real equality of opportunity.

Distributive Justice, Fairness, and Rights

Another way of framing the problem of environmental justice comes from theories of distributive justice devised by philosophers who grapple with issues such as how to distribute benefits and burdens, how expectations of equality are to be satisfied, and what ethical principles can guide natural resource policy making. Notions of distributive justice guide our thinking about such questions as: What definition of equity do we use in attempting to develop an equitable distribution in the location of polluting facilities or equitable access to natural resources? Does equity mean the polluter pays—that those who benefit from pollution should bear the burden of disposing of the accompanying wastes? If so, then should those who consume more have more polluting facilities near them, or pay others to bear that risk? The polluter-pays principle appeals strongly to a sense of fairness that links benefits and burdens. But following this principle presents numerous challenges, such as determining who should bear the burdens, what those burdens are, how those burdens should be valued, and what additional costs should be imposed on producers and purchasers. All this suggests the importance of prior knowledge of effects and the importance of environmental impact assessment and other requirements to disclose environmental harms and threats. It also makes clear the importance of preventing pollution so as to reduce environmental harms for all communities.

One form of distributive justice is geographic equity, which requires fairness in the physical distribution of hazardous facilities. Burying wastes or shipping them somewhere else are no solution; they simply impose the problem on future generations or on people elsewhere. However, geographic equity, in which each person is exposed equally to all environmental harms, is impractical. Most environmental harms travel a short distance from their source; others dissipate with distance as toxins are diluted by air or water. So it is unlikely that everyone would be exposed equally. One option is to give preference to those who have benefited less or have been burdened more in the past. Here, we face the same challenges faced by advocates of preferential treatment:

- Do we compensate actual victims of specific injustices, or do we compensate victims of general, societal discrimination?
- Do we compensate individuals or communities?
- How do we prove instances of past discrimination?
- How do we identify victims of societal discrimination?
- Are all members of an identifiable group (like people of color or other disadvantaged minorities) entitled to the same preference?
- Are low-income groups similarly deserving?
- How do we determine which persons are in fact entitled to the benefit?

Violations of principles or expectations of distributive justice also compel questions of providing compensation to victims of past injustices. Should those who have benefited from access to those resources or from reduced exposure to risk pay those who have been denied benefits or borne higher risks? Perhaps so, but the calculations of who must pay and who receives compensation are complex.

One of the most prominent forms of distributive justice is utilitarianism. Utilitarianism calls for a distribution of benefits, opportunities, and burdens that generates the greatest welfare for the greatest number. It is defended from at least two perspectives. First, utilitarianism is consistent with economic efficiency; a failure to maximize benefits would be unjust because it leaves an unrealized potential for generating wealth and its consequential well-being. Second, utilitarianism can be defended as egalitarian: every person's utility or interests are given equal weight. Utilitarianism here is consistent with democratic theories of individual equality and majority rule.

Utilitarianism often shows up in environmental policy in the form of cost-benefit analysis. Cost-benefit analysis is a widely used analytic tool that appeals to common sense notions and has deep roots in natural resource policy making (Gramlich 1990, 2). Yet, like any tool, it has shortcomings. The shortcomings of cost-benefit analysis and utilitarian calculations have been most prominent in natural resource and environmental law and policy. These shortcomings usually take one of two forms. First, many values cannot be easily quantified in dollars, and those values that can be more precisely and unambiguously quantified and monetized will be given priority over others, even if the others would actually enhance overall utility more. More precise economic costs, for example, may be given more weight than imprecise estimates of the value of ecosystem health, ecological services, public health, or aesthetics. Cost-benefit analysis's bias against values that are not easily quantified can be overcome by resisting quantification and laying out in qualitative terms the values to be compared. Systematic qualitative identification of the costs and benefits of alternatives can be a very useful decision-making tool and can help illuminate the consequences of policy choices, but its inability to generate an unambiguous bottom line—whether the benefits are greater than the costs—makes it less useful, at least to some users.

A second shortcoming of cost-benefit analysis is particularly important for environmental justice because it may produce unfair outcomes. A cost-benefit analysis is based on an *aggregate* of relevant costs and benefits, but these consequences may not be distributed equally. A facility that generates benefits to an entire community, for example, may also pose greater risks to some residents—such as those who live near enough to inhale toxic emissions—than others. More problematic is the case in which benefits largely accrue to one group while burdens are primarily imposed on others. Even if the aggregate benefits clearly and strongly overwhelm the costs, it is hard to defend as fair a stark mismatch between those who bear the burdens and those who enjoy the benefits of a particular activity. Utilitarianism does not prevent the designation of a minority of people to bear costs or risks in order for a majority of people to enjoy the benefits.

Utilitarianism underlies much of current environmental and natural resource law, and its consequences for how natural resource and environmental benefits and burdens are distributed have done much to spark interest in environmental justice. Other theories of justice challenge utilitarianism and suggest other ways benefits and burdens should be distributed. A rights-based theory of justice, for example, requires that no one be subjected to certain burdens, adverse impacts, or restraints, regardless of the overall benefits. Individuals may possess rights, such as the right to breathe clean air or have a safe environment, that trump utilitarian calculations of aggregate net benefit. Even where there are no constitutional rights to a clean or safe environment, environmental laws create statutory rights and general expectations that individuals will be protected from unreasonable risks or that their health will be protected with an adequate margin of safety.

The dominant American understanding of individual rights is that rights are so important that, in the words of John Rawls, they cannot be outweighed by majority will: "rights secured by justice are not subject to political bargaining or the calculus of social interests" (Rawls 1999, 25). Rawls argued that rights provide a framework that ensures individuals have the freedom to pursue their own vision of the good life, as long as they respect the similar freedom of others. Government is to remain neutral toward specific ends in respecting the capacity of individuals to choose for themselves their own beliefs and values. Liberals, following Kant, argue that society should protect rights and liberties rather than promote "good" values. No one way of life should be affirmed or mandated, but society should be neutral in terms of by what values individuals choose to live. Individual rights are trumps that people possess against the majority.

Rawls's theory of justice is an alternative to the dominant role of utilitarianism in moral philosophy. But Rawls provides no clear guidelines for determining when environmental injustices have occurred or how to remedy them. His theory of justice calls for interventions to remedy environmental or other injustices that disadvantage those who are already less well off than others. Priority must be given to the status of the least well off, as long as this can be done without violating basic personal and civil liberties. People are disadvantaged by social structures for which they are not responsible. The more fortunate should only benefit from social, political, and economic arrangements if the less fortunate benefit more. But liberal or individualist theories of justice may not provide a sufficient basis for the kind of shared morality that is best suited to deal with collective problems like environmental pollution and the preservation of natural resources.

Other conceptions of distributive justice suggest different definitions of egalitarianism. Perhaps the simplest notion is that benefits and burdens are to be distributed equally across all affected parties; everyone receives the same level of benefit, such as access to natural resources, and is exposed to the same level of environmental risk or pays the same cost. Alternatively, equality can mean that those who are similarly situated are treated the same way, and those who are differently situated have those differences taken into account. That is, there may be some factors that justify different treatment, although they should be applied consistently to all the individuals affected by that factor. Under this understanding of distributional justice, those who benefit from a risky activity should bear the associated costs. Or equality can be understood to require a minimum level of equality in access to benefits or imposition of burdens or risks. A commitment to equality may conflict with simple utilitarian calculations and suggest different distributions to different persons according to their merit, conditions, or needs. A socialist formulation links benefits and needs: everyone is to receive a level of benefits consistent with their needs even as their contributions vary according to their abilities. In contrast, a merit-based approach requires that benefits be distributed according to effort and contribution. Correspondingly, those who make only partial contributions should receive only partial benefits (Paul 1995, 27).

The variability of risk and the circumstances in which persons are exposed to it are complicating but important factors here. Risks that are voluntarily assumed, particularly after a well-informed choice, pose less of an equity problem than risks involuntarily assumed because they were imposed by others. The choice of individuals to live on the oceanfront and voluntarily accept the increased risk of damage or death from hurricanes and other storms does not pose a challenge to this notion of distributive justice. Conversely, a decision to live next to a toxic emitting factory or incinerator is problematic because it may be "voluntary" in only a very narrow sense; low-income persons may have few options other than living in an area where land or housing prices are low because environmental risks are high.

There are other forms of justice besides the distributional version that should be mentioned here, and these are sometimes used to identify examples of environmental injustices and to suggest remedies. Corrective or compensatory justice seeks to compensate victims of injustices in order to restore victims to the condition they were in before the injustice occurred or make them whole, to remedy the damage inflicted, or to provide fair recompense for the injury suffered. Obviously, some harms can be remedied and conditions restored—hazardous sites can be cleaned up, for example—but in many cases, where life or health has been lost, cash payments are a limited surrogate for making the victim whole. The repeated violation of treaties with Native Americans or the history of colonial exploitation, for example, may trigger demands for compensatory justice that have implications for access to natural resource policy.

The Public Participation Framework

Ensuring effective participation by those who are not represented well in political forums is an essential part of environmental justice. However, there is no consensus over what kind of participation is required because there are different expectations or theories of procedural fairness and justice. One standard is that a "choice made without prior consideration of the interest of all sections of the community would be open to criticism as merely partisan and unjust" (Hart 1961, 162). Justice may require the right to participate in a decision-making process, the right to have one's interests included in the analysis, or the right to be represented by others. Participation may range from commenting on proposals formulated by others to being involved in the process of generating the proposals themselves and selecting from among options.

For many, environmental justice is driven by aspirations for community empowerment, accountability of political power to those who are affected by it, and real democratic participation. For some advocates of public participation, the ultimate goal is to ensure that low-income and minority communities have the opportunity to participate effectively in decision making and to ensure their views are taken into account. These advocates emphasize the importance of ensuring that those who have been underrepresented in past decision making, because of racial or other discrimination, are empowered to participate fully and effectively. For others, public participation is less about remedying specific examples of discrimination and more about pursuing a strong, inclusive, egalitarian form of democracy that gives voice to every member of a community across a broad range of issues that are important to all members, particularly those who have lacked a strong voice in the past.

Full public participation creates procedural rather than substantive expectations for natural resource policy making: if fair procedures are established and all interests represented, then the results, whatever they may be, are acceptable. This view is consistent with pluralist politics: policy making is to include all relevant interests; they have the incentive to represent their interests the best they can; and out of the competitive clash of interests emerges the public interest. But critics have long warned that interest group politics has an upper-class bias because low-income groups and people of color are not well represented. Pluralist expectations can be more closely approximated, however, by empowering everyone through broadening public access to technical information and other resources that will ensure they can participate effectively in deliberative processes as equal participants, or at least to be competitive with those who have technical resources.

Christopher Foreman (1998, 5) argued that environmental justice advocates' real concerns "lie in the eternal yearnings for a more democratic and egalitarian society comprised of livable communities." Their discourse of justice, fairness, community, and related terms clashes with the technocratic language that dominates environmental policy as well as the clash of environmental and industry groups that dominate its politics. He stated,

> For many activists, environmental justice is mostly about accountability and political power rather than the more technical issue of environmental risks facing communities. A major reason why one simply cannot accept advocacy claims of risk at face value is that they are often anchored, ultimately, not in the dangers posed by a site or substance ostensibly at issue, but rather in a desire for transformed power relationships to be achieved on behalf of politically energized and engaged communities. (1998, 58–59)

In Foreman's view, simply holding more meetings and hearing more voices is not sufficient to produce a more just distribution of environmental burdens. It also requires fundamental changes in the way in which economic and political power are distributed.

One of the major debates in environmental justice is whether procedural expectations are sufficient or whether justice calls for certain substantive standards to be satisfied as well, as with the distribution of benefits and burdens discussed earlier. But some argue that a lack of consensus concerning the kinds of policies to adopt and the role of government in economic and social activities may make judging policies on substantive grounds nearly impossible. Without objective measures or widely agreed upon standards by which public policies can be evaluated, we turn to procedural values of pluralism, openness, and representation. Advocates of pluralist policy making in the United States have argued that because there is often little agreement over substantive goals, the best we can hope for is to design fair processes for making natural resource and other policies. If procedural norms are satisfied, then we judge policies to be largely justified.

Defenders of the public participation solution argue that if it is truly inclusive and grants access to decision makers, it can empower people to make their own decisions and does not rely on paternalistic policy making by government. People can decide for themselves how to balance environmental risks and economic benefits rather than having those decisions made by others. This community decision ideal is also attractive because it does not require policy makers to come up with a nationwide set of substantive principles to guide all decisions but instead allows participants to shape local solutions that meet their specific circumstances.

The public participation solution also has limitations. Critics of pluralism in existing societies have emphasized that because all groups are not equal in resources and ability to shape outcomes, the results of pluralist politics are unequal and unfair (Lindblom 1977). Although this concern could be addressed through redistribution or political mobilization, even the most equal forms of participatory decision making have limitations. Solutions that communities devise may be acceptable to everyone in them, but they may have spillover effects that threaten others elsewhere who were not part of the decision-making process, or they may leave out future generations. We may decide as a society that broader institutions of governance are required to intervene to protect those interests. We may decide that there are fundamental rights at play here, such as a right to a healthy environment, that people should not be allowed to negotiate away or be forced to compromise because of poverty. Negotiations may have results that yield acceptable cost-benefit ratios for those members of the community willing to be exposed to greater risks in exchange for more benefits but leave others in the community unhappy either because they assess risks differently or because they oppose such trade-offs. Advocates of pollution prevention might argue that we should not allow people to negotiate some levels of acceptable pollution or waste generation; rather, communities should be required to accept no pollution or waste so that producers will be compelled to prevent pollution. For all these reasons, ensuring a more fair, balanced, and representative decision-making process may not be enough to solve problems of environmental and natural resource injustices.

The Social Justice Framework

Advocates of the social justice framework typically regard environmental injustices and disparities in access to natural resources or the benefits that flow from their development as a manifestation of broader social inequities, including the interaction of poverty and race, the relative political powerlessness of low-income and minority groups, political inequality, and restricted participation. Thus, for many activists, environmental justice is really about the fundamental distribution of political power not the environmental risks facing communities. Although this is a view shared by some advocates of more inclusive public participation, the critique reaches much deeper than race to address fundamental issues of class. For the critics, social injustices go beyond disproportionate environmental risks and lack of access to natural resource benefits to include jobs, housing, education, public services, health, and other areas in which people of color or lower income are disadvantaged. The critics see all these problems as interrelated because they are functions of racism, exploitations of the politically powerless, cultural and social practices that favor majority interests, laws formulated to benefit those who are already advantaged and can afford to invest in the political process and campaigns, and a host of other factors. These critics also insist that solutions to the complex problems of social justice require fundamental structural changes in political, economic, and social institutions.

Securing such changes is obviously beyond the scope of environmental and natural resource law and policy. The question here is whether environmental and natural resources law and policy can play some role, however modest, in addressing these broader economic, political, and social concerns. If we can reduce environmental injustices, that is a step forward toward reducing injustice as a whole, and it might inspire other efforts to redress other injustices.

Critical legal scholars have argued that legal institutions, doctrines, and decisions "work to buttress and support a pervasive system of oppressive, inegalitarian relations" (Minda 1995, 206). Law is not neutral but rather is rooted in subjective and political choices that favor the interests of dominant political, economic, and social elites. Many critical theorists argue that conventional legal principles serve to obstruct the goals of democracy, and these theorists move beyond deconstructing societal practices to prescribing how law must be radically transformed to advance the realization of participatory democracy. They have emphasized that laws rest on an underlying layer of meaning that is not objective but rather depends on and reflects dominant cultural and social beliefs, and these are largely beliefs that elites summarize and interpret for society as a whole.

Critical race theory is based on the experience, traditions, culture, and perspective of people of color or at least how intellectuals try to characterize those experiences. It offers a race-conscious perspective by which legal doctrines and decisions are critiqued. Critical race theorists reject the notion of a color-blind law in favor of race consciousness, analysis rooted in the history of American race relations. Race consciousness recognizes major economic differences between white and black communities and seeks to develop a distinctive set of legal theories and principles rooted in those differences. This requires greater participation by minority scholars in the development of civil rights law because they have experiences of racial oppression that gives their assessments the "authority of racial distinctiveness" (Minda 1995, 172). Some critical race theorists call for the rejection of the integrationist goal of some proponents of racial equality, and these theorists favor a more culturally diverse, contextualized set of standards that recognize the uniqueness of minority experience (Minda 1995, 177). The different experiences of racial groups in dealing with problems such as disproportionate exposure to environmental hazards, should, according to this view, become the basis for formulating and implementing natural resources law and policy. These approaches would contrast with conventional ideas such as economic efficiency and rationality as the basis for determining optimal levels of pollution and suggest more of a commitment to pollution prevention and remedying the effects of past injustices.

Reducing environmental injustices can be a part of a much broader effort to address social injustices, but it is not clear that environment-related efforts will have much of an impact on these more systemic shortcomings. Broader efforts to address poverty and poverty-related issues will get more directly at root causes of social injustice. A social justice framework also suggests that, although reducing or eliminating pollution hazards and environmental burdens that prevent the disadvantaged from exercising choices is important in itself, there is also need for other actions to promote choice and freedom more broadly among people who have traditionally had very limited options.

Expectations created by different notions of justice among people do not exhaust the philosophical ideas that can serve as the basis for identifying cases of unfairness in natural resource policies and in fashioning remedies. Many of these ideas overlap significantly with the more critical variations of social justice theories discussed here. Some environmental ethics writers suggest how environmental policy should be shaped by notions of equality among all species as well as by commitments to a biospheric, rather than anthropocentric, perspective—commitments that are reflected in ideas of deep ecology (Stone 1987). Because the focus in deep ecology is on the rights of and duties to non-humans, the relevance for environmental justice here is indirect, as these ethical theories seek to broaden our thinking about the consequences of environmental and natural resource decisions. Also relevant are critical theories rooted in ecological economics, ecofeminism, socialism, and other critiques of modern, industrial, male-dominated, high-consumption societies that offer alternative visions of environmental ethics that are rooted in equality, nurturing, and postmodern challenges to ideas of progress and materialism (Merchant 1994; Princen, Maniates, and Conca 2002).

The Ecological Sustainability Framework

Advocates of ecological sustainability argue that environmental injustices are sometimes a result of the way in which environmental policies are formulated and implemented. The injustices are not necessarily an intentional outcome of these policies but rather are a result of political compromises, limited resources, incomplete understanding, and other shortcomings that nevertheless contribute to unfair outcomes and impacts. For example, many environmental laws have been criticized for shifting pollution from one environmental medium to another rather than reducing or preventing it. Politically connected individuals are often quite successful in manipulating the political system to ensure that most pollution and environmental risks occur far from where they live. Their success in getting pollution moved somewhere else may produce injustices, as poor and minority communities are simply late in joining the political debate over how to deal with environmental risks. It is usually cheaper, at least in the short run, to shift pollutants from one environmental medium (such as air) to another form (such as solid waste), which then poses a new set of problems and risks, often to other groups of people and other ecosystems. The traditional approach to environmental regulation has also contributed to environmental injustice because it emphasizes treating rather than preventing pollution, thus taking the easy path because treating pollution is, at least in the short run, usually less expensive than preventing it in the first place. Advocates of preventing pollution argue that there are significant long-term economic advantages to reducing waste and improving efficiency. However, the investments needed are costly initially, and unless all parties are compelled to make those investments, the ones who do not (thereby externalizing some of their costs) will gain competitive advantages. So collective action is required. Yet advocates of pollution prevention are also quick to point out the advantages for addressing the problem of injustice: if threats are eliminated, then there is no disproportionate risk to be fobbed off on the powerless.

Part of what is most valuable here is endorsing the idea of true costs—prices should include the *real* or *true* costs of production, including the environmental and health consequences and impacts, rather than allowing sellers and purchasers to externalize those costs to others. In a system committed to markets as a way of allocating scarce resources, determining value, and making choices from competing needs and wants, ensuring that prices provide accurate information about the true costs of what is being sold is critical. As real costs become better understood, those affected by them can have more of the information needed to decide about trade-offs and balance competing concerns such as environmental protection and economic development (Prugh, Costanza, and Daly 2000, 28–29).

The idea of sustainability goes beyond reforming particular environmental and natural resource laws to make them more effective; it also includes addressing the values underlying all activities of production and consumption. It respects the maxim, "everything is connected to everything else," which is at the heart of ecology (Commoner 1990), and requires that we deal with a broad range of problems—sprawl, traffic, air pollution, open spaces, access to recreation, overcrowding, and other ills that threaten our quality of life (Kahn 2006; Flint 2006).

Sustainability links up with notions of justice because it is concerned with the distribution of wealth and material resources, both in terms of intergenerational equity—including the wealth and wealth-generating opportunities preserved for future generations—and distribution within the current generation. Wealth matters because the lack of it causes people to engage in ecologically damaging practices to survive. But sustainability also requires appreciating limits and appropriate scale as well as the distribution of resources. Sustainability requires moderating the growth of consumption as well as that of the total human population. It is not enough to stabilize population growth because the ecological impact of population is a function of the kinds of technologies that are prevalent and the levels of consumption. Sustainability also points in the same direction as the concern for justice: it indicates that the poor must be able to increase their access to the goods and services basic to human life even as humanity as a whole decreases the aggregate levels of pollution generated and nonrenewable resources used.

Environmental Justice Among Nations

The same frameworks that guide discussions of environmental justice within countries can be applied, with the modifications necessary for shifting from the individual, household, or local level, to environmental justice among countries. The same concerns with siting of dangerous facilities or toxic waste disposal centers, unequal environmental impact of consumption between the wealthy and the poor, and intergenerational equity can be raised at the level of the nation-state.

In one version, national self-interest leads developed countries to prefer continuing the traditional approach to economic development that, in many ways, treats developing countries primarily as a source of cheap raw materials. Developing countries are increasingly identifying the Washington Consensus—the economic policies that have become the prerequisite for foreign aid—as nothing more than, as writer Naomi Klein put it, "a clever rebranding effort, a way for former northern colonial powers to continue to drain the southern countries of their wealth without being inconvenienced by the heavy lifting of colonialism" (Klein 2009, 56).

Early in the first decade of the twenty-first century, a coalition of developing countries refused to meet the demands of the wealthy countries to further liberalize their economies. Instead, they began to insist that the developing world live up to its advocacy of markets by ending the various subsidies that protect the Northern Hemisphere producers from foreign competition—particularly in agriculture. While advanced primarily within a "trade not aid" agenda, ending some of the subsidies would have environmental and health benefits. Critics of large-scale agriculture in the USA note that public policies have encouraged growth of "monocultures of corn and soy in the field and cheap calories of fat, sugar, and feedlot meat on the table" (Pollan 2008, 3). Public policy, influenced by strong produce-grower lobbies based in California and Florida, required that farmers receiving subsidies for grain cultivation abandon growing fruits and vegetables. This helped keep the prices of those foods high while prices of foods based on or derived from grain (the high fructose corn syrup now ubiquitous in processed foods of all types) fell. Though an increase in South-North trade in food and agricultural commodities raises concerns about shifts to cash crops in developing countries, increased or renewed dependence on imported food, and the transfer of high-chemical, high-energy use modes of agriculture to the Third World, developing countries and environmentalists sometimes find themselves on the same side in debates about wealthy countries' agricultural subsidies.

The sustainability emphasis on the disparities of environmental impact between the high-energy use, high-consumption, high-waste lifestyles of the industrial world and the low-energy use, insufficient consumption, low-waste lifestyles of the poorest countries is simply the demand for environmental justice reframed globally. On no issue are demands for environmental justice between countries sharper than on questions of hazardous wastes and toxic substances. Bans on the international shipment of hazardous wastes to Africa as well as limits on the subsequent shipments to secondary destinations have been based on a combination of demands that the rich clean up their own messes at home and on concerns that low administrative capacity in many third world countries means that any regulations included in international regimes will not be enforced adequately. Growing demands by developing countries for greater information disclosure and stronger prior informed consent when trading in pesticides and other toxic chemicals reflect environmentalist success at presenting chemical use as posing dangers to workers as well as to the environment.

The protests in Seattle that scuttled the 1999 World Trade Organization meeting, the 2001 World Conference on Racism held in Durban, South Africa, and other events also focused attention on the issue of development and race. From the perspective of the developing world, the colonial period was really the first era of globalization, an era when the wealth of the North was built, to a great extent, by the theft of indigenous lands, the institution of slavery, and the forced transfer of natural resources. Rather than the developing countries owing the rich world the money that had been lent in recent decades, in reality, they argue, the North owes an enormous debt to the South, and these demands for reparations have been the subject of UN meetings and conventions.

In parallel to discussions of race within countries, poor countries have raised demands for redress of past race-based injustice. They have demanded that wealthy nations acknowledge slavery and colonialism as "crimes against humanity" and sought either explicit monetary reparations or to promote the notion of a Western "moral debt" that could be used to leverage concessions in areas such as canceling Africa's foreign debt or launching a massive African-focused financial assistance program similar to those that the United States provided to Japan and Western Europe after World War II. However, these efforts often get sidetracked by other political developments. The first Durban World Conference on Racism concluded on September 9, 2001, and was quickly overshadowed by the September 11 terrorist attacks against the United States. The Durban II conference, held in April 2009, was then sidetracked by Islamic demands that Israel be labeled a racist state. The only head of state to attend the conference was Iranian president Mahmoud Ahmadinejad, whose address was a broad attack against Israel. Israeli groups had convinced the United States and other powerful nations to boycott the conference, which coincided with the interest of those countries in avoiding a discussion of what little had been done to combat racism since the original meeting (Klein 2009, 57, 62–63).

Environmental Justice and Climate Change

The idea of environmental justice helps clarify the ethical issues underlying climate change and compels action to reduce the threat even in the face of uncertainties as well as to help poor nations with the costs of adapting to disruptive climate change. People who are responsible for few emissions and have not enjoyed much of the benefits derived from burning fossil fuels will bear the brunt of climate change impacts, and these same people have few resources to adapt to disruptive changes. The converse is also true: those who are most responsible for emissions and have enjoyed great wealth arising from fossil fuel use have the resources to adapt to many of the consequences of climate change.

Reports from the United Nation's Intergovernmental Panel on Climate Change (IPCC) and many other scientific bodies conclude that the earth and its inhabitants are already experiencing the effects of human-induced climate change. The IPCC's November 2007 synthesis report pointed to a number of signs that global warming is occurring, including a decline of mountain glaciers and snow cover in both hemispheres; an increase of precipitation in the eastern parts of North and South America, northern Europe, and northern and central Asia; and a decline of precipitation in the Sahel, Mediterranean, southern Africa, and parts of southern Asia. "Observational evidence from all continents and most oceans," the authors of the report wrote, "shows that many natural systems are being affected by regional climate changes, particularly temperature increases" (IPCC Nov. 2007, 1).

Adaptive capacity is intimately connected to social and economic development but is unevenly distributed across and within societies. Areas of the world already susceptible to the effects of adverse weather and environmental problems and lacking resources to deal with these challenges will likely find such problems greatly magnified in the future by climate change. Adapting to the disruption of water supplies will require water policies and integrated water resource management efforts such as increased harvesting of rainwater, water storage, conservation, water reuse, desalination, and efficiency investments. Agricultural adaptations are likely to include adjusting planting dates and crop variety, relocating crops to more hospitable areas, planting more trees, and taking other measures to reduce soil erosion. Other efforts toward adaptations will involve research and development aimed at producing drought-resistant crops and new strains that flourish in new climates, expanding crop insurance programs to help farmers cope with climate-driven crop failures, and reforming land tenure or ownership to open new opportunities for marginalized farmers. However, many developing countries lack the resources to pursue such policies.

In their comprehensive study of the impacts of climate-related (not necessarily climate change–driven) disasters, Roberts and Parks (2007,

74–79) found that the poor nations of Asia, Africa, and Central America repeatedly suffer the greatest number of casualties from weather-related catastrophes such as flooding, droughts, severe windstorms, and heat waves. The only weather-related disasters producing relatively high levels of casualties in developed countries are heat waves, such as those in Chicago in 1995 and Europe in 2003. Between 1980 and 2002 weather-related disasters claimed nearly 301,000 lives in Ethiopia, a fatality rate of 4.78 per thousand. During that same time, they rendered homeless some 62 million Bangladeshis—almost 46 percent of the total population. The twenty countries that suffered the largest number of fatalities from these kinds of disasters were all developing countries, except the United States, which ranked tenth in terms of the number of people killed (7,617) during this time. Although these weather-related disasters were not necessarily driven by global warming, they demonstrate the magnitude of the impacts and their tremendous effects on poor countries.

Specific examples of communities threatened by climate change suggest how expensive adaptation will be. Global warming has been blamed for warming the air and melting the sea ice in Alaska in ways that threaten to cause houses and other buildings to fall into the sea from storms and to crumble the ground on which they are built. One village, Kivalina, located on a barrier reef in the Chukchi Sea north of the Arctic Circle, is home to the Inupiat. The cost of relocating the village is estimated to be about US$400 million, or about US$1 million for each of the village's 400 residents (Gardner 2008; Barringer 2008; Cole 2008). Estimating the actual costs of rebuilding or moving a community is relatively straightforward; determining how to address the loss of lives or the threat to indigenous communities whose culture, identity, and existence as a community are intertwined with their traditional lands is much more difficult.

Both procedural and distributive justice provide standards and guidance for designing and evaluating policies. The distribution of the effects of climate change is quite unequal and will become even more pronounced in the future. The vulnerability to climate change impacts is similarly distributed unfairly around the world: those in the South are much more vulnerable than those in the wealthy world. Adaptation strategies also raise issues of justice and fairness because of the ways in which they will increase or decrease vulnerabilities (Adger et al. 2006, 4). In 2006 the World Bank estimated that US$10 to US$40 billion dollars a year will be needed to help developing countries adapt to climate change (World Bank 2006a), whereas Oxfam International put the annual need at US$50 billion (Oxfam International 2007). Despite acceptance in principle of the long-standing demands from developing countries that wealthy countries—that have benefited from environmental spoliation—pay most of the cost of remedying or adapting to it, relatively little money has been forthcoming. Although parties to the UN Framework Convention on Climate Change did agree to impose a 2 percent tax on the Clean Development Mechanism—the program by which governments and companies in industrial countries can get emissions credits by investing in carbon dioxide emission reduction projects in developing countries, this is expected to raise only US$100 to US$500 million a year (Ayers and Huq 2009).

The issues involved in adaptation include determining responsibility for climate change impacts, setting the level and burden-sharing of assistance to developing countries for adaptation, allocating assistance between countries and adaptation measures, and promoting equal participation in planning and making decisions on adaptation (Adger et al. 2006, 276–77). Roberts and Parks emphasize that inequality makes cooperation more difficult because it generates divergent views and expectations, contributes to mistrust, and makes it difficult to fashion agreements about what constitutes fairness and justice in international agreements and efforts (Roberts and Parks 2007, 6–7). Climate change takes place within the context of international development and the decades of efforts in developing countries to draw attention to their environmental problems, including a lack of safe drinking water, indoor and urban air pollution, soil erosion, and desertification as well as the intersection of these problems with the poverty, poor health, malnutrition, and other challenges they face. The issues that most concern the wealthy world, such as climate change, ozone depletion, and loss of biodiversity, are much less pressing concerns for the developing countries. But the wealthy world's agenda dominates, and global agreements push the South to take on the environmental issues that are of lowest priority and importance to them—much less immediate than the pressing needs of survival and basic quality of life.

There has been relatively little political discussion of how to pay for the costs of adapting to climate change. The United Nations Framework Convention on Climate Change (1992) spawned several multilateral funds to help developing countries adapt to climate change. The Least Developed Country Fund was created to help that set of countries in

2001; as of mid-2007 it had spent US$9.8 million on small-scale projects. The Special Climate Change Fund, open to all developing countries, began operating in 2005 and has disbursed US$1.4 million in two years for projects related to long-term adaptation to climate change. The Strategic Priority on Adaptation, started in 2004, spent US$14.8 million on ecosystem management projects. The separate Adaptation Fund, which aids the most vulnerable countries, is funded through a 2 percent levy on credits generated through the Clean Development Mechanism (which allows developed countries to offset their emissions by funding projects in developing countries that reduce GHG emissions), but disagreements over governance issues delayed the start of operations. Altogether, these funds had provided US$26 million in adaptation funding through mid-2007, an amount that, over six years, equaled what the United Kingdom spends each week on flood control (United Nations Development Programme 2007, 188–89).

The modest beginning of these special multilateral funds is not surprising given the history of development assistance. Few countries have actually followed through with their promise to dedicate 0.7 percent of their GDP to developing countries. Assistance declined dramatically in the 1990s, rebounded in the early years of the twenty-first century in response to several global meetings, then again fell by 5 percent in 2006 (United Nations Development Programme 2007, 185–87). Current and recent spending on development assistance in general as well as on these climate adaptation funds fail to address even a fraction of the adaptation needs that have been identified. As impacts become more visible and global accords are strengthened, these funds may be dramatically expanded. But little assistance is now available from these sources. All this suggests the importance of the two levels of problems—the tension between levels of consumption in the industrialized and developing nations and the differences of wealth within nations. However, the rapid growth in the emerging economies in Asia and elsewhere suggest the limited value of the traditional industrialized–developing nation distinction in guiding policy formulation.

Helping the victims of disruptive climate change adapt to those changes and deal with the damages that occur will require massive transfers of resources to victims, particularly those in developing countries. Revenues from carbon taxes and auctioning emission allowances for cap-and-trade programs are two promising ways to raise funds for adaptation, but those funds may also be earmarked for subsidizing and encouraging energy efficiency, renewable energy, and other mitigation efforts. Additionally, relying on revenues from a carbon tax to pay for adaptation may be counterproductive. For the carbon tax to succeed in its primary purpose of triggering a reduction of emissions, it must be high enough that it actually compels sources to reduce their emissions. If it does succeed, revenues will decline as emissions decline. If emitters simply continue to release GHGs and pay the tax, there will be funds for adaptation, but the primary goal of reducing concentrations of GHGs in the atmosphere will not be attained.

Climate change liability lawsuits such as those that have been brought in the United States (Barringer 2008) are no substitute for major global programs aimed at funding the kinds of adaptive measures that are already needed on a large scale. Nevertheless, they are helping to clarify the responsibility of major GHG emitters and are pressuring those who enjoy the goods and services produced by those emissions to pay the cost of the consequences of those emissions in the prices they pay for the goods and services produced. Because the common law tradition prevails in other countries as well, the potential of such suits to trigger change is not limited to the United States but could also occur through courts elsewhere. A comparative study could help illuminate whether these kinds of cases are being brought elsewhere and what the prospects are for encouraging them in other nations. Another fruitful area of study is to examine how international tribunals could also provide a forum for discussing and evaluating ways of framing the obligation of GHG emitters and those who benefit from those emissions to help pay for the cost of adapting to a warmer and, in many places, a much less hospitable world.

Applying Environmental Justice Frameworks

The five frameworks are not independent ways of approaching the problem of injustices; they overlap in many ways. Advocates of environmental justice will find that elements of each can contribute to their goal. Some remedies may come from within one framework, whereas others will be built through the interaction of different approaches. No one framework is sufficient, but understanding all of them helps in recognizing the perspectives of those with other views and increases the possibility of creative solutions that bring together alternative approaches. The traditional, civil rights approach, for example, is compelling and has a strong history on which it can extend its efforts. Advocates of this approach can find allies who approach the problem from other directions. Expectations of distributive justice pull powerfully on many people. Enhanced public participation by all members of a community is widely viewed as an essential part of any response to injustice, and it is valuable in promoting democratic politics. Social justice addresses the essential needs of all members of a community to live lives of freedom, dignity, and promise. Advocates of solutions to problems such as access to adequate water supplies and exposure to toxic mine tailings can seek legal remedies rooted in civil rights or pursue more fundamental social and economic reforms that promise to give people more power over their lives.

The agenda laid out by the idea of ecological sustainability is particularly important for addressing natural resource injustices. Sustainability is intertwined with political and governmental renewal, which encourages citizens to participate and engages them in identifying problems and designing and implementing solutions. A strong sense of political efficacy encourages people to become involved in devising solutions to environmental problems. A robust commitment to community motivates people to reduce adverse impacts that they impose on others and to contribute to a shared quality of life. The kinds of changes that are required by sustainability require motivation and commitment that are more likely to come from people who feel a sense of responsibility and accountability for how their actions affect others' quality of life. The changes also require engagement and empowerment, so that participants devise solutions with which they are then willing to comply. A spirited, vibrant civil society, composed of effective government and committed nongovernmental organizations, works together to ensure that the common interests of all are realized.

Chapter Six
TOWARD A SUSTAINABLE WORLD

The greatest political challenge we face in thinking about global environmental threats is the dominance of short-term pressures and imperatives. Not just in the United States but all around the world, democracies are highly responsive to immediate problems but have great difficulties developing long-term solutions to enduring problems. Yet authoritarian governments appear to be no better; they, too, are pressured to satisfy immediate concerns if they are to remain in power. The political incentives facing any kind of regime seem inevitably to favor putting off solutions to enduring problems as long as possible. These incentives are strengthened by the pervasive belief in the possibility of economic growth. As an unnamed investment banker put it, "The story of endless economic growth, now driven by China and other key emerging markets, is a dream that dies hard" (quoted in Foroohar 2009, 47).

The dominance of the short term can change through leaders both inside and outside government who see that the long-term interests of their nation lies in effectively addressing global environmental threats. The emphasis on long-term interests is exactly the kind of thing that requires visionary leadership. The science is clear: although some environmental conditions have improved in recent decades, the most important environmental problems—global warming, loss of biodiversity, depletion of fresh water and other natural resources—are becoming more severe. Although environmental problems presently primarily plague the poor countries most severely, they will increasingly affect the wealthy world in coming decades. Governments and publics in the wealthy world will eventually come to see that it is in their own interest to take action, but that may not occur until changes are so threatening and extensive that prevention is impossible and adaptation is all that is left.

It is clear that countries can act expeditiously and effectively when they perceive immediate peril to their key interests. Mobilization to fight world wars is a clear but extreme example of radical transformation of economies in the face of immediate, unambiguous threats. Wealthy countries mobilized trillions of dollars to counter the meltdown of banks and other financial institutions in 2008 and 2009—evidence of national leaders' ability act quickly and in concert when they believe that their countries' interests are threatened. Yet up to now leaders have failed to act sufficiently aggressively to remedy environmental threats.

That does not deny that there has been collective action against environmental problems. Dozens of global environmental treaties have been negotiated and ratified, as have hundreds of bilateral and regional accords. But few of the global treaties have been able to inspire actions that have significantly remedied environmental problems. They typically address environmental threats that different countries view with different degrees of urgency, so their policy prescriptions are often modest so as to attract wider participation. They also typically lack effective enforcement mechanisms. A few do have implementation committees able to muster peer pressure, but the continuing decentralization of global politics means there is no worldwide equivalent to the powerful administrative agencies that exist in the better organized states. In contrast, bilateral agreements tend to contain clearer policy prescriptions because the parties typically deal with more focused problems and threats that they perceive as immediate, such as cleaning up a polluted common border resource such as a river. Because both parties also see that they have a strong interest in effective cooperation to address the problem, they mobilize their national agencies to that end. Not surprisingly, there has only been a modest response to the problems posed by climate change, loss of biodiversity, water shortages, and a host of other broadly dispersed but very serious ecological challenges.

Chapter 2 explored the reasons for nations' focus on immediate threats. Realism, still the best account of why nations do what they do, suggests that they only address threats that they perceive as directly affecting them. Although nations are increasingly prepared to provide economic development assistance and humanitarian aid in emergencies, they undertake no large sustained effort unless they perceive a clear threat to their own core interests. The rational choice approach often used to analyze policy making within states provides a supplementary explanation. Their relatively large number, vastly differing capacities, and primary concern with self-interest mean that states are particularly prone to free-riding or providing minimal contributions to collective efforts. Inaction or low action can sometimes be overcome through provisions of side payments like financial aid or concessions on other issues, but the amounts of money wealthy countries are willing to provide and the number of potential concessions in other issues is small compared to the need.

Yet constructivist approaches to world politics suggest that states are not inevitably and unalterably committed to calculations of their immediate material interests; they can learn and act on new beliefs about how the world works or new normative commitments. Political theory provides some resources for moving political and economic elites toward a better understanding of the deep embeddedness of human life and activity in nature as well as a more adequate response to the major environmental challenges of this era.

Three Elements of Creating a Changed World

This book has sought to supply three sources of inspiration for beliefs about the world and normative commitments that will carry humanity forward into a new ecological age. The first, making markets work, can be seen as "economic" because it focuses primarily on production and exchange of goods and services. However, it transcends the conceptual boundaries of neoclassical and neoliberal economics by taking nature and human connections with nature seriously. The second, ensuring that developing countries develop more sustainably, is part of a wider shift in thinking needed to make ecological sustainability the lodestar for orienting human activity that affects nature. The third, helping the most vulnerable deal with the effects of global environmental problems, raises the broader question of environmental justice.

Making markets work, the subject of Chapter 3, requires reconceptualizing economic activity and markets to better address environmental concerns. The key here is ensuring that economic activity is evaluated by new metrics that take the environment and natural resources into full account. On the cost side this means giving greater weight both to the fact that extracting a nonrenewable resource is a one-time opportunity as well as avoiding overexploitation of renewable resources, preventing or minimizing pollution, and maximizing end-of-use retrieval of materials. On the benefit side it means calculating the value of having unpolluted air, water, and soil; maintaining biodiversity; and stabilizing the global climate. Many of the analytical tools required to do so already exist. The primary challenge, then, is political and social: overcoming resistance from the many organizations and individuals who benefit from continuing "business as usual" because that allows them to externalize environmental costs and ignore environmental benefits. The broader discussions of the need for government regulation to make markets work well, inspired by the global financial crisis of 2007–2008, may provide an opening for shaking the blind ideological belief in "free markets," but policy debates in the United States during 2009 and early 2010 suggest that countering that ideology effectively will continue to require hard work.

Sustainable development and the broader notion of sustainability on which it draws is the subject of Chapter 4. An old political saying maintains that "you can't oppose something with nothing"—signaling a warning that replacing a counterproductive policy requires formulating and winning support for a better one. "Getting prices right" suggests a set of particular remedies but does not provide the more general orienting principle that helps identify when prices are "right." For many, particularly those who place their faith in unfettered markets, efficiency is the economic lodestar, the key criterion for evaluating the relative merit of competing choices. Sustainable development rests on a very different lodestar principle: sustainability. Sustainability often incorporates efficiency: more efficient use of resources, more efficient use of energy, more efficient use of water can all contribute to environmental improvement and ecological sustainability. As Herman Daly wrote when he endorsed the Happy Planet Index, "Economists like the concept of efficiency and the Happy Planet Index is the ultimate efficiency ratio—the final valuable output divided by the original scarce input" (Daly 2009, 2). Yet sustainability goes beyond efficiency, even in its ecological economics version, by adopting a long-term focus and paying attention to the ways in which impacts of human activity can ramify through all the interconnected parts of the ecosystem.

A few skeptics regard sustainable development as simply the latest excuse for outsiders to impose their priorities on developing countries—another element of a "colonialism without formal colonial rule" that would perpetuate North-South differences and leave the global South dominated by the global North. Yet in its better formulations it is a thoughtful effort to reconcile poor countries' justifiable desire to escape from the cramped material and mental conditions of poverty with the long-term need to maintain a habitable planet. As the spread of environmental concern among grassroots movements around the world attests, concern for sustainability does not divide North from South; rather, it divides every national society into "green" (environmentally conscious) and "brown" (environmentally oblivious) fractions. In every country in the world, some citizens' groups pursue environmental initiatives, some portions of the business community take the environment seriously, and some government agencies established to protect the environment struggle to leverage (or, when leverage is lacking, to persuade) the other government agencies managing resources or regulating economic activity to incorporate environmental considerations. When those in the North who are working to achieve sustainability at home take up this challenge, the notion of sustainable development becomes a common rallying point for advocates of new ways in South and North alike.

Serious efforts to help the most vulnerable—whether small countries threatened with inundation by rising sea levels or poor people living in shantytowns or on marginal lands—are most likely to occur when people are animated by a sense of environmental justice. Helping vulnerable people who are not seen because they live far away requires a strong sense of human connection. Thus, chapter 5 builds on the insight that ecological sustainability is politically and socially sustainable only when it is accompanied by fairness and justice. Environmental justice has been defined in at least as many ways as ecological sustainability, ranging from a focused concern on redressing unequal exposures to pollution and other environmental hazards to a broad vision of egalitarian participatory communities. Defining the ecologically sustainable is complex; one must take into account the interconnections of natural systems and the impact of human activity on those natural systems over extended periods of time. Scientific methods for observing the current state of the physical environment, understanding the workings of natural systems, identifying their interconnections, and anticipating the impact of changes in human activity have improved considerably in recent decades. Scientific disputes still turn on particular questions, but the methods for settling those disputes—or at least separating the scientifically plausible from the scientifically implausible answers—have advanced. Arguments about how to define fairness and justice, which lack the observable human-independent phenomena that bring discipline to human speculation about the natural world, continue unabated. The end of the Cold War marked the collapse of one way of attempting to implement a vision of justice: totalitarian revolutionary vanguard parties proved in the long term to be poor mechanisms for bringing about socialist visions of participatory, egalitarian, spontaneously cooperating communities. It did not discredit the whole socialist vision, however, which continues to inspire many people around the world. The anti-globalization movement's "another world is possible" is not a replica of Marx's "workers of the world unite," but it is the twenty-first century-version of the same hope for a fairer and more just world that animated all factions of the nineteenth-century workers' movement.

Possible Futures

Imagine three scenarios for the year 2050, a widely used reference point in assessments of the environmental health of the planet and efforts to protect it. In the first scenario, dramatic technological breakthroughs in clean energy technology produce a fundamental transformation of energy production and use. Fossil fuel use falls to a tiny fraction of what it was in 2010 because engineers developed a variety of renewable energy sources from solar panels to wind farms to fusion energy. (Jacobson and Delucchi [2009] plausibly project such an energy future in the United States.) Access to water is no longer a problem because of breakthroughs in desalination processes, making them so inexpensive that they are deployed routinely around the world. Countries freely share markets in the best technologies, and assistance to developing countries, allowing them access to cheap and clean energy, drives development and reduces poverty.

The second scenario is very much like life in 2010. Developing countries suffer the most from environmental problems, but the wealthy world remains largely insulated from them. Climate change is gradual, its impacts softened by steady incremental progress in developing and deploying renewable energy sources. Countries make incremental progress in policies that prompt innovation, discourage the release of carbon and other greenhouse gases, and promote modest changes in behavior. Population levels off, and increased consumption in the developing world is accommodated through incremental progress in food

production, the creation of new jobs, and the establishment of new social services that provide better health care and contribute to the social
order.

The third scenario for 2050 is quite bleak. Disruptive climate
changes have become so ubiquitous that fossil fuel energy has been curtailed even though alternative energy sources are not widely available,
and the poor in both rich and poor countries lack access to them. Coping with climate changes is a dominant public concern, with the trillions
of dollars being spent on adaptation crowding investment in new energy
technologies out of the national budgets. Climate becomes a permanent
emergency that governments struggle with or use to expand their powers at the expense of economic and political freedom. Wealthy countries
continue to have the resources to insulate themselves from some of the
effects, but floods of refugees, political instability, and conflicts over scarce
resources make the world a very dangerous place to live.

This third scenario may be unavoidable if breakthroughs in clean
technologies do not materialize or are not widely adopted, environmental problems continue to grow, climate change spins out of control and
magnifies other problems such as drought and food production, and
ecosystem services collapse. If it prevails, political conflict will dominate
international relations as countries fight to preserve what environmental
resources they possess and to gain access to others that they need. Politics within countries would be affected as well if environmental degradation occurred much more rapidly than technological, policy, and cultural changes are possible. The result both globally and nationally would
be a permanent chaos and conflict, for which theories of political science, economics, and other social sciences offer little guidance.

Thus, the central question in global environmental policy making is
whether environmental problems and threats can be successfully managed. One version of the question assumes that the needed technical
changes can be made in time and asks whether humanity will muster the
necessary political will to adopt them. Much of liberal and constructivist
international relations theory is ultimately an optimistic enterprise
because it assumes that contemporary environmental problems will be
remedied as self-interest is redefined to encompass broader concerns or
is checked by additional motivations for preserving the well-being of
future generations and protecting those who are most vulnerable to environmental harms. An alternative answer to the question leaves no ground
to be optimistic that the necessary political will can be mustered in time.

This answer rests on the belief that because all previous civilizations have collapsed, ours is destined for the same fate. In this conception the primary issue is not the health of the planet but the survivability of civilization as we know it. Dealing with collapse poses tremendous challenges that dwarf the difficulties that conventional environmental politics seeks to address and takes us into realms of existence poorly conceptualized in current theorizing about international relations.

The likelihood of civilizational collapse has been explored by a number of scholars (Tainter 1990; Diamond 2005; Homer-Dixon 2006; Brown 2008). The case for believing that collapse is likely is based on several arguments:

- *Complexity.* As new problems surface, societies must become increasingly more complex, but complexity breeds fragility as more and more layers of administration or bureaucracy are added. Society becomes so tangled in bureaucracy that no person or organization can understand how the system works and thus manage it effectively.
- *Increasing Connectedness.* As complexity increases, decision making becomes more distributed or decentralized into networks, causing some to conclude that complexity becomes manageable. But as network systems become more tightly tied together, failures spread more easily and networks transmit rather than absorb shocks.
- *Diminishing Returns.* As layers of complexity increase, more energy is required to solve problems. The amount of usable energy produced per unit of energy invested in production declines. Eventually all the available energy is required just to maintain the status quo. Then, when a major crisis or disturbance occurs, institutions are so stretched that they snap. The same is true of other key resources besides energy.
- *Tipping Points.* Some progress is being made in developing new energy technologies and ecologically sustainable economies. The key may be which occurs first—the emergence of an alternative economy or crises that topple into a collapse? Social stability may be illusory; society and/or the environment may be stressed but appear sustainable until key factors reach that hard-to-predict tipping point that triggers cascades that in turn trigger the unraveling of society.

If collapse occurs, urban areas will be the hardest hit, and an unimaginable loss of life could occur. Those who fare best in collapse may be subsistence farmers, for whom conditions could conceivably improve, prompting one writer to recall scripture and observe that perhaps the meek really will inherit the Earth (MacKenzie 2008, 35).

For those who deny the inevitability of collapse, the key question becomes whether collapse can still be avoided. The rapid spread of the financial crisis in 2007–2008 and of swine flu in 2009 are examples of how quickly problems can fan out in our interconnected global political economy and threaten the stability throughout the world. One approach to maintaining stability is to increase redundancy—increase the resources available to deal with a crisis. This is clearly not a market-driven value because it is by definition inefficient: resources are invested in a duplicative manner as a kind of insurance. In the long run, given the threat of collapse, redundancy is a rational response because it provides more resiliency in the face of disruption, but it clearly clashes with short-term calculations of economic efficiency. Another approach is reducing the scale of connections, thereby providing insulation from turbulence. Radical decentralization of food and energy production would not only reduce energy use dramatically, but it would also decrease the chance of catastrophic disruptions in supply (MacKenzie 2008, 35). Insulation would reduce the likelihood of massive social disorder outright.

Climate Change and the Road Ahead

The December 2009 conference on climate change in Copenhagen provided an illuminating view of the current state of global environmental politics. At the last minute, after a small group negotiation left a number of governments complaining about the exclusivity and opacity of the process, the major greenhouse gas emitting countries agreed on the goal of ensuring no more than a 2°C rise in average global temperatures during the twenty-first century. They did so while aware of the projections that this will require an 80 percent cut in emissions from developed nations and a 50 percent reduction from developing nations. Achieving these goals will require shifting energy production from fossil fuels to renewable resources. The technologies needed for making that transition are already available. Energy from them is more expensive than current prices for fossil fuel energy, but renewable energy sources will be economically viable if carbon emissions are priced in a way that reflects their environmental costs. The investments required are within the ability of countries to pay if they are willing to shift their priorities.

The real barriers to reducing greenhouse gas emissions are not technological or even economic, but political. They exist at both the international and the national levels. At the international level, the key question is persuading China to maintain limits on its emissions. The Chinese are typically slow to accept any legally binding international commitments, and this reluctance is reinforced by their high dependence on their abundant and cheap, though highly polluting, coal. Yet some Chinese enterprises have made great strides in developing cutting-edge renewable energy technology. Furthermore, persuading China becomes doubly important because the U.S. Congress has made Chinese commitment to limits a precondition for accepting limits on U.S. emissions. Because economic activity in these two countries currently produces 40 percent of global carbon dioxide emissions, having them committed to limits, even of a soft law sort, is crucial to avoiding serious global warming.

The Copenhagen conference also put on display all of the unwieldiness of UN-sponsored negotiations among 191 states requiring consensus for decisions. The situation was complicated by the fact that negotiations were proceeding in two related but distinct tracks—one among all the parties to the UN Framework Convention on Climate Change and the other among the somewhat smaller set of parties to the Kyoto Protocol on Greenhouse Gas Emissions. Yet any effective extension of limits on emissions past the 2012 expiration date of the Kyoto Protocol depends on bringing states that are not parties to Kyoto into the detailed negotiations regarding emissions limits, financing mechanisms, carbon trading, and related matters. It remains to be seen whether the additional conferences to be held in 2010 will put the UN negotiations back on track or whether effective limitation of greenhouse gas emissions will occur outside the UN framework.

The domestic political barriers are no less serious. These are most obvious in the United States, where the constitutional separation of powers requires coordination between the president and Congress and between the two Houses of Congress. Though the House has a Democratic Party majority ready to commit the country to significant action on limiting greenhouse gas emissions and investing in renewable energy technologies, action in the Senate can be stymied by the forty-one-strong Republican Party minority through the use of a rule requiring sixty votes to break a filibuster so that a proposal can be brought to a vote. Congressional Republicans are not enthusiastic about taking action; many continue to believe the climate change skeptics who deny that human-induced global warming poses any serious environmental threat, and none face a groundswell of public opinion in their home state or district strong enough to push them to support action. Although a stalemate persists at the federal level, states and localities are continuing the climate change policies they initiated during the George W. Bush administration; political decentralization is allowing communities that are particularly concerned about the issue to experiment with a range of greenhouse gas emission reduction efforts.

Other countries also face domestic hurdles. Though the terms of discussion are not public, it is possible to infer the existence of a heated policy debate within China between those wedded to continuing to exploit the nation's vast coal reserves and those desiring to give new technologies a boost and reduce China's infamous air pollution by shifting to other energy sources. Even among EU members—generally regarded as leaders on climate change—full compliance with EU decisions implementing agreed upon emissions limits is not foreordained. Despite considerable criticism from environmentalists, the government of South Africa is supporting government-owned Eskom's plan to build a large coal-fired power plant in Limpopo to serve undersupplied rural areas.

At present, humanity appears to be stuck with continued emissions that necessitate adaptation and mitigation. Though the willingness to act is increasing, whether action will come in time to prevent environmental damage that will make adaptation traumatic is unclear. For committed environmentalists this is a gloomy prospect, one that can easily induce despair or contempt for politics.

Human Life

Yet politics exists because human societies need to make collective decisions to ensure their continuance. Human life, like all life, seeks to perpetuate its own kind. Hence, a key purpose of human society is to form and orient the lives of individuals in each generation so that they realize human life well (enjoy a favorable life outcome) while they also live and contribute to perpetuating human life without decline. Because human beings are social beings—they live together in groups or societies that develop common ways of life—perpetuating human life means more than giving birth to the next generation; it also means being involved as an integral part in helping to maintain the community and its way of life (or prized parts of it) and perpetuating human life.[1]

A key role of law and policy, and thus of politics, is to reinforce this normative culture. One of the most compelling aspirations we can embrace is the profound and equally intrinsic worth of each individual life, fostering everyone's nature to be free and shape their own lives. Defining the fundamental commitment to the ideal of equality in this way suggests that it applies across time as well as across individuals. Each individual life at every stage of existence is related to every other life in every generation. As such, each present generation sees future generations as they see themselves and realize that the lives of future generations is as important as their own lives were for past generations. For the present generation, future generations' ability to live freely is as important as our own ability to do so as well. Thus, past, present, and future generations are knit together as one people.

Yet every fundamental law contains possibilities of its own degeneration. If perpetuating human lives is no longer an integral part of realizing human life—if a critical mass of current humans enjoy their lives in way that neglect or eschew the possibility of future lives—the integral and intimate relations between themselves and their posterity degenerates. If present generations begin treating their own lives as more important than that of future generations, the basic glue of human society dissolves. Failing to arrest environmental decline is a clear violation of this commitment to the equal intrinsic worth of each individual life, past, present, and future.

This commitment to the equal intrinsic worth of current and future lives means that human freedom is limited freedom. All persons have a right to enjoy the maximum degree of freedom that is consistent with the same degree of freedom for all. Thus, the bounds of one person's freedom are set by the existence of other peoples' freedom. Properly understood, the phrase "same freedom for all" includes successive generations of a free people. This also means that the relations between present and future generations should be such that present generations enjoy their life in freedom in ways compatible with ensuring that future generations can also enjoy lives in freedom; actions that extend future generations' ability to live a free life are an integral part of living a free life today. Thus, a commitment to individual freedom is part of a larger commitment to the continuation of life.

Human life is environmentally situated. It depends for its existence and well-being on being effectively situated in the natural environment. Every generation in the unfolding of generations has an equal claim on the use of the natural environment in order to realize and perpetuate without decline the free life. The natural environment belongs to all generations in the continuation of lives; a culture of the natural environment is a basic part of any viable society's larger normative culture and its fundamental laws and policies. A culture of the natural environment plays a critical role in forming and orienting the lives of succeeding generations so they can realize life fully and perpetuate it for those who follow. The challenge for law and policy, therefore, is to order the uses of the natural environment so that the integrity of that environment is preserved and that free life continues without decline. It is the duty of every living generation to not use renewable natural resources faster than they can be renewed, to adopt the most efficient uses of nonrenewable natural resources, and live within the ecological carrying capacity of the earth.

One of environmentalism's most attractive and compelling characteristics is its commitment to making abstract commitments to intergenerational equity and fairness a policy reality. This book seeks to encourage ways of pursuing this commitment to the future through environmental policies that impose constraints and costs on current generations in order to secure a more environmentally sustainable future for those to come.

NOTES

Chapter 2

1. The discussion of regimes is based on Bryner 2001.

Chapter 3

1. The most important presidential actions have been Exec. Order 12,291, 3 C.F.R. 127 (1982); Exec. Order 12,498, 3 C.F.R. 323 (1986); and Exec. Order 12,866, 3 C.F.R. 638 (1994).

Chapter 6

1. I acknowledge my colleague Don Sorensen for developing these ideas on which I rely here concerning the obligations of each generation to perpetuate the preconditions for the free life.

REFERENCES

Adger, W. Neil, John Paavola, Saleemul Huo, and M. J. Mace, eds. 2006. *Fairness in adaptation to climate change*. Cambridge, MA: MIT Press.

Adler, Jonathan. 2008. Warming up to water markets—Will global warming force us to adopt sensible resource policies? *Regulation* 31 (4):14–17.

Alonso, Alfonso, Francisco Dallmeier, Elise Granek, and Peter Raven. 2007. *Biodiversity: Connecting with the tapestry of life*. 2nd ed. Washington, DC: Smithsonian Institution/Monitoring and Assessment of Biodiversity Program.

American Association for the Advancement of Science. 2000. *AAAS atlas of population & environment*. Berkeley: University of California Press.

Anderson, Terry L., and Pamela Snyder. 1997. *Water markets: Priming the invisible pump*. Washington, DC: Cato Institute.

Armquist, Sarah. 2009. The new old age. *New York Times*, August 4, D8.

ASEAN (Association of Southeast Asian Nations Secretariat). 2000. *Second ASEAN state of the environment report*. Jakarta: ASEAN.

Asia—An astonishing rebound. 2009. *The Economist* 392 (8644):9.

Ayers, Jessica M., and Saleemul Huq. 2009. The value of linking mitigation and adaptation: A case study of Bangladesh, *Environmental Management* 43 (5):753–64.

Barringer, Felicity. 2008. Flooded village files suit, citing corporate link to climate change. *The New York Times*, February 27.

Bell, Daniel. 1960. *The end of ideology*. Glencoe, IL: The Free Press.

Bergesen, Helge Ole, Georg Parmann, and Oystein B. Thommessen, eds. 1998. *Yearbook of international co-operation on environment and development*. London: Earthscan Publications.

Blatter, Joachim, and Helen Ingram. 2001. *Reflections on water: New approaches to transboundary conflicts and cooperation*. Cambridge, MA: MIT Press.

Borman, F. Herbert, and Stephen R. Kellert. 1991. *Ecology, economics, ethics: The broken circle*. New Haven, CT: Yale University Press.

Brook, Daniel. 2007. Mall of America: The architecture of our privatized government. *Harper's Magazine*, July. www.harpers.org/archive/2007/07/0081593.

Brown, Lester R. 2001. *Eco-economy: Building an economy for the earth*. New York: W. W. Norton.

Brown, Lester. 2008. *Plan B 3.0: Mobilizing to save civilization*. New York: W. W. Norton.

Brown, Lester et al., eds. 2000. *State of the world 2000*. New York: W. W. Norton.

Bryner, Gary C. 1995. *Blue skies, green politics: The Clean Air Act of 1990 and its implementation*. Washington DC: CQ Press.

Bryner, Gary C. 1997. *From promises to performance: Achieving global environmental goals.* New York: W. W. Norton.

Bryner, Gary C. 2001. *Gaia's wager: Environmental movements and the challenge of sustainability.* Lanham, MD: Rowman and Littlefield.

Bullard, Robert D. 1993. Anatomy of environmental racism and the environmental justice movement. In *Confronting environmental racism: Voices from the grassroots*, ed. Robert D. Bullard, 15–40. Boston: South End Press.

Burger, Joanna, and Michael Gochfeld. 1998. The tragedy of the commons: 30 years later. *Environment* 40 (10):4–27.

Camacho, David E. 1998. *Environmental injustices, political struggles: Race, class, and the environment.* Durham, NC: Duke University Press.

Carruthers, David V. 2008. *Environmental justice in Latin America: Problems, promise, and practice.* Cambridge, MA: MIT Press.

Carter, Neil. 2007. *The politics of the environment: Ideas, activism, policy*. Cambridge: Cambridge University Press.

Cashmore, Benjamin, Graeme Auld, and Deanna Newsom. 2004. *Governing through markets.* New Haven, CT: Yale University Press.

Cassidy, John, 2009. *How markets fail: The logic of economic calamities*. New York: Farrer, Straus and Giroux.

Chang, Ha-Joon. 2008. *Bad Samaritans: The myth of free trade and the secret history of capitalism*. New York: Bloomsbury Press.

China and America—The odd couple. 2009. *The Economist* 393 (8654):15.

Clapp, Jennifer, and Peter Dauvergne. 2005. *Paths to a green world: The political economy of the global environment*. Cambridge, MA: MIT Press.

Clark, Mary E. 1989. *Ariadne's thread: The search for new modes of thinking.* New York: St. Martin's Press.

Cline, William R. 2007. *Global warming and agriculture: Impact estimates by country.* Washington, DC: Center for Global Development.

Cole, Luke. 2008. Integrating environmental justice into policy, regulation, and litigation. Paper presented at University of Denver Law School Symposium on Global Climate Change, February 15.

Collins, W. D., V. Ramaswamy, M. D. Schwarzkopf, Y. Sun, R. W. Portmann, Q. Fu, S. E. B. Casanova, et al. 2006. Radiative forcing by well-mixed greenhouse gases: Estimates from climate models in the Intergovernmental Panel on Climate Change (IPCC) Fourth Assessment Report (AR4). *Journal of Geophysical Research* 111 (D14317):1–15.

Commoner, Barry. 1990. *Making peace with the planet.* New York: Pantheon.

Conca, Ken. 2006. *Governing water: Contentious transnational politics and global institution building.* Cambridge, MA: MIT Press.

Daily, Gretchen C. 1997. *Nature's services: Societal dependence on natural ecosystems.* Washington, DC: Island Press.

Daly, Herman. 1996. *Beyond growth: The economics of sustainable development.* Boston: Beacon.

Daly, Herman. 2009. Foreword. In *The unhappy planet index 2.0: Why good lives don't have to cost the earth,* ed. S. Abdallah, S. Thompson, J. Michaelson, N. Marks, and N. Steuer. www.neweconomics.org/sites/neweconomics .org/files/The_Happy_Planet_Index_2.0_1.pdf.

Daly, Herman E, and John B. Cobb. 1994. *For the common good: Redirecting the economy toward community, the environment, and a sustainable future.* Boston: Beacon Press.

Daubon, Ramon. 2002. A grassroots view of development assistance. *Grassroots Development* 23 (1):1–8.

DeSombre, Elizabeth, and Joanne Kauffman. 1996. The Montreal protocol multilateral fund: Partial success story. In *Institutions for environmental aid,* ed. Robert O. Keohane and Marc A. Levy, 89–126. Cambridge, MA: MIT Press.

De Villiers, Marq. 2000. *Water: The fate of our most precious resource.* Boston: Houghton Mifflin.

Diamond, Jared. 2005. *Collapse: How societies choose to fail or succeed.* New York: Penguin.

Diamond, Jared. 2008. What's your consumption factor? *New York Times,* January 2.

Dionne, E. J. 1998. *Community works: The revival of civil society in America.* Washington, DC: The Brookings Institution.

Donnelly, Jack. 2003. *Universal human rights in theory and practice.* Ithaca, NY: Cornell University Press.

Ehrlich, Paul R., and Anne H. Ehrlich. 2004. *One with Nineveh: Politics, consumption, and the human future.* Washington, DC: Island Press.

European Environment Agency. n.d. Biodiversity. www.eea.europa.eu/themes/ biodiversity.

Fairman, David. 1996. The global environmental facility: Haunted by the shadow of the future. In *Institutions for environmental aid: Pitfalls and promise,* ed. Robert O. Keohane and Marc A. Levy, 55–88. Cambridge, MA: MIT Press.

FAO (Food and Agriculture Organization of the United Nations). 2009. *Diouf calls for rapid elimination of hunger.* www.fao.org/news/story/en/item/36350/icode/.

Ferguson, Brett. 2000. Implications of restoration project on minority, poor citizens should be weighed, panel told. *Environmental Reporter* 31, 443–44.

Ferroukhi, Lyes, and Alejandra Aguilar Schramm. 2003. *Municipal forest management in Latin America.* Ottawa, Canada: International Development Research Centre.

Finnemore, Martha. 1996. *National interests in international society.* Ithaca, NY: Cornell University Press.

Flint, Anthony. 2006. *This land: The battle over sprawl and the future of America.* Baltimore, MD: Johns Hopkins University Press.

Florini, Ann. 2005. *The coming democracy: New rules for running a new world.* Washington, DC: Brookings Institution.

Foreman, Christopher. 1998. *The promise and peril of environmental justice.* Washington, DC: Brookings Institution.

Foroohar, Rana. 2009. Boom and gloom. *Newsweek*, November 9, 44–47.

Foster, Sheila. 1998. Justice from the ground up: Distributive inequities, grassroots resistance, and the transformative politics of the environmental justice movement. *California Law Review* 86 (4):775–841.

French, Hilary F. 1997. Learning from the ozone experience. In *State of the World 1997*, ed. Lester R. Brown et al. New York: W. W. Norton.

Friedberg, Aaron L. 2005. The future of U.S-China relations: Is conflict inevitable? *International Security* 30 (2):7–45.

Friedman, Benjamin M. 2005. *The moral consequences of economic growth.* New York: Vintage.

Fukuyama, Francis. 1993. *The end of history and the last man.* New York: Free Press.

Gardner, Daniel. 2008. *The science of fear. Why we fear the things we shouldn't—and put ourselves in greater danger.* New York: The Penguin Press.

Gibney. Mark. 2008. *International human rights law: Returning to universal principles.* Lanham, MD: Rowman and Littlefield.

Gladwell, Malcolm. 2000. *The tipping point: How little things can make a big difference.* Boston: Little, Brown.

Gleick, Peter H. 2003. Water use. *Annual Review of Environment and Resources* 28:275–314.

Gleick, Peter H, William C. G. Burns, Elizabeth L. Chalecki, Michael Cohen, Katherine Kao Cushing, Amar Mann, Rachel Reyes et al. 2002. *The world's water: 2002–2003.* Washington, DC: Island Press.

Glennon, Robert. 2009. *Unquenchable: America's water crisis and what to do about it.* Washington, DC: Island Press.

Global Environment Facility. n.d. The restructured Global Environment Facility. www.worldbank.org/html/gef/intro/revqa.htm.

Go forth and multiply a lot less. 2009. *The Economist* 393 (8655):29–32.

Goodstein, David. 2004. *Out of gas: The end of the age of oil.* New York: W. W. Norton.

Gramlich, Edward M. 1990. *A guide to benefit-cost analysis.* 2nd ed. Prospect Heights, IL: Waveland Press.

Group of 20. 2009. Leaders' statement, the Pittsburgh Summit. Conference, Pittsburgh, PA, September 24–25.

Group of Green Economists. 1992. *Ecological economics.* London: Zed.

Haas, Peter M. 1992. Introduction: Epistemic communities and international cooperation. *International Organizations* 46 (1):1–35.

Haas, Peter M., Robert O. Keohane, and Marc A. Levy. 1993. *Institutions for the earth: Sources of effective environmental protection.* Cambridge, MA: MIT Press.

Hansen, James. 2008. *Global warming twenty years later: Tipping points near.* June 23. www.columbia.edu/~jeh1/2008/TwentyYearsLater_20080623.pdf.

Hansen, James, Makiko Sato, Pushker Kharecha, David Beerling, Valerie Masson-Delmotte, Mark Pagani, Maureen Raymo et al. 2008. *Target atmospheric CO2: Where should humanity aim?* www.columbia.edu/~jeh1/2008/Target CO2_20080407.pdf.

Harris, Jonathan M., Timothy A. Wise, Kevin P. Gallagher, and Neva R. Goodwin. 2001. *A survey of sustainable development: Social and economic dimensions.* Washington, DC: Island Press.

Harrison, Neil E., and Gary Bryner. 2004. Thinking about science and politics. In *Science and politics in the international environment*, ed. Neil E. Harrison and Gary C. Bryner, 1–15. Lanham, MD: Rowman and Littlefield.

Hart, H. L. A. 1961. *The concept of law.* Oxford: Clarendon Press.

Heal, Geoffrey. 2000. *Nature and the marketplace: Capturing the value of ecosystem services.* Washington, DC: Island Press.

Heilbroner, Robert. 1991. *An inquiry into the human prospect.* New York: W. W. Norton.

Hempel, Lamont C. 1999. Conceptual and analytic challenges in building sustainable communities. In *Toward sustainable communities: Transition and transformations in environmental policy*, ed. Daniel A. Mazmanian and Michael E. Kraft, 43–74. Cambridge, MA: MIT Press, 1999.

Holdren, John P. 2001. The energy climate challenge: Issues for the new U.S. administration—Government management of energy resources in prevention of climatic changes. *Environment: Science and Policy for Sustainable Development* 43 (5, June):8–25. http://ftp.whrc.org/resources/published_literature/pdf/ HoldrenEnv.01.pdf.

Hollander, Jack M. 2003. *The real environmental crisis: Why poverty, not affluence, is the environment's number one enemy.* Berkeley: University of California Press.

Homer-Dixon, Thomas. 2006. The end of ingenuity. *New York Times*, November 29, 27.

Hossay, Patrick. 2006. *Unsustainable: A primer for global environmental and social justice*. London: Zed Books.

Hunter, David, James Salzman, and Durwood Zaelke. 2002. *International environmental law and policy*. 2nd ed. New York: Foundation Press.

Hyer, Eric. 2009. Alternative perspectives on U.S.-China relations. Paper presented at the People's Republic of China at 60: Internal and External Challenges conference, Buckness University.

IISD (International Institute for Sustainable Development). 1997. Summary of the nineteenth United Nations General Assembly special session to review implementation of Agenda 21. *Earth Negotiations Bulletin* 5 (88). www.iisd.ca/linkages/csd/enb0588e.html#1.

International Energy Agency. 2008. *World energy outlook*. Paris: Organisation for Economic Cooperation and Development.

International Environment. 1999. Montreal Protocol parties reach accord on three-year, $440 million package. *International Environment* (December 8):978.

IPCC. Feb. 2007. Summary for policymakers. In *Climate change 2007: The physical science basis*. Contribution of Working Group I to the Fourth Assessment Report of the Intergovernmental Panel on Climate Change. Cambridge, UK: Cambridge University Press. www.ipcc.ch/pdf/assessment-report/ar4/wg1/ar4-wg1-spm.pdf.

IPCC. Mar. 2007. Summary for policymakers. In *Climate change 2007: Impacts, adaptation, and vulnerability*. Contribution of Working Group II to the Fourth Assessment Report of the Intergovernmental Panel on Climate Change. Cambridge, UK: Cambridge University Press. www.ipcc.ch/pdf/assessment-report/ar4/wg2/ar4-wg2-spm.pdf.

IPCC. Apr. 2007. Summary for policymakers. In *Climate change 2007: Mitigation*. Contribution of Working Group III to the Fourth Assessment Report of the Intergovernmental Panel on Climate Change. Cambridge, UK: Cambridge University Press. www.ipcc.ch/pdf/assessment-report/ar4/wg3/ar4-wg3-spm.pdf.

IPCC. Oct. 2007. Press release. ipcc.ch/press/prpnp12oct07.htm.

IPCC. Nov. 2007. Summary for Policymakers. In *Climate change 2007: Synthesis report*. Contribution of Working Group III to the Fourth Assessment Report of the Intergovernmental Panel on Climate Change. Cambridge, UK: Cambridge University Press. www.ipcc.ch/pdf/assessment-report/ar4/syr/ar4_syr_spm.pdf.

IPCC. 2007a. *Climate change 2007: Mitigation of climate change*. Contribution of Working Group III to the Fourth Assessment Report of the Intergovernmental Panel on Climate Change, ed. B. Metz, O. R. Davidson, P. R. Bosch, R. Dave, L. A. Meyer. Cambridge UK: Cambridge University Press.

IPCC. 2007b. *Climate change 2007: Impacts, adaptation, and vulnerability.* Contribution of Working Group II to the Fourth Assessment Report of the Intergovernmental Panel on Climate Change, ed. M. L. Parry, O. F. Canziani, J. P. Palutikof, P. J. van der Linden, and C. E. Hanson. Cambridge, UK: Cambridge University Press.

IPCC. 2007c. *Climate change 2007: The physical science basis.* Contribution of Working Group I to the Fourth Assessment Report of the Intergovernmental Panel on Climate Change, ed. S. Solomon, D. Qin, M. Manning, Z. Chen, M. Marquis, K. B. Averyt, M. Tignor, and H. L. Miller. Cambridge, UK: Cambridge University Press.

IUCN (International Union for Conservation of Nature). 2007. The red list. http://www.iucnredlist.org/.

IUCN. 2008. IUCN Red List reveals world's mammals in crisis. Press release, Gland, Switzerland, October 6.

Jackson, Robert, and Georg Sorensen. 2003. *Introduction to international relations: Theories and approaches.* Oxford: Oxford University Press.

Jacobson, Harold K., and Edith Brown Weiss. 2000. A framework for analysis. In *Engaging countries: Strengthening compliance with international environmental accords,* ed. Edith Brown Weiss and Harold K. Jacobson, 1–18. Cambridge, MA: MIT Press.

Jacobson, Mark Z., and Mark A. Delucchi. 2009. A path to sustainable energy by 2030. *Scientific American* 301 (5):58–65.

Jamieson, Dale. 1996. Sustainability and beyond. Natural Resources Law Center Discussion Paper Series PL 02. Boulder, CO: University of Colorado School of Law, 1996.

Jasanoff, Sheila, and Marybeth Long Martello, eds. 2004. *Earthly politics: Local and global in environmental government.* Cambridge, MA: MIT Press.

Joint Science Academies' Statement: Global response to climate change. 2005. *The Times Online,* June 7. www.timesonline.co.uk/tol/news/world/article 530945.ece?token=null&offset=0&page=1.

Kahn, Matthew E. 2006. *Green cities: Urban growth and the environment.* Washington, DC: Brookings Institution.

Keck, Margaret E., and Kathryn Sikkink. 1998. *Activists beyond borders: Advocacy networks in international politics.* Ithaca, NY: Cornell University Press.

Kennedy, Donald. 2006. *Science magazine's state of the planet, 2006–2007.* Washington, DC: Island Press.

Keohane, Nathaniel O., and Sheila M. Olmstead. 2007. *Markets and the environment.* Washington, DC: Island Press.

Keohane, Robert O. 1986. *Neorealism and its critics.* New York: Columbia University Press.

Keohane, Robert O., and Marc A. Levy, eds. 1996. *Institutions for environmental aid.* Cambridge, MA: MIT Press.

Keohane, Robert O., and Joseph S. Nye. 2001. *Power and interdependence.* New York: Longman.

Kerr, Richard A. 2007. Climate change: Pushing the scary side of global warming. *Science* 316 (5830, June 8):1412–15.

Kingdon, John W. 1984. *Agendas, alternatives, and public policies.* Boston: Little, Brown and Company.

Kirkby, John, Phil O'Keefe, and Lloyd Timberlake. 1995. *The Earthscan reader in sustainable development.* London: Earthscan.

Klein, Naomi. 2007. *The shock doctrine: The rise of disaster capitalism.* New York: Metropolitan Books.

Klein, Naomi. 2009. Minority Death Match—Jews, blacks, and the "post-racial" presidency. *Harpers*, September, 53–67.

Krasner, Stephen D., ed. 1983. *International regimes.* Ithaca, NY: Cornell University Press.

Kuehls, Thom. 1996. *Beyond sovereign territory: The space of ecopolitics.* Minneapolis: University of Minnesota Press.

Lafferty, William M. 1996. The politics of sustainable development: Global norms for national implementation. *Environmental Politics* 5 (2):185–208.

Lafferty, William M., ed., 2004. *Governance for sustainable development: The challenge of adapting form to function.* Cheltenhan, UK: Edward Elgar.

Lafferty, William M., and Eivind Hovden. 2003. Environmental policy integration: Towards an analytic framework. *Environmental Politics* 12 (3):1–22.

Lafferty, William, and James Meadowbrook, eds. 2000. *Implementing sustainable development: Strategies and initiatives in high consumption societies.* Oxford: Oxford University Press.

Lenton, T. N., and N. E. Vaughn. 2009. The radiative forcing potential of different climate geoengineering options. *Atmospheric Chemistry and Physics* 9 (August 6):2559–608. www.atmos-chem-phys.net/9/5539/2009/acp-9-5539–2009.pdf.

Leopold, Aldo. 1966. *A sand county almanac.* New York: Ballantine Books.

Limbaugh, Mark. 2009. Minimizing and resolving conflict is the key. *The Environmental Forum* 26 (5):51.

Lindblom, Charles. 1977. *Politics and markets: The world's political-economic systems.* New York: Basic Books.

Lindzen, Richard S. 2006. There is no "consensus" on global warming. *The Wall Street Journal*, June 26. www.cfa.harvard.edu/~wsoon/ArmstrongGreen Soon08-Anatomy-d/Lindzen06-June26-WSJonConsensus.pdf.

Litfin, Karen T. 1994. *Ozone discourses: Science and politics in global environmental politics.* Cambridge, MA: MIT Press.

Litfin, Karen T., ed. 1998. *The greening of sovereignty in world politics.* Cambridge, MA: MIT Press.

Loh, Sandra Tsing. 2008. Should women rule? *The Atlantic,* November, 120–30.

Lomborg, Bjorn. 1998. Metodologisk vurdering af borger/bruger-undersøgelser i Århus Amts kommuner 1995–96 [Methodological evaluation of surveys in the Århus area municipalities 1995–96]. *Nordisk Administrativt Tidsskrift* 79(1):93–120.

Lomborg, Bjorn. 2001. *The skeptical environmentalist.* Cambridge, UK: Cambridge University Press.

Lomborg, Bjorn, ed. 2004. *Global crises, global solutions.* Cambridge, UK: Cambridge University Press.

Lomborg, Bjorn. 2007. *Cool it: The skeptical environmentalist's guide to global warming.* New York: Alfred A. Knopf.

Low, Nicholas, and Brendan Gleeson. 1998. *Justice, society and nature.* London: Routledge.

Lowi, Theodore J. 1998. Think globally, lose locally. *Boston Review,* April/May, 4–10.

Lowi, Theodore J. 1999. Globalization, the state, democracy: Vision of a new political science. Paper presented at the International Workshop of Development of Political Science: Universal and Regional Models, Faculty of Philosophy, Moscow State University, March 25.

Lowi, Theodore. n.d. Commentaries on politics and markets. Unpublished manuscript.

Mackay, Richard. 2009. *The atlas of endangered species.* Berkeley: University of California Press.

MacKenzie, Debora. 2008. Why the demise of civilization may be inevitable. *New Scientist,* April 2, 32–35.

MacNeill, Jim, Pieter Winsenium, and Taizo Yakushiji. 1991. *Beyond interdependence: The meshing of the world's economy and the earth's ecology.* New York: Oxford University Press.

Malaysia, Government of. 2007. Malaysia's forest management with reference to Ramin. The Hague, Netherlands.

Maniates, Michael. 2005. The politics of sacrifice in an ecologically full world. Draft briefing paper presented at the Annual Meeting of the International Studies Association, San Diego, March 2006.

McMillan, John. 2002. *Reinventing the bazaar: A natural history of markets.* New York: W. W. Norton.

Mearsheimer, John, J. 2001. *The tragedy of great power politics.* New York: W. W. Norton.

Merchant, Carolyn. 1992. *Radical ecology: The search for a livable world.* London: Routledge.

Merchant, Carolyn. 1994. *Ecology.* Atlantic Highlands, NJ: Humanities Press.

Merchant, Carolyn. 1995. *Earthcare: Women and the environment.* London: Routledge.

Michaels, Patrick J., ed. 2005. *Shattered consensus: The true state of global warming.* Lanham, MD: Rowman and Littlefield.

Milanovic, Branko. 2005. *Worlds apart: Measuring international and global inequality.* Princeton, NJ: Princeton University Press.

Milbrath, Lester W. 1989. *Envisioning a sustainable society: Learning our way out.* Albany: State University of New York Press.

Miles, Edward L., Arild Underdal, Steinar Andresen, Jon Bierger Skjaerseth, and Elaine M. Carlin. 2002. *Environmental regime effectiveness: Confronting theory with evidence.* Cambridge, MA: MIT Press.

Miller, Morris. 1991. *Debt and the environment: Converging crises.* New York: United Nations Publications.

Minda, Gary. 1995. *Postmodern legal movements.* New York: NYU Press.

Mishkin, Frederic S. 2006. *The next great globalization: How disadvantaged nations can harness their financial systems to get rich.* Princeton, NJ: Princeton University Press.

Murray, Mark. 2000. Seeking justice in roads and runways. *National Journal,* March 4, 712–13.

Nadeau. Robert L. 2003. *The wealth of nations: How mainstream economics has failed the environment.* New York: Columbia University Press.

New Economics Foundation. 2006. The (un)happy planet index. www.new economics.org.

New Economics Foundation. 2010. The (un)happy planet index 2.0. www .happyplanetindex.org/public-data/files/happy-planet-idex-2.0.pdf.

New Vista Communities. n.d. www. newvistas.com.

Nickel, James W. 1987. *Making sense of human rights: Philosophical reflections on the universal declaration of human rights.* Berkeley: University of California Press.

Nivola, Pietro S. 1999. *Laws of the landscape: How policies shape cities in Europe and America.* Washington, DC: Brookings Institution.

Okun, Arthur M. 1975. *Equality and efficiency: The big tradeoff.* Washington, DC: Brookings Institution.

Ophuls, William, and A. Stephan Boyan, Jr. 1992. *Ecology and the politics of scarcity revisited.* New York: W. H. Freeman.

Orr, David. 1992. *Ecological literacy: Education and the transition to a postmodern world.* Albany: State University of New York Press.

Orski, C. Kenneth, and Jane S. Shaw. 2005. Whatever happened to smart growth? *PERC Reports,* June, 3–5.

Oxfam International. 2007. *What's needed in poor countries, and who should pay?* London: Oxfam International.

Paehlke, Robert C. 2003. *Democracy's dilemma: environment, social equity, and the global economy.* Cambridge, MA: MIT Press.

Panayotou, Theodore. 1993. *Green markets: The economics of sustainable development.* San Francisco, CA: Institute for Contemporary Studies.

Paul, Ellen Frankel. 1995. Set-asides, reparations, and compensatory justice. In *Environmental protection and justice*, ed. Kenneth A. Manaster. Cincinnati, OH: Anderson Publishing Co.

Pear, Robert. 2007. Bush directive increases sway on regulation. *New York Times*, January 30. www.uri.edu/artsci/ecn/starkey/ECN342/bush_regulation.pdf.

Pellow, David, and Robert J. Brulle. 2005. *Power, justice, and the environment: A critical appraisal of the environmental justice movement.* Cambridge, MA: MIT Press.

Perlez, Jane. 1991. African dilemma: Food aid may prolong war and famine. *The New York Times*, May 12, A1.

Pinker, Susan. 2008. *The sexual paradox: Men, women, and the gender gap.* New York: Scribner.

Pirages, Dennis, ed. 1996. *Building sustainable societies.* Armonk, NY: M. E. Sharpe.

Pirages, Dennis, and Ken Cousins, ed. 2005. *From resource scarcity to ecological security: Exploring new limits to growth.* Cambridge, MA: MIT Press.

Plantlife International. 2008. *Medicinal plants in conservation and development.* Salisbury, UK: Plantlife International.

Pogge, Thomas. 2002. *World poverty and human rights.* London: Polity.

Pollan, Michael. 2008. *In defense of food: An eater's manifesto.* New York: The Penguin Press.

Porter, Gareth, Janet Welsh Brown, and Pamela S. Chasek. 2000. *Global environmental politics.* 3rd ed. Boulder, CO: Westview Press.

Princen, Thomas. 2005. *The logic of sufficiency.* Cambridge, MA: MIT Press.

Princen, Thomas, Michael Maniates, and Ken Conca, eds. 2002. *Confronting consumption.* Cambridge, MA: MIT Press.

Prugh, Thomas, Robert Costanza, and Herman Daly. 2000. *The local politics of global sustainability.* Washington, DC: Island Press.

Rawls, John. 1999. *A theory of justice.* Rev. ed. Cambridge, MA: Harvard University Press.

Revenga, Carmen, and Greg Mock. 2000. Dirty water: Pollution problems persist. *Pilot Analysis of Global Ecosystems: Freshwater Systems.* http://earthtrends.wri.org/pdf_library/feature/wat_fea_dirty.pdf.

Revkin, Andrew C. 2008. A shift in the debate over global warming. *New York Times*, April 6. www.nytimes.com/2008/04/06/weekinreview/06revkin.html.

Ringquist, Evan J. 2000. Environmental justice: Normative concerns and empirical evidence. In *Environmental policy*, 4th ed., ed. Norman J. Vig and Michael E. Kraft, 232–56. Washington, DC: CQ Press.

Roberts, J. Timmons, and Bradley C. Parks. 2007. *A climate of injustice: Global inequality, North-South politics, and climate policy.* Cambridge, MA: MIT Press.

Roberts, Paul. 2004. *The end of oil: On the edge of a perilous new world.* Boston, MA: Houghton Mifflin.

Rockström, Johan, Will Steffen, Kevin Noone, Asa Persson, F. Stuart Chapin III, Eric F. Lambin, Timothy M. Lenton et al. 2009. A safe operating space for humanity. *Nature*, September 24:472–475, 461.

Roodman, David Malin. 1995. Public money and human purpose: The future of taxes. *WorldWatch* 8 (September–October):10–19.

Rothfeder, Jeffrey. 2001. *Every drop for sale: Our desperate battle over water in a world about to run out.* New York: Tarcher/Putnam.

Ruggie, John Gerard. 1998. What makes the world hang together? Neoutilitarianism and the social constructivist challenge. *International Organization* 52 (4):855–85.

Sachs, Jeffrey D. 2005. *The end of poverty: Economic possibilities for our time.* New York: Penguin Books.

Samuelson, Robert J. 2008. Globalization's Achilles heel. *Newsweek*, July 21, 53.

Sandel, Michael. 1996. *Democracy's discontent.* Cambridge, MA: Harvard University Press.

Sandler, Ronald, and Phaedra C. Pezzullo. 2007. *Environmental justice and environmentalism: The social justice challenge to the environmental movement.* Cambridge, MA: MIT Press.

Sandler, Todd. 1997. *Global challenges.* Cambridge, UK: Cambridge University Press.

Schaefer, Mark. 2008. Water technologies and the environment: Ramping up by scaling down. *Technology in Society* 30 (3):415–22.

Schaper, David. 2008. States still struggle with bridge upkeep. *All things considered*, August 1. Minnesota Public Radio.

Schelling, Thomas C. 2006. *Strategies of commitment and other essays.* Cambridge, MA: Harvard University Press.

Sen, Amartya. 1999. *Development as freedom.* New York: Knopf.

Serageldin, Ismail. 1995. Third Annual World Bank Conference on environmentally sustainable development. Paper prepared for the Third Annual World Bank Conference on Environmentally Sustainable Development, Washington, DC, October.

Shabecoff, Philip. 1996. *A new name for peace: International environmentalism, sustainability development, and democracy.* Hanover, NH: University Press of New England.

Shindell, Drew, and Geg Faluvegi. 2009. Climate response to regional radiative forcing during the twentieth century. *Nature Geoscience*, March 22.

Simmons, Matthew. 2005. *Twilight in the desert: The coming Saudi oil shock and the world economy.* Hoboken, NJ: John Wiley.

Simpson, R. David, Michael A Toman, and Robert U. Ayers, eds. 2005. *Scarcity and growth revisited: Natural resources and the environment in the new millennium.* Washington, DC: Resources for the Future Press.

Solomon, Susan. 2009. Irreversible climate change due to carbon dioxide emissions. *Proceedings of the National Academy of Sciences*, February 10.

Soroos, Marvin. 1998. Global institutions and the environment. In *The global environment: Institutions, law, and policy*, ed. Norman J. Vig and Regina S. Alexrod, 27–51. Washington, DC: CQ Press.

Speth, James Gustave. 2005. *Red sky at morning: America and the crisis of the global environment.* New Haven, CT: Yale University Press.

Speth, James Gustave, and Peter M. Haas. 2006. *Global environmental governance.* Washington, DC: Island Press.

Stanger, Allison, and Omnivore. 2007. Foreign policy, privatized. *New York Times*, October 5. www.nytimes.com/2007/10/05/opinion/05stanger.html.

Sterling-Folker, Jennifer, ed. 2005. *Making sense of international relations theory.* Boulder, CO: Lynne Reinner.

Stiglitz, Joseph E. 2009. *Freefall: America, free markets, and the sinking of the world economy.* New York: W. W. Norton.

Stone, Christopher D. 1987. *Earth and other ethics: The case for moral pluralism.* New York: Harper and Row.

Stoner, Nancy. 2009. America's water future: There's a better way. *The Environmental Forum* 26 (5):53.

Tainter, Joseph. 1990. *The collapse of complex societies.* New York: Cambridge University Press.

Terrill, Ross. 2003. *The new Chinese empire and what it means for the United States.* New York: Basic Books.

Toffel, Mike, and Reid Lifset. 2007. Sustainability. In *Encyclopedia of Earth*, ed. Cutler J. Cleveland. Washington, DC: Environmental Information Coalition, National Council for Science and the Environment. www.eoearth.org/article/Sustainability.

Torchia, Andrew. 2009. China drought deprives millions of drinking water. *Reuters*, February 7.

Transboundary Freshwater Dispute Database. 2007. www.transboundarywaters.orst.edu/database/.

UNEP (United Nations Environment Programme). 1997. *Global environmental outlook.* New York: Oxford University Press.

UNEP (United Nations Environment Programme). 2002. *Global environment outlook 3.* London: Earthscan.

UNEP (United Nations Environment Programme). n.d. *Global outlook 3*, www.unep.org/geo/geo3/english/pdfs/synthesis.pdf.

UNESCO. n.d. *World water assessment programme.* www.unesco.org/water/wwap/facts_figures/protecting_ecosystems.shtml.

UN Food & Agricultural Organization. n.d. Reported at World Resources Institute. www.wri.org/trends/deforest.html.

UNFPA. 2001. *The state of the world's population 2001.* www.unfpa.org/swp/2001/english/ch03.html#3a.

United Nations. 1992. *The United Nation framework convention on climate change.* http://unfccc.int/resource/docs/convkp/conveng.pdf.

United Nations. 2002. *Global challenges, global opportunities: Trends in sustainable development.* www.johannesburgsummit.org/html/documents/summit_docs/criticaltrends_1408.pdf.

United Nations. 2007. *Human development report 2007/08, Fighting climate change: Human solidarity in a divided world.* New York: Palgrave Macmillan.

United Nations Commission on Sustainable Development. 2001a. *Agriculture, land, and desertification 2001.* http://ods-dds-ny.un.org/doc/UNDOC/GEN/N01/312/96/PDF/N0131296.pdf?OpenElement.

United Nations Commission on Sustainable Development. 2001b. *Global status of biological diversity.* http://ods-dds-ny.un.org/doc/UNDOC/GEN/N01/292/34/PDF/N0129234.pdf?OpenElement.

United Nations Commission on Sustainable Development. n.d. *Global status of biological diversity.* http://ods-dds-ny.un.org/doc/UNDOC/GEN/N01/292/34/PDF/N0129234.pdf?OpenElement.

United Nations Conference on Trade and Development. 2002. *E-commerce and development report 2002.* www.unctad.org/en/docs/ecdr2002_en.pdf.

United Nations Development Program. 2007. *Human development report 2007/2008.* New York: Palgrave Macmillan.

United Nations Division for Sustainable Development. n.d. *Agenda 21: Chapter 12.* www.un.org/esa/sustdev/documents/agenda21/english/agenda21chapter12.htm.

United Nations General Assembly. 1997a. Overall review and appraisal of the implementation of Agenda 21. Nineteenth special session, Agenda item 8, June 27, II. Assessment of progress made since the United Nations Conference on Environment and Development, paragraphs 7–8. gopher://gopher.un.org:70/00/ga/docs/S-19/plenary/AS19-29.TXT.

United Nations General Assembly. 1997b. Overall review and appraisal of the implementation of Agenda 21. Nineteenth special session, Agenda item 8, June 27, UNGASS, III. Implementation in Areas Requiring Urgent Action.

U.S. Fish and Wildlife Service. 2008. http://ecos.fws.gov.

Velders, Guss J. M., et al. 2009. The large contributions of projected HFC emissions to future climate forcing. *Proceedings of the National Academy of Sciences Online,* June 22.

Victor, David G., Kai Raustiala, and Eugene B. Skolnikoff. 1998. *The implementation and effectiveness of international environmental commitments: Theory and practice.* Cambridge, MA: MIT Press.

Victor, David G., and Eugene B. Skolnikoff. 1999. Translating intent into action: Implementing environmental commitments. *Environment* 4 (2):16–20, 39–44.

Vig, Norman. 1999. Introduction: Governing the international environment. In *The global environment: Institutions, law, and policy*, ed. Norman Vig and Regina Axelrod, 1–26. Washington, DC: CQ Press, pp. .

Walker, Brian et al. 2009. Looming global-scale failures and missing institutions. *Science* 325 (5946):1345–46.

Wapner, Paul 1996. *Environmental activism and world civic politics.* Albany: State University of New York.

Waring, Marilyn. 1988. *Counting for nothing.* San Francisco, CA: Harper.

Weiss, Edith Brown. 1999. The emerging structure of international environmental law. In *The global environment: Institutions, law, and policy*, ed. Norman J. Vig, Regina S. Axelrod, 98–115. Washington, DC: CQ Press.

Weiss, Edith Brown, and Harold K. Jacobson. 1998. *Engaging countries: Strengthening compliance with international environmental accords.* Cambridge: MIT Press.

Wetlands International. n.d. *The socio-economics of wetlands.* www.wetlands.org/pubs&/pub_online/SocioEcs/Part1.pdf.

Whoriskey, Peter. 2007. Report says corps miscalculated on levees. *Washington Post*, March 22. www.washingtonpost.com/wp-dyn/content/article/2007/03/21/AR2007032101963.html?nav=emailpage.

Wildavsky, Aaron. 1997. *But is it true? A citizen's guide to environmental health and safety issues.* Cambridge, MA: Harvard University Press.

Wilkinson, Clive, ed. 2000. *The status of coral reefs of the world.* Cape Ferguson, Queensland: Australian Institute of Marine Science.

World Bank. 1995. *Monitoring environmental progress: A Report on work in progress.* Washington, DC: The World Bank.

World Bank. 2001. Executive summary of the WWDR. Washington, DC: World Bank.

World Bank. 2003a. *Globalization guide, 2003.*

World Bank. 2003b. *World development report 2003: Sustainable development in a dynamic world.* www.wds.worldbank.org/servlet/WDSContentServer/WDSP/IB/2002/09/06/000094946_02082404015854/Rendered/PDF/multi0page.pdf.

World Bank. 2006a. *An investment framework for clean energy and development: A progress report.* Washington, DC: World Bank.

World Bank. 2006b. *World development indicators.* http://devdata.worldbank.org/wdi2006/contents/index2.htm.

World Bank. n.d. *Globalization, growth, and poverty.* http://econ.worldbank.org/files/2899_ch4.pdf.

World Commission on Environment and Development. 1987. Towards sustainable development. In the *Report of the World Commission on Environment and Development: Our Common Future.* www.un-documents.net/wced-ocf.htm.

World Resources Institute. n.d. Earthtrends.

World Resources Institute. 1994. *World resources 1994–95.* Washington, DC: WRI.

World Resources Institute. 1995. *Power, responsibility, and accountability: Rethinking the legitimacy of institutions for climate finance.* http://pdf.wri.org/working_papers/power_responsibility_accountability_2009-11.pdf.

World Resources Institute. 1998. Wasting the material world: The impact of industrial economies. http://earthtrends.wri.org/pdf_library/feature/ene_fea_materials_complete.pdf.

World Resources Institute, in collaboration with the United Nations Development Programme, United Nations Environment Programme, and World Bank. 2005. *World resources 2005: The wealth of the poor.* Washington, DC: WRI.

World Scientists' Warning to Humanity. 2003. www.worldtrans.org/whole/warning.html.

Worldwatch Institute. 2007. *Vital signs: The trends that are shaping our future.* New York: W. W. Norton.

Worldwatch Institute. 2008. *State of the world: Innovations for a sustainable economy.* New York: W. W. Norton.

World Wildlife Fund. 2002a. *Annual Report 2002.* www.panda.org/downloads/general/rapport02eng.pdf.

World Wildlife Fund. 2002b. *Living planet report 2002.* www.panda.org/downloads/general/lpr2002summary.pdf.

Yeatman, William. 2008. Bali follies: The benefits of failure. *Planet: Advancing liberty from the economy to ecology* 21(1):6. http://cei.org/pdf/6410.pdf.

Young, Oran, ed. 1997. *Global governance: Drawing insights from the environmental experience.* Cambridge, MA: MIT Press.

Young, Oran, 1998. *Creating regimes: Arctic accords and international governance.* Ithaca, NY: Cornell University Press.

Young, Oran. 1999. *Governance in world affairs.* Ithaca, NY: Cornell University Press.

Young, Oran, et al. 2002. *The institutional dimensions of environmental change: Fit, interplay, and scale.* Cambridge, MA: MIT Press.

ADDITIONAL READING

Adato, Michelle. 2000. *Final report: The impact of PROGRESA on community social relationships.* Washington DC: International Food Policy Research Institute.

Adegbidi, Anselme, Esaia Gandonou, and Remco Oostendorp. 2004. Measuring the productivity from indigenous soil and water conservation technologies with household fixed effects: A case study of the hilly mountainous areas of benin. *Economic Development and Cultural Change* 52:313–346.

Alix-Garcia, Jennifer, Alain de Janvry, and Elisabeth Sadoulet. 2005. A tale of two communities: Explaining deforestation in mexico. *World Development* 33:219–235.

Ayala-Carcedo, Fransisco J., and Manuel Gonzalez-Barros. 2005. Economic underdevelopment and sustainable development in the world: Conditioning factors, problems and opportunities. *Environment, Development, and Sustainability* 7 (1):95–115.

Behrman, Jere R., and Emmanuel Skoufias. 2006. Mitigating myths about policy effectiveness: Evaluation of Mexico's antipoverty and human resource investment program. *Annals of the American Academy of Political and Social Sciences* 606 (1):244–275.

Beitz, Charles. 2009. *The idea of human rights.* New York: Oxford University Press.

Berner, Erhard, and Benedict Phillips. 2005. Left to their own devices? Community self-help between alternative development and neo-liberalism. *Community Development Journal* 40:17–29.

Bhagwati, Jagdish. 2004. *In defense of globalization.* New York: Oxford University Press.

Bond, Patrick. 2006. Global governance campaigning and MDGs: From top-down to bottom-up anti-poverty work. *Third World Quarterly* 27: 339–54.

Bourguignon, Francois, and Satya R. Chakravarty. 2003. The measurement of multidimensional poverty. *Journal of Economic Inequality* 1:25–49.

Bryner, Gary C. 2004. Global Interdependence. In *Environmental governance reconsidered: Challenges, choices, and opportunities*, ed. Robert F. Durrant, Daniel J. Fiorino, and Rosemary O'Leary, 69–104. Cambridge, MA: MIT Press.

Burns, Justine, Malcolm Keswell, and Murray Leibbrandt. 2005. Social assistance, gender, and the aged in south africa. *Feminist Economics* 11:103–115.

Caldes, Natalia, David Coady, and John A. Maluccio. 2006. The cost of poverty alleviation transfer programs: A comparative analysis of three programs in Latin America. *World Development* 34:818–837.

Caldwell, Lynton Keith. 1999. Is humanity destined to self-destruct? *Politics and the Life Sciences* 18 (2):3–14.

Campbell, Catherine, and Catherine MacPhail. 2002. Peer education, gender, and the development of critical consciousness: Participatory HIV prevention by South African youth. *Social Science and Medicine* 55:331–345.

Chambers, Robert. 1997. *Whose reality counts? Putting the first last.* London: Intermediate Technology Publications.

Chess, Caron. 2000. Evaluating environmental public participation: Methodological questions. *Journal of Environmental Planning and Management* 43:769–84.

Coady, David, Margaret Grosh, and Josh Hoddinott. 2004. Targeting outcomes redux. *The World Bank Researcher Observer* 19:61–85.

Conning, Jonathan, and Michael Kevane. 2002. Community-based targeting mechanisms for social safety nets: A critical review. *World Development* 30: 375–394.

Cornwall, Andrea. 2003. Whose voices? Whose choices? Reflections on gender and participatory development. *World Development* 31:1325–1342.

Costanza, Robert et al. 1997. The value of the world's ecosystem services and natural capital. *Nature* 387 (6630):253–60.

De Beer, Frik, and Marinda Marais. 2005. Rural communities, the natural environment and development—Some challenges, some successes. *Community Development Journal* 40:50–61.

Despommier, Dickson. 2009. The rise of vertical farms. *Scientific American* 301 (5):80–87.

Dowla, Asif. 2006. In credit we trust: Building social capital by Grameem Bank in Bangladesh. *The Journal of Socio-Economics* 35:102–122.

Dryzek, John S. 1997. *The politics of the earth: Environmental discourses.* Oxford: Oxford University Press.

Elahi, Khandakar Q., and Constantine P. Danopoulos. 2004. Microfinance and third world development: A critical analysis. *Journal of Political and Military Sociology* 32:61–74.

Esfahani, Hadi Salehi, and Maria Teresa Ramirez. 2003. Institutions, infrastructure, and economic growth. *Journal of Development Economics* 70:443–77.

Eversole, Robyn. 2003. Managing the pitfalls of participatory development: Some insight from Australia. *World Development* 31:781–95.

Finan, Frederico, Elisabeth Sadoulet, and Alain de Janvry. 2005. Measuring the poverty reduction potential of land in rural Mexico. *Journal of Development Economics* 77:27–51.

Flannery, Tim. 2005. *The weather makers: How man is changing the climate and what it means for life on earth.* New York: Atlantic Monthly.

Fonjong, Lotsmart N., Ngwa Nebasina Emmanuel, and Charles C. Fonchingong. 2004. Rethinking the contribution of indigenous management in small-scale water provision among selected rural communities in Cameroon. *Environment, Development and Sustainability* 6:429–51.

Gaiha, Raghav, Katsushi Imai, and P. D. Kaushik. 2001. "On the targeting and cost-effectiveness of anti-poverty programmes in rural India." *Development and Change* 32 (2):309–42.

Gertler, Paul. 2004. Do conditional cash transfers improve child health? Evidence from PROGRESA's control randomized experiment. *Health, Health Care, and Economic Development* 94:336–41.

Gibson, John, and Scott Rozelle. 2003. Poverty and access to roads in Papua New Guinea. *Economic Development and Cultural Change* 52:159–85.

Global Policy Forum. 2002. *WTO watch: Piles of poison in Mexico.* www.global policy.org/globaliz/special/2002/0510poison.htm.

Goodhart, Michael, ed. 2009. *Human rights: politics and practice.* New York: Oxford University Press.

Griffin, James. 2009. *On human rights.* Oxford: Oxford University Press.

Grima, A. P. Lino, Susan Horton, and Shashi Kant. 2003. Introduction: Natural capital, poverty, and development. *Environment, Development and Sustainability* 5:297–314.

Halder, Shantana R., and Paul Mosley. 2004. Working with the ultra-poor: Learning from BRAC experiences. *Journal of International Development* 16:387–406.

Hannah, Gordon. 2006. Maintaining product-process balance in community antipoverty initiatives. *Social Work* 51:9–17.

Hariss, John. 2002. The case for cross-disciplinary approaches in international development. *World Development* 30:487–96.

Heinrich, Carolyn J. 2007. Demand and supply-side determinants of conditional cash transfer program effectiveness. *World Development* 35:121–43.

Homer-Dixon, Thomas. 2008. *Catastrophe, creativity, and the renewal of civilization.* Washington, DC: Island Press.

Hulme, David, and Andrew Shepherd. 2003. Conceptualizing chronic poverty. *World Development* 31:403–23.

Julia, Maria, and Mary E. Kondrat. 2005. Health care in social development context. *International Social Work* 48:537–52.

Kleymeyer, Charles David, ed. 1994. *Cultural expression and grassroots development.* Boulder, CO: Lynn Reinner.

Kolbert, Elizabeth. 2006. *Field notes from a catastrophe: Man, nature, and climate change.* New York: Bloomsbury.

Kutting, Gabriella. 2006. The politics of sacrifice: Whose sacrifice? Sustainable fashion, the North-South divide and global politics. Paper presented at the Annual Meeting of the International Studies Association, San Diego, March.

LaRochelle, Serge, and Fikret Berkes. 2003. Traditional ecological knowledge and practice for edible wild plants: Biodiversity use by the Rarámuri in the Sierra Tarahumara, Mexico. *International Journal of Sustainable Development and World Ecology* 10:361–75.

Leary, Neil, James Adejuwon, Vicenty Barros, Ian Burton, Jyoti Kulkarni, and Rodel Lasco. 2008. *Climate change and adaptation.* London: Earthscan.

Leary, Neil, Ceclia Conde, Jyoti Kulkarni, Anthony Nyong, and Juan Pulhin. 2008. *Climate change and vulnerability.* London: Earthscan.

Levy, Santiago. 2006. *Progress against poverty: Sustaining Mexico's opportunidades program.* Washington, DC: Brookings Institution.

Loomis, Terrence M. 2000. Indigenous populations and sustainable development: Building on indigenous approaches to holistic, self-determined development. *World Development* 28:893–910.

Marschke, Melissa, and Fikret Berkes. 2005. Local level sustainability planning for livelihoods: A Cambodian experience. *International Journal of Sustainable Development and World Ecology* 12:21–33.

McKibben, Bill. 2003. *Enough.* New York: Henry Holt.

Meadows, Donella, Jorgen Randers, and Dennis Meadows. 2004. *Limits to growth: The 30-year update.* White River Junction, VT: Chelsea Green Publishing Co.

Michaels, Patrick J. 2004. *Meltdown: The predictable distortion of global warming by scientists, politicians, and the media.* Washington, DC: Cato Institute.

Micklewright, John, and Sheila Marnie. 2005. Targeting social assistance in a transition economy: The Mahalla in Uzbekistan. *Social Policy and Adminitration* 39: 431–47.

Mohaheng, T. 2005. Problems of implementation in the Lesotho Fund for Community Development. *Africanus* 35:28–39.

Mukjerjee, Sanjukta, and Todd Benson. 1998. The determinants of poverty in Malawi. *World Development* 31:339–58.

Muñoz-Piña, Carlos, Alain de Janvry, and Elisabeth Sadoulet. 2003. Recrafting rights over common property resources in Mexico. *Economic Development and Cultural Change* 52:129–58.

Narayan-Parker, Deepa, Raj Patel, Kai Schafft, Anne Rademacher, and Sarah Koch-Schulte. 2000. *Voices of the poor: Can anyone hear us?* New York: Oxford University Press.

Narayan-Parker, Deepa, and Patti Petesch, eds. 2002. *Voices of the poor: From many lands.* New York: Oxford University Press.

Njie, A. B. Hatib. 2001. Poverty and ill health: The Ugandan national response. *Development* 44:93–98.

Osborn, Timothy J., and Keith R. Briffa. 2006. The spatial extent of 20th-century warmth in the context of the past 1200 years. *Science* 311 (5762):841–44.

Pagiola, Stefano, Agustin Arcenas, and Gunars Platais. 2005. Can payments for environmental services help reduce poverty? An exploration of the issue and the evidence to date from Latin America. *World Development* 33:237–53.

Parker, Susan W., and Graciela M. Teruel. 2005. Randomization and social program evaulation: The case of Progresa. *Annals of the American Academy of Political and Social Sciences* 59:199–219.

Perez, Nina. 2002. Achieving sustainable livelihoods—A case study of a Mexican rural community. *Community Development Journal* 37:178–87.

Pew Oceans Comissions Report. *State of America's Oceans.* www.pewoceans .org/oceans/downloads/state_oceans.pdf.

Putnam, Robert. 2001. *Bowling alone: The collapse and revival of American community.* NY: Simon and Schuster.

Renkow, Mitch, Daniel G. Hallstrom, and Daniel D. Karnaja. 2004. Rural infrastructure, transactions costs and market participation in Kenya. *Journal of Development Economics* 73:349–67.

Resurreccion, Bernadette P., Mary Jane Real, and Panadda Pantana. 2004. Officialising strategies: Participatory processes and gender in Thailand's water resources sector. *Development in Practice* 14:521–33.

Rioja, Felix K. 2003. The penalties of inefficient infrastructure. *Review of Development Economics* 7:127–37.

Ruggeri-Laderchi, Caterina, Ruhi Saith, and Frances Stewart. 2003. Does it matter that we do not agree on the definition of poverty? A comparison of four approaches. *Oxford Development Studies* 31:243–74.

Sadoulet, Elisabeth, and Benjamin Davis. 2001. Cash transfer programs with income multipliers: PROCAMPO in Mexico. *World Development* 29:1043–56.

Serr, Klaus. 2004. Voices from the bottom. *Australian Social Work* 57:137–49.

Shah, Amita, and D. C. Sah. 2004. Poverty among tribals in South West Madhya Pradesh: Has anything changed over time? *Journal of Human Development* 5:249–63.

Shaw, D. J. 2005. Dimensions of poverty: Status and solutions towards the millenium development goals. *Development Policy Review* 23:499–523.

Singer, Fred, and Dennis T. Avery. 2008. *Unstoppable global warming.* Lanham, MD: Rowman and Littlefield.

Skoufias, Emmanuel. 2005. PROGRESA and its impacts on the welfare of rural households in Mexico. Washington, DC: International Food Policy Research Institute.

Skoufias, Emmanuel, Benjamin Davis, and Sergio de la Vega. 2001. Targeting the poor in Mexico: An evaluation of the selection of households into PROGRESA. *World Development* 29:1769–84.

Steger, Manfred B. 2008. *The rise of the global imaginary: Political ideologies from the French Revolution to the global war on terror.* Oxford: Oxford University Press.

Streeten, Paul. 1998. Beyond the six veils: Conceptualizing and measuring poverty. *Journal of International Affairs* 52(1):1–31.

Swallow, Brent. 2005. Potential for poverty reduction strategies to address community priorities: Case study of Kenya. *World Development* 33:301–21.

UNEP (United Nations Environment Programme). 2001. *State of the world's cities report 2001: Urban pollution.* www.unchs.org/Istanbul+5/68.pdf.

UNEP (United Nations Environment Programme). 2002. *UNEP in 2002.* www.unep.org/home/UNEP_Annual_Report_2002.pdf.

UNESCO. *World water assessment programme.* www.unesco.org/water/wwap/facts_figures/water_industry.shtml.

Veeman, T. S., and J. Politylo. 2003. The role of institutions and policy in enhancing sustainable development and conserving natural capital. *Environment, Development, and Sustainability* 5: 317–32.

Victor, David G. 2004. *Climate change: Debating America's policy options.* New York: Council on Foreign Relations.

Vig, Norman J., and Regina Alexrod, eds. 1999. *The global environment: Institutions, law, and policy.* Washington, DC: CQ Press.

Vig, Norman J., and Michael G. Faure, eds. 2004. *Green giants: Environmental policies of the United States and the European Union.* Cambridge, MA: MIT Press.

Villano, David. 2008. A future of less. *Miller-McCune.com* September, 60–69.

Volkery, Axel, Darren Swenson, Klaus Jacob, Francois Bregha, and Laszlo Pinter. 2006. Coordination, challenges, and innovations in 19 national sustainable development strategies. *World Development* 34:2047–63.

Wagle, Udaya. 2002. "Rethinking poverty: Definition and measurement." *International Social Science Journal* 54:155–65.

Wagstaff, Adam, Flavia Bustreo, Jennifer Bryce, Mariam Claeson, and the WHO-World Bank Child Health and Poverty Working Group. 2004. Child health: Reaching the poor. *American Journal of Public Health* 94:726–36.

Waltz, Kenneth N. 1979. *Theory of international politics.* New York: McGraw Hill.

Weart, Spencer R. 2003. *The discovery of global warming.* Cambridge, MA: Harvard University Press.

Weaver, Thomas. 2000. Changes in forestry policy, production, and the environment in Northern Mexico: 1960–2000. *Journal of Political Ecology* 7:1–18.

Wester, Philippus, Douglas J. Merrey, and Marna de Lange. 2003. Boundaries of consent: Stakeholder representation in river basin management in Mexico and South Africa. *World Development* 31:797–812.

White, Howard. 1999. Global poverty reduction: Are we heading in the right direction? *Journal of International Development* 11:503–19.

World Bank. 2004. *Poverty in Mexico.* Washington, DC: World Bank.

World Resources Institute. n.d. http://earthtrends.wri.org/conditions_trends/feature_select_action.cfm?theme=7.

World Resources Institute. n.d. www.wri.org/trends/index.html.

World Resources Institute, http://earthtrends.wri.org/conditions_trends/feature_select_action.cfm?theme=6.

World Resources Institute. www.wri.org/trends/index.html.

World Resources Institute. www.wri.org/trends/deforest.html.

World Resources Institute. www.wri.org/trends/wasting.html.

World Resources Institute. www.wri.org/trends/soilloss.html.

World Resources Institute. www.wri.org/trends/fishloss.html.

Yunus, Muhammad. 2003. *Banker to the poor: Micro-lending and the battle against world poverty.* New York: PublicAffairs.

Zbinden, Simon, and David R. Lee. 2005. Paying for environmental services: An analysis of participation in Costa Rica's PSA program. *World Development* 33:255–72.

INDEX

ABOUT THE AUTHOR

Gary C. Bryner was, until his death, Professor of Political Science at Brigham Young University. He also served as Director of the Natural Resources Law Center at the University of Colorado School of Law. He authored and edited many books dealing with the global environment, public policy, and political theory, among them *Gaia's Wager: Environmental Movements and the Challenge of Sustainability* (2001) and *Blue Skies, Green Politics: The Clean Air Act of 1990* (1993, 1995). He completed two book-length manuscripts in the last year of his life while fighting cancer.

0 1341 1379105 4

DATE DUE	RETURNED
JAN 0 3 2012	JAN 0 3 2012
JAN 0 2 2014	DEC 1 3 2013